NOBODY'S LEGEND

NOBODY'S LEGEND

Let Go of Who You Were, Rewrite Your Story, and Take Back Your Life

Jason Ferguson

Published by Best Seller Publishing®, St. Augustine, FL
Best Seller Publishing® is a registered trademark.
Printed in the United States of America.

ISBN: 978-1-966395-73-7

This publication is designed to provide accurate and authoritative information with regard to the subject matter covered. It is sold with the understanding that the publisher is not engaged in rendering legal, accounting, or other professional advice. If legal advice or other expert assistance is required, the services of a competent professional should be sought. The opinions expressed by the author in this book are not endorsed by Best Seller Publishing® and are the sole responsibility of the author rendering the opinion.

For more information, please write:
Best Seller Publishing®
1775 US-1 #1070
St. Augustine, FL 32084
or call 1 (626) 765-9750
Visit us online at: www.BestSellerPublishing.org

Table of Contents

Author's Note 1

Introduction... 3

Chapter 1: How Did I Get Here? 5

Chapter 2: Thoughts Become Things........................ 9

Chapter 3: The Rabbit 15

Chapter 4: A New Voice.. 25

Chapter 5: Get Hit.. 35

Chapter 6: Be Obsessed, or Be Average 43

Chapter 7: You Want to Make God Laugh? 57

Chapter 8: Yellow Shorts....................................... 67

Chapter 9: Hurricane Henry................................... 79

Chapter 10: The Pathological Optimist 91

Chapter 11: Goodbye 103

Chapter 12: Aloha 109

Chapter 13: Those Four Words 123

Chapter 14: One Snap, and Clear 135

Chapter 15: Danza 149

Chapter 16: Ready for War 159

Chapter 17: Scar Tissue....................................... 169

Chapter 18: The Wild Wolf................................... 181

Chapter 19: What Quitting Actually Looks Like 195

Chapter 20: The Holy Grail 207

Chapter 21: Divine Intervention 223

Chapter 22: Victory House 233

Chapter 23: Glacier Freeze 253

Chapter 24: We All Take the Stairs...........................275

Chapter 25: Disneyland for Executives 291

Chapter 26: Sabotage...305

Chapter 27: My Origin Story................................321

Chapter 28: The Life Contract..............................333

Chapter 29: Today...349

Acknowledgments 365

About the Author..373

Author's Note

What's up, family?

If you're holding this book in your hands, you've already taken the first step into a story that is as raw as it is real. This is an unfiltered journey through nearly every triumph I have celebrated and dark secret I have wrestled with. By the time you finish, you will not just know my story, but you will know why it matters. And if you are here, we are already connected. So yeah, at this point, we're family.

Writing this book has been one of the most emotional, challenging, and rewarding journeys of my life. What started as an idea in the early days of the pandemic became a four-year process of reflection, vulnerability, and growth. Each chapter, each word, represents facing fears, pushing past self-doubt, and sharing my truth in the most authentic way I know how.

I won't sugarcoat it. There were moments I didn't think I could do this. Imposter syndrome flooded my thoughts, whispering that my voice didn't belong on these pages or that my story wasn't worth telling. I kept asking myself: *Would there really be a reader interested in this?* I wrestled with fears of judgment, of not being a good-enough writer, and of the potential shame and embarrassment that can come with exposing too much. But those fears became my compass, guiding me toward the truth I needed to tell.

If even one person sees a reflection of themselves in these words and feels inspired to keep fighting, keep dreaming, or simply keep going, then every sleepless night, every edit, and every vulnerable moment has been worth it.

This isn't just a story about me. It's about the people and experiences that shaped me, the triumphs, the heartbreaks, the lessons learned, and the mistakes made along the way. Out of respect for those who have been part of my journey, I've changed names to protect their anonymity while still giving you an unflinching look into my world.

Writing this book has been deeply therapeutic, helping me make sense of my past while holding space for my future. And in the end, maybe that's the beauty of sharing stories. They are not just reflections of where we've been; they are bridges—connecting people, experiences, and understanding. The lessons we carry from our experiences are not meant to stay locked away. They have the power to spark belief in someone else that transformation is possible. Even the hardest moments, when shared, can reshape lives.

To anyone who has ever doubted themselves, felt unseen, or struggled to rise above life's obstacles: this book is for you. If my story can be a reminder that change is possible and that resilience lives in us all, then I've done what I set out to do.

Thank you for picking up this book, for allowing me to share this journey with you, and for walking alongside me as I step into this space not just as a storyteller but also as a fellow traveler on the path of growth and self-discovery.

With love and gratitude,
Jason Ferguson

Introduction

We all have moments in life that define us. Moments when everything changes and we are forced to face the truth of who we are, what we have been through, and what we are willing to fight for. This book is about those moments. It is about resilience, transformation, and the pursuit of something greater, despite every setback, mistake, or moment of self-doubt that stands in the way.

If you are holding this book in your hands, it means you are searching for something. Maybe it is hope. Maybe it is clarity. Maybe it is proof that change is possible even when it feels out of reach. Whatever brought you here, I am glad you showed up. Because while this is my story, it is also about what is possible for you.

Nobody's Legend is not just about chasing a dream. It is about fighting through the noise to figure out who you are and what you are made of. It is about the kid who grew up with more dreams than resources, the athlete who had to work twice as hard for half as much, and the man who fell apart only to discover how to rebuild himself, piece by piece. It is about wrestling with demons, staring down failure, and clawing back from the brink of losing everything I thought defined me.

Life is messy, and so is this journey. But that is the point. It is through the chaos, the pain, and the moments when we feel like giving up that we learn what is possible. We all face struggles, no matter the arena of life we are in. It's this shared experience that inspired me to write this book. I wrote it for the underdogs, the dreamers, and the fighters. It is for the high achievers, the hitters who recently realized there are cracks in the foundation that nobody else sees but them.

I wrote this to remind us all that the hardest moments in life do not define us; they refine us. I know because I have been there. I know what it feels like to wonder if change is even possible. That is why I wanted to share the lessons I have learned, to show that transformation is not just for some of us. It is for all of us.

The story starts now, and I promise you, it's worth the ride.

1

How Did I Get Here?

APRIL 2009

Ask an addict what his worst nightmare is and he'll tell you: having money for drugs but no one to buy from. And right now, I'm trapped in that hell.

Morning light seeps through the blinds as I sit alone in my brother's apartment. Withdrawal looms like a dark storm on the horizon, and my head's a chaotic mess.

I'm glued to the couch, paralyzed by the gnawing craving for a fix. I need something, anything, to put me out of my misery and cure me of the sickness that intensifies by the second.

By midafternoon, the sweats flood in. Nausea begins to twist my stomach. My body aches like I've been hit by a freight train. I'm deteriorating, and I'm utterly alone.

What the fuck do I do?

I can't stop the thoughts from spiraling, each one more desperate than the last. Zeroing in on the right idea feels impossible; it's like I'm trying to catch water with a net. The panic of withdrawal intensifies, choking me.

Where do I go?

There's no escape, no way out. It's just me and this unbearable need, tearing me apart from the inside.

I'm desperate for a pill.

Just one to stop the shaking, to alleviate the pain. The craving drowns out everything: logic, reason, fear. It's crawling under my skin like a swarm of fire ants, relentless and unforgiving. I know this is killing me, but the pull is too strong. I don't care about the consequences; I care only about the relief that's just out of reach, taunting me with the promise of peace. It's the only thing that feels real.

Then it hits me—the mom-and-pop pharmacy down the street. I can easily walk there. They've gotta have all the Oxy and Percocet I need to put me out of my misery.

I could ... rob them?

I know where my brother keeps his revolver, a massive silver .357 magnum. And I'm not interested in their cash. I just want every opioid they've got.

I drag myself off the couch, adrenaline and desperation fueling my every move. I pace the room, jumping up and down like I'm psyching myself up for a football game.

You've got this, Filly.

I throw on some basketball shorts and a hoodie, and lay my brother's gun on the coffee table. I'm not completely sure how it works, and I'm too scared to check for bullets in case it accidentally goes off. I don't actually plan on using it anyway, so it doesn't really matter, right? Right?!?

Drenched in sweat, trying to think clearly about what I'm about to do, I ask myself out loud, "How the fuck did I even get here?"

The question echoes in my head, banging against the walls of my sanity.

This isn't me. I wasn't always an addict.

I had dreams, goals, passions.

There was a time when my life was simple ... when my biggest concern was nothing more than a game.

2
Thoughts Become Things

SEPTEMBER 1998

I'm 13, and my family has taken me to my first University of Southern California (USC) football game. I don't know it yet, but it'll become one of the most impactful moments in my life.

My senses today are heightened. The sharp scent of citrus from the car's air freshener smells more potent than usual. I can feel the hum of engines vibrating through our vehicle as cars roar past us. I'm restless, hyperaware of everything around me as we drive down the freeway, heading for the game.

The excitement is bubbling up inside me, and I can't help but wonder just how big these players will look in real life. At 5'2" and 125 pounds, I've never played tackle football before, but I've been obsessed with the sport since I was five. While most kids slept with a blanket or stuffed animal, I used to sleep with a football clutched in my arms, like it was a part of me.

This is my first college football game, and the anticipation is electric, almost overwhelming. My thoughts start to swirl: *How fast are these players? How physical will the game be up close?* I picture myself out on that field, wondering if one day, I could be the one everyone is cheering for. There's a mix of awe and nervousness building inside me, like a kid on his way to a theme park for the first time—unsure of what to expect, but knowing it's going to be unforgettable.

We exit the freeway, and it's like colliding head-on with a force field from the football gods, stopping us dead in our tracks. The enormity of the event hits me all at once—the sea of people flowing in waves of nothing but crimson and gold, bobbing along toward the stadium. It's hard to believe that all of us are here for the same thing. Not just the fans—everyone. There are guys stationed on every block with glow sticks in their hands; there are people in front of their apartment buildings waving us in, directing us to park in their private lots. There's even an elotes lady standing curbside, cheffing up some of the best Mexican corn the city has to offer.

USC jerseys hang neatly on a fence next to the parking lot, where an older gentleman hustles Carson Palmer jerseys to passing fans. He reminds me of the OGs you run into at the barbershop. Confident and witty, with energy that immediately puts a smile on your face. Everyone seems to play a role in making this event what it is, each person contributing to the buzzing atmosphere that defines college football.

On our hike to the stadium, I'm in the zone. Completely focused. There's music everywhere, loud and inviting, cultivating a party vibe. People have been here since the crack of dawn, setting up their tarps, tables, grills, and coolers. The smell of BBQ owns the airwaves. I watch in awe as complete strangers exchange food with one another. Families sit in circles debating the state of college football and making predictions about today's game. Right away, it's clear to me who the students are. They, too, are tailgating, but their focus isn't on BBQ or football politics. They're preoccupied by how many beers they can shotgun before kickoff.

USC is located in an area notorious for being somewhat dangerous, but that isn't the case today. Today, there are nothing but smiles, and the positive energy is infectious. What I'm witnessing feels only possible through sports. Where else do you see people from all walks of life, different backgrounds, and even rivalries, coming together like this? It's not just about the game; it's about the sense of community, the shared passion, and the collective experience that transcends everyday life. Sports have a unique way of dissolving barriers, at least for a few hours, and uniting people in a way that few other things can.

As I climb the steps to my seat, my eyes lock on the field, and I can't tear them away. It's stunning. The grass is a perfect canvas, its vibrant green glows under the sunlight, and every blade is trimmed to perfection. The chalk lines are sharp and crisp, and it looks like they were etched with a ruler. My gaze follows the yard markers that stretch across the grass, drawing me into the smaller details that somehow make the whole field look even bigger. The hash marks, those tiny lines used to position the ball, resemble the stitching of a masterpiece, pulling everything together into what feels like a statement. In the center of the field, the word *Trojan* is painted in flowing cursive, with the letters *S* and *C* boldly beneath it. It's impossible to look away, a symbol of pride and heritage that feels larger than life.

From any angle you view it, it's bold, unyielding, and full of character, as if the field itself is declaring its legacy. This is more than just a game; it's a history, a tradition, a hallmark of excellence.

Its perfectly manicured state is almost intimidating. This is one of the biggest stages in the world, and I feel like an ant among giants. I'm too wired to sit down and too awestruck to look away.

The USC band strikes up their fight song, and the Trojan faithful rise in unison, throwing two fingers over their heads and floating their arms back and forth to the beat of the band. I have no clue what they're doing, but I immediately join in, feeling special, like I'm one of them.

Something compels me to walk to the tip-top of the stadium for an aerial view of all of it. My mom had bought me one of those Kodak FunSaver 35 mm disposable cameras. It came with 27 pictures, and after each shot, you had to wind the reel to set up for the next picture. I angle myself so I can capture the entire field and a good chunk of the stadium in the background.

I take two pictures, then tilt my head toward the sky, eyes closed, focused on the sound of the crowd. I breathe in the wind on my face. The smell of BBQ still lingers in the air as the southern California sun smiles down on all 80,000 of us in attendance.

Suddenly, the fans kick it up a notch, as if something amazing has happened. I open my eyes to find the USC players emptying out of the tunnel onto the field. Some of my favorite college football players are there, in real life. Kareem Kelly, Chad Morton, and Carson Palmer. The game itself is a blur.

When we get home after a nail-biting USC win over San Diego State, I immediately start bugging my mom about developing the pictures on my camera. Remember, there are no photos on cell phones at this time. Shit, I don't even have a cell phone. I have to wait a week for the film to be developed at the grocery store.

But eventually, I get them. And they are perfect. As I pour over my pictures, a surge of emotion runs through me. It's chilling. I know deep down in my soul that this is my destiny. I'm hooked, and there is no cure for the bug I've caught. I want to play on this field, rocking that same crimson and gold. I want parking lot attendants to direct fans who've come to see me play. I want the jersey hanging on the fence to say "Ferguson 22."

Everything is so clear. When you know, you just know. Even at a young age.

*   *   *

That night, I taped those pictures directly above my bed, making them impossible to ignore. They weren't just decorations; they were silent demands, promises etched into my mind. Every morning when I woke up, they were the first thing I saw. Every night before I fell asleep, they stared right back at me. They were so much more than just pictures; they were fuel.

Every time I looked at them, I wasn't just seeing the vision; I was committing to whatever it would take to get there. Visualization became my weapon, but discipline was the shield that protected the dream.

Looking back, I see why it was so important. Those pictures were rewiring me. Every time I saw them, my brain filtered out distractions and locked in on what mattered most.

My mom used to tell me all the time: "Thoughts become things: Think it, see it, say it, believe it, then do it." At the time, I didn't fully grasp what she meant, but now it makes total sense. There's actual science behind it.

Your brain has something called the reticular activating system, or RAS. It's a bundle of nerves that sits in your brainstem, acting as a gatekeeper for your focus. Out of the thousands of things happening around you every day, your RAS decides what gets through.

Ever start thinking about buying a certain car and suddenly see it everywhere? That's your RAS in action, pulling your attention toward what you've told it is important. In the same way, when you set a goal or visualize a dream, your RAS begins to spotlight opportunities and resources that align with that vision, often things you might have otherwise overlooked.

When you combine visualization with intentionality, you train your RAS to work in your favor, sharpening your focus on what truly matters. Neuroscientists like Dr. Andrew Huberman, Stanford University professor and popular podcaster, explain that visualization engages key areas of your brain in ways that mirror real-life experiences. It's like a mental dress rehearsal, strengthening neural pathways and preparing you to take action.

I experienced this firsthand every time I looked at those USC pictures. My RAS was at work, constantly pulling my focus back to my goal. But those pictures were just the spark. Turning thoughts into reality requires something more, a bridge between intention and achievement. That bridge is action. Consistent, deliberate action. Or what I like to call "massive action."

Those USC pictures weren't magic. They didn't drag me out of bed at 5 a.m. or push me through grueling workouts. What they did was remind me, every single day, of what I was chasing.

The lesson is simple but powerful: *visualize intentionally, act relentlessly.* Your brain might open the door, but it's your effort that gets you through it.

3
The Rabbit

It's the summer of '99, and Los Angeles is scorching. The city pulses with life amid a relentless heat wave, and the beautiful people contribute to the vibrant summer energy. Everyone is outside. Women stroll in packs, wearing low-cut shirts or colorful sundresses. Teenagers, shirtless and carefree, dash through the streets on bikes and skateboards.

And the trees—man, the palm trees are flourishing. They sway back and forth on the islands dividing our roads. In the summer, they're more noticeable than ever, with the sun hovering effortlessly, casting a golden glow that defines L.A. summers.

Most kids are eager to run the streets with their friends, but not me. I'm singularly focused on one thing: finally getting my own football equipment. I daydream about the feel of pads on my shoulders and the view of the field from inside a helmet, gazing through the bars of my face mask.

Today is the day I meet my coach, receive my gear, and embark on my high school football journey at summer camp.

My stepdad, Danny White—or D-Weez, as I've always called him—drives me to practice today, just like he has for years. He's always been one of my biggest supporters.

I vividly remember the first time I realized something serious was brewing between him and my mom. I was about ten years old, and D-Weez was the assistant coach of my Amateur Athletic Union (AAU) basketball team.

He'd drive me to and from practice, often with his seven-year-old son, Donovan, in tow. Without him, I might not have even played. My mom's grueling work schedule made it nearly impossible to get me to practice regularly during the week.

One day after practice, instead of just dropping me off at home, he came upstairs and stayed for dinner—it was Taco Tuesday. Donovan and I spent most of the evening playing video games with my brother Ryan, lost in our own world. But after about an hour, curiosity got the best of me. I went looking for Danny and found him in the living room, deep in conversation with my mom. She was smiling from ear to ear, and that's when it hit me—this was something more.

I like to joke that Danny brought me home from practice one day, stayed for Taco Tuesday, and hasn't left since. He went from being my basketball coach, Coach Danny, to becoming D-Weez, my stepdad. Donovan and Dominic, Danny's oldest son who's two years older than me, went from being just kids I knew from the park to becoming my actual brothers.

D-Weez was easy to like right out of the gate. He was the most popular coach at the park and a limitless source of wisdom, with unmatched energy. He's patient and generous.

He's also extremely sarcastic. Everything turns into a joke or catchphrase with him and winds up sticking around as an inside family joke. He's calculated in how he communicates—rather than directly answering a question, he likes to teach and guide you into uncovering the answer yourself.

And when he knows you're lying, rather than calling you out, he prefers to hit you with a barrage of questions, slowly, giving you just enough rope to unravel your own story without ever having to call you a liar. Classic D-Weez. He's far from perfect but perfect for us—exactly what I needed as a little boy growing up without a father in the home.

Merging families wasn't easy. My brother Ryan and I had to adjust, just like Donovan and Dominic. We all had to handle the changes together. For an entire year, the four of us kids shared the same bedroom. For the most part, it was like a 12-month slumber party—cracking jokes, wrestling, talking about girls, and playing video games.

But it wasn't all fun. We fought and bickered, each of us struggling in our own ways to adjust to this new world that included one another. We had our good days and bad days, but through it all, we bonded into what we are now—brothers. It also helped all of us develop thick skin, something I've relied on again and again when life started throwing things at me.

This was our new vibrant family dynamic, and it was only right for D-Weez to be the one to take me to my first practice on that day.

He parks the car right in front of the field, and we walk over to meet Coach Shane Cox. Coach Cox is starting his first year as the head coach at Fairfax High School. He's here to turn the football program around—with a team one season away from setting a record for the most consecutive losses in California. Coach Cox needs talent, a new culture, and kids ready to adopt a winning mindset. He needs kids like me.

Initially, I didn't even want to go to Fairfax. All my middle school friends were going to L.A. High, and I wanted to be with them. But football was my top priority, and my mom knew better. She insisted, and I had to trust her.

Word of my middle school flag football skills had reached Coach Cox. He'd heard about this quick, hardworking little running back. We'd never met, but he was willing to take a chance on me.

As D-Weez and I head over to greet Coach Cox, I look around at a pretty underwhelming field. The grass isn't green but light brown. It's dry and patchy, with mini mountains of dust everywhere. There are no lines on the field, and we're sharing it with the girls' softball team. The dugouts on opposite ends spill dirt into our practice area. It's a mess.

I guess it's not surprising that the facilities reflect the school record, but *God damn,* I think, *Is this really where we practice? My allergies are never gonna survive this.*

The whole team is already on the field practicing. A knot forms in my stomach as I stand there. I feel every emotion all at once. I'm nervous about making the right first impression, on edge about whether I'll be as good in tackle football as I was in flag football. This moment has been the center of my obsession for as long as I can remember, and now here I am, standing face-to-face with my high school coach.

A hint of fear creeps in. I have never played tackle football before, never taken a real hit, and I am easily the smallest player here, maybe in all of California. My stomach churns, but it is not just nerves; it is anticipation, pure and electric. Deep down, I know how quick I am, how slippery I can be when I have the ball in my hands. I have spent years imagining this moment, and now it is here. This is my chance, not just to prove something to everyone else, but to prove it to myself.

D-Weez shakes hands with Coach Cox, who nods and then turns to me. To all 5'2", 125 pounds of me. While most of my friends have hit their growth spurt this summer, my body has decided to take some time off. I haven't grown at all in height or weight. It almost feels like a cruel joke on this coach who has so much at stake.

As he looks me over, I take the chance to size him up too. Coach Cox is a medium-built guy—not small by any means, but his presence doesn't rely on his stature alone. He has a closely shaven goatee that frames his face with precision. His bald head wears a light red hue from hours spent under the relentless Southern California sun, a testament to his commitment to coaching. Coach Cox is a White man, but he carries himself with an urban swagger that instantly sets him apart. You can tell he spends a lot of time around Black and Latino communities, and it reveals itself in the way he speaks—not in a forced, awkward, White-guy-trying-to-act-Black kind of way, but with an authentic edge that comes from real-life experience. He's real, he's raw, and he's direct. His coaching style is loud, but it's never unnecessary noise. He builds you up with positive reinforcement, fueling your confidence with the right words at the right time. But he's just as quick to cuss you out and bring your ass back down to earth when your ego needs a check. He's exactly the kind of coach I need.

Our introduction is brief, and the vibe gets awkward fast. D-Weez gives me a hug goodbye and heads back to the car, leaving me feeling slightly abandoned—like I've been dumped on an empty island and left to fend for myself. Despite my roller coaster of emotions, I try to project extreme confidence.

Coach Cox and I head into the equipment room to get me sized up. And when I say "equipment room," I mean an old storage room converted into a makeshift space for JV and Varsity football gear. Standing there, the reality of the situation begins to set in. The excitement that had fueled my imagination all morning crashes hard against the sight of this makeshift room. It's a blow to the image I had in my head. I'm faced with the harsh truth that nothing is ever as perfect as you envision it, and this realization feels like a gut punch, stripping away any trace of my naive expectations.

As I stand at the foot of the door, peering into the equipment room, I see helmets hanging from nails on the far side of the wall. Shelves are overflowing with massive piles of shoulder pads, haphazardly crammed into every available inch, teetering on the edge as if one wrong move could send them toppling down.

As I absorb the reality of this cramped space, my eyes lock on the shoulder pads, and suddenly, it hits me. I'm really about to get my own. They look much bigger and way more clunky in person.

As I snap back into focus, I notice the rest of the space around me. Boxes are scattered across the floor, twisting the narrow pathways into a maze. Each step requires careful navigation, and I can't even begin to guess what's packed inside of them. The entire space feels suffocated by clutter, with gear piled up in every corner, making the room feel smaller with every glance.

I think my immature mind envisioned a grand, pristine equipment room where helmets hang from the wall, buffed and polished, sparkling with a finishing touch. Shoulder pads would be stacked neatly, like rows of perfectly aligned books on a shelf, each one waiting to be picked up and put to use. Everything would have its place, organized and spotless, reflecting the pride and precision I associated with football. Instead, I'm standing in this cramped room, surrounded by a mess that's a far cry from the flawless image in my head.

Coach Cox grabs a helmet off the wall and says, "Here, try this one on." There's no measuring of my head. It's clear I'm gonna stand here trying on helmets one by one until we find one that fits. When we finally do, we pump it with air until it's nice and snug.

At first, it feels kind of heavy on my head. The pressure from the air forces the padding across the front of the helmet to dig into my forehead—hella uncomfortable. The bars on the face mask obstruct my view, and I feel uneasy about the way it restricts my peripheral vision.

The maroon paint on the helmet that once represented the school's colors is a distant memory, and it's now severely chipped all over, like the previous owner might have been in multiple head-on collisions. Maybe even a car accident. And given the condition of the helmet, he may not have survived it.

Once my helmet is situated, we move on to shoulder pads, using the same strategy. I try on pads, one by one, jumping up and down and making quick cuts to see how they feel. Not surprisingly, everything feels way too big. They slide around on my back and flap heavily on my shoulders.

This can't be right, I think. That morning I'd woken up so excited to join the team, to finally get my gear. But nothing is playing out like I thought it would. The field is shitty. The equipment is worse. And yet somehow, I know I'm exactly where I'm supposed to be.

*   *   *

Back on the field, my helmet padding is still digging into my forehead. My shoulder pads slide around, but at least now I have a practice jersey doing a decent job of holding them down. I'm uneasy about the flapping sound of the pads when I move, and I'm still concerned about my face mask messing with my vision.

I do my best to blend in with the other players who are transitioning from one drill to another. The skill position players go one way, while the linemen go the other. I follow them over to where several cones are set up for the next drill.

I recognize this drill from flag football. The offensive player starts with the ball, and his job is to make the defender miss and get through the cones without getting his flag pulled. At least, that's how it worked in flag football. I've done this drill before and always excelled at it, but never with pads on or someone trying to tackle me.

Still, I know what I'm capable of. I've been shaking defenders for as long as I can remember, and there isn't a better way to show this team what I can do. My nerves are steady, replaced by a quiet confidence that builds with every passing second. A tiny smile forms beneath my face mask.

The first runner makes a feeble attempt to get past the defender. It's as if he has bricks zip-tied across the top of his cleats, forcing him to slog forward. The weight of those invisible bricks slows him down with every step, making his legs look heavy as he gives his best attempt to juke left then right.

The defender, awkward and clumsy at best, lurches forward with flailing arms and very little coordination. He charges toward the ball carrier as if he already expects to miss the tackle. If I'm honest, they both look terrible, and the exchange is lackluster. It's the same with the second and third runners. Everyone looks awful. It's embarrassing. I start to wonder if getting past these cones might be a lot harder in pads than it was with just a flag.

Several coaches hover around the drill to observe the talent pool. Each leans forward with hands on their knees, whistles dangling from their mouths, awaiting some sort of fireworks that just aren't happening.

Now it's my turn. I jog over to my position and pick up the ball. I pop in my mouthpiece and place the tip of the ball firmly in my palm, using my forearm and bicep to secure a better grip. I take my stance and focus on the defender, who is easily twice my size. He has no clue who I am or what I'm capable of. It feels like he doesn't want to go up against me because I'm so small, like he thinks he's gonna hurt me or something. This really pisses me off. It makes me want to earn the respect of my teammates even more.

I'm focused, waiting for the whistle. When it blows, I burst toward the defender like I've been shot out of a cannon. I fake left, then wiggle right. The defender charges at me with almost zero body control, lunging like he's gonna try to run through me. My sudden shift in direction forces him to reach for my jersey. I make one last quick move back to the left and run right past him untouched. He never even gets a finger on me.

I hear the "oohs" and "ahhs" from the sideline. I hear one of the coaches yell out, "Oh shit, he's like a little rabbit—that's Rabbit." The nickname hangs in the air. He just called me the most unthreatening, nonintimidating animal on the planet. Rabbits are skittish, harmless, and the furthest thing from a predator. Yet somehow, it was electric and alive, and it sparks an instant connection with everyone watching. It's Day 1, and I've already got a nickname.

This has to be a good sign, right?

I get back in line to await my next turn and think to myself: *Rabbit, huh? Fuck it. I can live with that.*

*   *   *

As a kid, I never doubted my ability to play football, regardless of my size. My size was never a concern for me; it was only a concern for others. Their doubts, their projections, their whispered what-ifs had no space in my world. Every time I touched the ball, something magical happened. My body instinctively knew what to do and my legs always kept pace with my mind.

Every time I was out on that field, it felt right. I felt at home. It was about not just what I could do but also how it felt when I did it. I call it being in your element, where passion and ability collide. When you're in your element, nothing else matters, and the doubts of others fade into the background.

But not everyone sees it that way. Humans have a way of projecting their own limitations onto others, defining what's possible not by someone's potential but by the boundaries of their own fears and insecurities. It's less about what we can or can't do and more about what they struggle to imagine.

The trick is simple. Refuse to accept those projections. *What others see as your weakness might just be your strength.*

When you stop letting their doubts define you, you create space to embrace your element. When you own your element, their doubts lose all power. And when they underestimate you, you have the chance to rewrite the rules in your favor.

4

A New Voice

Before this first summer camp, football is just a seasonal sport for me. I play flag football every year, which keeps me connected to the game, but it's nothing like what's coming. Until now, basketball has been a year-round commitment, offering me the chance to compete against some of the best athletes in my age group on the nation's top middle school team, the Southern Cal All-Stars (SCA). This is the same AAU program that developed NBA stars like Baron Davis and Tyson Chandler. In fact, the team I played for went on to beat LeBron James's team in the 14-and-under (14u) national championship game.

Surrounded by such elite talent in a program known for producing top-tier athletes, I began to think beyond high school, setting my sights on a college scholarship. While basketball wasn't my primary focus for a scholarship, the experience of playing AAU ball sparked that ambition within me. Basketball, my second love, was always more accessible, and through it, I started to see the bigger picture of where sports could lead me.

Heading into freshman camp, my training isn't football-specific; it's mostly basketball. I'm in great shape, but it's a different kind of shape—quick sprints up and down the court, lateral bursts, cutting and weaving through defenders, all within the comfort of an air-conditioned gym. The grind of basketball drills focuses on agility and endurance, but football demands something else entirely. The intensity and physicality of football camp is a world I have yet to step into.

This first summer camp turns out to be brutal. We practice nearly every day under the relentless Southern California sun, including during Hell Week. The difference between running suicides on the court and grinding through full-contact drills under the blistering sun quickly becomes clear.

For those unfamiliar, Hell Week is dedicated to conditioning drills where coaches intentionally push players to their limits. It's an effective method used to weed out the weak and build mental toughness and camaraderie as the team endures the pain together. I'm talking 200-yard bear crawls, 100-yard linemen's sled pushes, 100-yard sprints, and 200-yard rolls. Yes, rolls—where you lie on your stomach and roll sideways across the entire field. Performing these drills in 100-degree heat is pure torture, and frankly, this type of stuff would never fly in today's climate. But remember, this is 1999.

Although hardcore coaching isn't Coach Cox's usual style, he has it in him to put his foot in your ass when necessary. He recognizes the need to break us down that summer, making the whole experience feel like one long, grueling Hell Week.

Before we know it, it's time for the first game of the season. I'm a freshman, penciled in to start at running back for the Junior Varsity team. My best friend Devin bet me that I wouldn't score ten touchdowns that season. And I'm determined to prove him wrong.

*　　*　　*

At this time, I'm a big-time Barry Sanders fan. Naturally, I try to imitate his style. (If you don't know who Barry Sanders is, take a second, jump on YouTube, and enjoy. You're welcome!)

Barry Sanders was the starting running back for the Detroit Lions. His ability to make defenders miss was unparalleled in the NFL. He'd break off 60-yard touchdown runs that began with him running backward 5 yards. I dream of being the next Barry Sanders.

I cut back and change directions on a play, thinking:

That's what Barry would do.

Because Barry is undersized like me, watching him is a constant reminder that limitations are self-imposed. My infatuation with him makes me feel more comfortable in my own undersized body.

If Barry can do it, I can do it.

Before that first football season starts, I take a Barry Sanders hat with a "BS" on one side and the number 20 on the other. I cut them out of the hat and wear them in my socks during every game. It may not give me the magic powers I hope for, but it serves its purpose.

In my mind, I have the cheat code tucked neatly into each sock and can't be stopped. Barry gives me someone to chase. He makes me believe I can be one of the greats, regardless of what anyone else thinks. He sets a bar for me, and my goal is to blow right past it.

But even with Barry in my socks, the season is brutal. Every game is a battle. We get so close to winning but just can't seem to make it happen. Despite the grind, something else is emerging—my style of play. It's becoming electric, the kind of football that keeps people on the edge of their seats.

There isn't anything I won't try. I spin out of a tackle and then end up running backward ten yards, weaving through defenders as I search for a lane to break a big play, only to gain a yard or two in the end. Running backward on a play is a big no-no in football, but I lean into my creativity, daring to defy the norm. I'd cut back in a heartbeat, inspired by Barry's wildest plays, all stored in my memory bank of possibilities. Each move is a calculated risk, channeling the master himself. And though the wins aren't coming, I'm starting to find my own groove on the field.

In addition to the constant losing, the physical toll is something I didn't anticipate. After my first game, I'm bruised and battered, and there's a sharp and unforgiving pain in my chest, like a knife wedged between my ribs. Breathing becomes a calculated effort—every inhale feels like a stab, and every exhale is a mix of relief and dread for the next breath. It felt like a fractured rib, but I hid it from my coach, determined not to miss any games.

Rest is really the only remedy for an injury to the ribs, but sitting out isn't an option. I start wearing a rib protector vest under my pads for the second half of the season and find a way to push through the pain.

As the weeks progress, the team begins to gel. The locker room culture shifts significantly; bonding between teammates evolves into a genuine brotherhood. We learn to trust and respect one another, growing stronger as a unit.

The losing, though, is difficult to accept. I come from a winning background where my hard work has usually paid off. But our team just continues to lose. I have a couple of multi-touchdown games, breaking off big electrifying plays. But I finish the season with only nine touchdowns, losing the bet with Dev.

Meanwhile, our Varsity team pulls off the impossible. With 43 straight losses looming over their heads, they manage to beat Hamilton High School late in the season—a monumental win for Coach Cox.

I witness the level of commitment Coach Cox puts into that season. I see how badly he wants it and the lengths he is willing to go to achieve it. So while it's just one win, it's the biggest win of his career and a necessary step toward greatness. It also really helps to turn our football program around.

Although our JV team doesn't win a single game, the lessons I learn from those losses are invaluable. I emerge battle tested. I know there is nothing soft about me. Yes, I'm small, but I can take a hit and I'm not afraid of contact. I help lead our team, even when it feels pointless. I never quit or turn my back on my teammates. I figure out exactly the kind of player I want to be.

*   *   *

So, yeah. Eventually, I learn a lot from the losses this season. But in the moment after losing the last game of the year, I'm a mess. I'm sitting in the locker room by myself, my mind racing.

Every ... fucking ... game?

I can't believe I let this happen.

The thought of all that effort ending in another loss feels unbearable. I feel so isolated in my frustration, like I'm the only one who cares this much.

My pads sit on the bench next to me, a silent reminder of the battle I just fought. The rest of my uniform is still on; I haven't even bothered to untie my cleats yet. My helmet's spinning on the floor on the opposite side of the room where I've just thrown it against a locker. My face is buried deep in the palms of my hands, hiding the uncontrollable flow of my tears.

I can't hold in the overwhelming sense of frustration and failure that fills me. I've never lost this much at anything. And even though we've lost continuously all season long, I'd never lost hope that we might pull off one victory.

As I sit there in silence, two of my teammates walk in. One asks if I'm okay. The other is chuckling over all the games we've lost. I ignore the question and look at the asshole who's laughing. I'm shocked at the nerve of this guy.

What can he possibly find amusing? How can any of this be funny to him?

We've just dedicated the last five months of our lives to this. We've sacrificed our summer. We've practiced in 100-degree heat. And this guy is laughing while I sit here in the dark, sobbing like a baby? *Are you fucking kidding me?*

His timing is horrendous. This isn't a laughing matter to me. I lock eyes with him, spring from the bench, and lunge at him with every ounce of energy I have left. I grew up in a household with three brothers. Fighting is something I'm very comfortable with.

In our house, we fought almost daily. With four competitive boys living under one roof, you could find almost anything to throw hands over. From losing a game of HORSE in the backyard to who ate the last Pop-Tart. Usually, three of us brothers would band together and roast the lone wolf who'd wind up catching rounds from all angles. Sometimes even D-Weez joined in on the roasting sessions with the other three, usually putting the icing on the cake. You had to have extremely thick skin in my house. I was small but feisty and not easily triggered.

But on this day, in the locker room, I'm a ticking time bomb. And this kid's untimely laughter lights the fuse. I snatch him up, take him down to the ground, and put him in a headlock. The other teammate does his best to break it up as Coach Cox races in the door. He grabs my arm and leads me outside.

I prepare myself for a lecture on leadership, on my behavior, on how I need to control my emotions. But it doesn't come. Instead, Coach Cox puts his arm around my shoulder and asks if I'm okay. I launch into my frustrations, explaining how much I care, and how badly I wanted to help turn things around this season. I'm embarrassed that he's seeing me like this. I don't want him to think that I'm unstable—an emotional wreck who fights with his teammates when things get difficult. So I take a minute to apologize for my behavior.

Coach Cox listens, then advises me not to dwell on the past. What he says next catches me completely off guard. I see his lips moving, but the words don't seem to connect. It sounds like he's saying, "You're with me next season." That can't be right. I pause, my mind scrambling to process the information. "Can you repeat that?" I ask, hoping my ears aren't deceiving me. He repeats, clearer this time, "You're with me next season."

As his words float in the air, puzzling yet exhilarating, I echo him, still grappling with the reality, "With you next season?"

"Yes, on the Varsity team," he confirms with a nod.

I'm floored. Coach Cox is all praises, acknowledging my grind and the way I handle business on the field. He's straight up with me, saying my size doesn't mean anything to him. He sees me as a major contributor in turning this program around. The future of Fairfax Football.

In that moment, I feel an unexpected shift. This kind of support is huge. It's like Coach Cox is saying, "I believe in you. I see something in you that you don't fully see in yourself yet." His words hit me harder than any tackle—it's the validation I didn't even know I was searching for.

I hadn't really considered playing Varsity football as a sophomore. It's not common for underclassmen to make the jump to Varsity so fast. Especially at my size. Although I've never let my size limit my ambitions, I assumed I'd be spending another season on the JV team to bulk up and hone my skills as a football player.

Coach Cox doesn't seem to care. His confidence in me is unwavering. It's clear he's given this a lot of thought. But then again, he hasn't discussed it with my mom yet. He can't possibly be prepared for how she's going to respond.

*   *   *

There's something you need to know about my mom. She's extremely overprotective. My mom is the most loving, caring, and affectionate person I know. She loves her children more than anything on this planet and would give up her life for ours in a heartbeat. But sometimes, her parenting can get in the way.

Because I'm much smaller than the other kids, my mom's always been fearful of me getting hurt, especially when it comes to football. That's why I was never allowed to play tackle football growing up—only flag football.

Coach Cox isn't just tasked with getting me ready physically and mentally for the next season; he's also burdened with convincing my mom I'm ready and capable of playing at the varsity level.

I've always been confident in my football abilities. Every time I stepped onto the field, I knew what I was capable of. But for some reason, at this point, the nonstop talk about my size finally begins to weigh on me. It's like a seed has been quietly planted without my knowing. For the first time in my life, I start to hear a voice in my head that I'm unfamiliar with: doubt.

The voice is cruel, whispering things in my ear I've never heard before—chilling and unfamiliar. *You're too small. You'll never be able to keep up. They're bigger, stronger, faster. Are you sure you're ready?* Over time, that voice grows louder and louder, but for now, it's just a whisper—a whisper that I can't seem to ignore.

Eventually, Coach Cox, D-Weez, and my mom come to an agreement. I can play varsity football, but Coach has to monitor the number of touches I get per game. I can't believe this is actually a thing, but it is. My mom literally has a conversation with my high school varsity football coach about how many times I can get the ball. *You've got to be shitting me!*

I play basketball and baseball during the off-season of my freshman year to keep myself busy. Once summer camp comes back around to kick off my sophomore season, I'm ready to go. And the stakes are high after the Varsity team has finally won its first game in years.

I'm now a whopping 5'4" and 130 pounds. Yeah, I grew an inch and put on five pounds. Whoop-de-doo. The confidence Coach Cox shows in me helps me make a seamless transition onto the Varsity team. He expects fireworks every time I touch the ball. So that's what I expect of myself.

That summer, I prove to be just as slippery on the field as I've always been. I manage to get through all of summer camp without heavy contact or any head-on collisions. If I can't make them miss, I go down to the ground a split second before contact. For me, this is an effective tactic that ruins the would-be tackler's attempt at a big-time hit on me.

But as our first game gets closer, that unfamiliar whisper of doubt in my head gets louder. And a hell of a lot more cunning.

5
Get Hit

It's the night before my first Varsity football game. I'm in my top bunk in the room I share with my little brother Donovan. The TV is off, and the fan in the corner of the room oscillates back and forth. I find myself focusing on the rhythm of the soft creaking sound it makes as it moves.

I'm completely still, my blanket pulled all the way up to my neck. My focus shifts to the light bulb on the ceiling. My mind is racing, and before I know it, I'm in a stare-down with this light bulb. I can't sleep. I stare at the light bulb for hours.

At some point, I finally realize I'm having a full-blown panic attack. I can't move. My mouth is dry, and I'm struggling to swallow. Spit collects in the corners of my mouth, and I don't think I've blinked for what feels like hours. My sheets are drenched in sweat.

I can't believe this is happening. Not once in my 15 years of life have I ever felt anything like this. The voice in my ear isn't whispering. It's not even talking. It's a full-blown scream. It muscles its way through the joy football usually brings me. All I can think about is getting hurt. When I close my eyes, I envision myself running full speed with the ball and getting hit so hard my pads unbuckle and my helmet pops off.

And then, as if the visions weren't enough, the flood of doubt rushes in, each thought hammering away at my confidence.

You can't do it.

This isn't like any game I've played before. I'm stepping into a world where everything is bigger, faster, and more brutal. What if I'm just not cut out for this?

You're not fast enough.

Speed has always been my advantage, but now I'm up against guys who are three years older, stronger, and fully developed. I've barely hit puberty. What if my speed isn't enough to keep up with these guys? What if it fails to translate at this level?

You're not big enough.

I'm painfully aware of how small I am compared to the guys I'll be facing. Their size alone could crush me. How can I compete with that?

You're going to get hurt. You'll never survive this.

The thought is relentless. I've seen the brutal hits, the injuries that leave players down and struggling to get up. The fear grips me: What if I'm not as tough as I've always thought I was? What if I don't make it through the season?

This level of fear that I feel is unlike anything I've ever experienced. It has a crippling effect on my confidence. I try to remember some of my best plays from last year. I try to sell myself on the idea that I am capable of playing at a very high level. But it doesn't work. I'm paralyzed. I start concocting a plan to get me out of playing in tomorrow's game.

While all of this is going on, I remain completely still. Completely silent. Looking at me, you'd never know I'm going through World War III in my mind. That my brain is executive producing a blood-stained battle of will versus fear. And that fear is kicking my ass.

I finally blink, and suddenly, it's morning. I've only managed to get about 15 minutes of sleep. My head feels heavy and my lower back is tight. Forcing myself out of bed feels like a micro-win. All I want to do is pull the covers up over my head and disappear. But my first Varsity football game is today, and my team is counting on me.

*   *   *

As soon as I get to school, the countdown begins. I stare at the clock in each class, feeling like I'm on death row, counting down the minutes to my execution. I'm so convinced I'm gonna get hurt that with every passing second, the pain feels more and more real.

The game's gonna be played at Jordan High School, which somehow makes matters worse. It's located in Watts, one of the most violent, gang-infested areas in Los Angeles. I've grown up hearing horror stories about Watts. This isn't me taking shots at Watts either. Nothing's ever that black-and-white. But in my 15-year-old mind, we're heading into a war zone. I picture their players being mean, aggressive, and extremely physical. I imagine the violence that once consumed the city revealing itself in their style of play.

As if to confirm my fears, when our bus exits the freeway, we need a police escort into the school. I can't believe this shit. Two cops on motorcycles lead our bus through the front gate toward the football field.

Should I tell Coach I'm sick and can't play?

Should I fake an ankle injury and start limping?

I need to get out of this. I've got to find a way out of this.

But quitting is a slippery slope. If I back out this time, it'll make it easy to back out of anything that makes me uncomfortable.

Running at the first sign of fear could become my new normal. Quitting might become my natural response to this voice of doubt in my ear. I can't let that become part of my DNA. I refuse to become synonymous with the words *I quit*, so I strap on my pads and tie my cleats.

My second micro-win of the day.

Then, it's game time. I'm the starting kick returner. We win the coin toss and elect to receive the ball. *Shit—just my luck, I'm up.* I run slowly onto the field to take my position, chomping down on my mouthpiece like it's chewing gum. I reach through my facemask and swipe away the sweat stinging my eyes. Once they're clear, I peer across the field to size up my competition. I look for the biggest, most intimidating figure on Jordan's kickoff team. Someone who stands out for their size and fearsome appearance.

Found him.

Fuck, he's huge.

My heart's racing. I can't stop my body from swaying back and forth. I try to appear calm and collected, but deep down inside, I'm a scared little boy.

Before I realize it's happened, the Jordan kicker drives his foot into the ball with an echoing thud, sending it directly toward me. It moves through the air in slow motion.

Oh my God.

The ball falls right out of the sky, landing directly in my arms. I leverage my pads to secure the catch without fumbling the ball. Then I tuck it into my arm and take off running like a bat out of hell. I can hear the sound of helmets violently clashing, reminding me that this is not a dream—this is actually happening. As I sprint at full speed, a trail of dust follows each step as my cleats dig into the dirt-heavy field.

My instincts take over. I close in on the wedge my offensive blockers have created for me and realize there's no hole for me to run through. I can feel the defensive players closing in, but I stay the course, scanning for a lane to squeeze my 5'4" frame through.

But the window isn't there. I feel like a kamikaze pilot, flying at full speed toward my inevitable death.

Suddenly, a forceful *crack* rings through my ears, echoing in my helmet. I tense up, gripping onto the ball with both hands and every ounce of strength I have. Holding on to it for dear life.

It takes me a second to regain my senses. When I force open my eyes, I am buried beneath a pile of defensive players three times my size. I hear the distant sound of a ref blowing a whistle. It dawns on me that the play is finally over.

I pop up off the ground, toss the ball to the referee, and stand there in shock. I'm confused, desperately trying to make sense of what just happened. Not only do I seem to have survived the play, but all of my limbs are still intact. My helmet is still on. My pads are still buckled tight.

Wait a minute ... Is that it?

Are you kidding me? Is that really it?

I'd just taken Jordan High School's best shot, a blindside hit I didn't see coming. And I was still alive.

That can't be it. How can that be the hit I agonized over all night? The one where my helmet goes flying, along with my mouthpiece, my pads, and I almost die? The hit that almost drove me to fake an ankle injury or create an illness to get out of playing the game?

I look down at my legs and give them each a quick wiggle to see if I'm missing something. I shake both arms, flexing my fingers to see if the injury is there, but my adrenaline is somehow masking the pain. I roll my neck clockwise, then counterclockwise, waiting to feel the hurt. But no; there's nothing, I mean, a-b-s-o-l-u-t-e-l-y nothing wrong with me.

I smile. Or maybe, I actually smirk. I've just had a profound breakthrough. What Oprah would call an "Aha" moment.

Though I can't quite articulate it yet, the 24 hours I've just lived through completely change my life and help me better understand my relationship with fear for years to come.

*   *   *

That hit, the one I had agonized over all night, turned out to be nothing. Getting hit showed me that fear itself was the real opponent. Fear thrives in inaction, but *action creates insight*. By engaging, by doing, we unlock a deeper understanding of our capabilities. The act of pushing forward reveals the truth. Most fears are paper tigers, illusions that fade when confronted.

Fear is often defined as an unpleasant emotion caused by the belief that something is dangerous, is likely to cause pain, or is a threat. For me, fear wasn't just a word or concept. It was something I felt in my body, something that took over when I faced the unknown. Most of my run-ins with fear up until that game came from moments where I lacked the knowledge or experience to understand what I was stepping into. Fear felt so real to me that it triggered a full-body panic attack and made me contemplate faking an injury and even quitting football.

What I didn't realize then is that fear isn't a sign of weakness; it's just our brain's way of trying to protect us. Neuroscience backs this up. The amygdala, a key part of the brain responsible for processing fear, categorizes unfamiliar or challenging situations as potential threats, triggering a fight-or-flight response. This survival instinct, though well-intentioned, isn't always helpful. Understanding this gave me a new perspective: fear wasn't my enemy. It was simply my brain doing its job.

But fear doesn't play fair. It crafts vivid illusions, worst-case scenarios, and paralyzing doubts to keep us safe. My brain wanted to protect me, but its dirty tricks nearly cost me the chance to chase my dreams.

This is when I learned the power of small, intentional wins. Each micro-win—stepping out of bed, suiting up, running onto the field—stacked into a breakthrough moment that rewrote my relationship with fear.

Getting hit that day wasn't about football. It was about facing every thought that whispered: *You can't.* It was about challenging the doubts that tried to limit me.

The key is this:

- Face your fears head-on. Don't let them dictate your actions.
- Stack those micro-wins. Small victories build the foundation for life-changing breakthroughs.
- Embrace the "get hit" moment. It's often in those moments that you realize just how capable you truly are.
- Remember that activity creates insight. Action is the antidote to fear.

Life will throw challenges your way, and you'll face situations in which doubt whispers: *Run.* But here's what I know for sure: When you choose to get hit, when you lean into fear instead of running from it, you discover the magic and power on the other side. That's how you win the battle against fear. One hit, one moment, one action at a time.

6

Be Obsessed, or Be Average

My sophomore football season on the Varsity team doesn't turn out the way I hope. While my "get hit" breakthrough profoundly impacts my mindset, things on the field don't change much. Our team struggles all season. I dream of dominating every game, manhandling my competition the way I once did in flag football. But that just isn't the case. On so many occasions, I am inches away from that huge, game-changing play my team desperately needs, but I fall short time and time again.

There are moments when I flash signs of greatness. I turn broken plays into electrifying runs, stopping on a dime to change direction, causing defenders to collide while reaching for my jersey and grabbing nothing but air. Numerous times, I start off running to the right side of the field, only to cut back and sprint to the left, making multiple defenders miss along the way.

But somehow, when it's time to kick it into another gear to finish the play, I'm missing that burst. My short, stocky legs lack the power and stride to gallop past that last defensive player between me and the end zone.

We do win three games that season, two more than the year before. I make second-team all-city, an award highlighting me as one of the top players in L.A., slowly gaining recognition as a wide receiver/running back with a bright future. College coaches even start asking questions about me. If I'm going to impress them, I'm going to have to dig deep during the off-season to tap into something else. I've got to find another gear.

I've always equated success with the idea of handing my mother the keys to a brand-new house. Seeing my mom work tirelessly for Ryan and me as a single parent before D-Weez became my stepdad was impossible to ignore. She did whatever it took to provide us with an amazing life, and at an early age, I felt a responsibility to pay it forward. I wanted to show her how grateful I was, acknowledging the hard work and sacrifice she endured by always putting us first. I would hear stories about athletes buying their parents mansions as their first big purchase after going pro, and I knew instantly that's what I wanted to do. For the first time in my young life, I start to see a road map to achieving that goal. I pay no mind to naysayers. Getting a Division I scholarship becomes my sole focus.

*   *   *

That focus drives every decision I make, and running track during the off-season becomes my secret weapon. It forces me to refine my form, shifting from running tight and rigid, with my shoulders drawn back and my chest pushed out, to running with ease and fluidity. The harder I tried before, the slower I seemed to move. But now, I've learned to relax, releasing the tension in my upper body and in my face, allowing my stride to open up naturally.

I begin to sprint with a smooth rhythm, making each step more powerful and efficient. My short, stocky legs, which once felt like they were fighting against me, now seem to fly across the track. Running track helps me develop the power and fast twitch muscles my lower body desperately needs to finish off those big plays I'm so close to making. It's not just my body that's transforming. This process is a testament to the discipline I've built over years of hard work.

I've always been a workhorse. I pride myself on being the first person on the field and the last to leave. If we're running conditioning drills, I want to finish first every time. If the team is slipping, I step up as a vocal leader to inspire everyone to go harder. For me, it's all about discipline, and I find that few around me are willing to make the sacrifices this mindset requires.

Which leads me to Sand Dune Park—a big-ass, 100-foot mountain of sand. Our running backs coach, Coach Redmond, suggests that I should do some extra training by waking up early and running up the massive dune in the morning before school.

So one day, I decide to do it. I feel a strong pull to test myself, to go beyond what's expected. It isn't just about physical tough-ness; it's about proving something to myself, about pushing my boundaries. It becomes a symbol for me, a symbol of mental toughness and commitment. I know no other kids in the city are crazy enough take on something like this. My hope is that if I make the dune a consistent part of my routine, it will help separate me from the pack.

*   *   *

People are quick to complain about the lack of time they have. In reality, if you wake up earlier, you can fit almost anything into your day. Hearing about people like Mark Wahlberg, who reportedly wakes up at 2:30 a.m. every day to lift weights, makes me realize how much more I can accomplish if I commit to using those early hours.

That's when I started teaming up with my friend, UCLA basketball great Josh Shipp. Josh lived five minutes away and was the definition of a gym rat. He never shied away from a workout, especially the grueling ones. At 4:15 a.m., I'd pick him up, and we'd head for the dune to get a session in before school.

Standing at the bottom, looking up, I'd always feel intimidated and immediately humbled. Full of respect. The early morning mist made the sand cold and wet between my toes. The air was thin and brisk, and my every breath was visible in the night sky. There was just enough light from a streetlight to make me feel safe and alert.

I'd tilt my head up to focus on the finish line. Although there was often a thin layer of fog floating around the top like a halo, there was nothing angelic about any of it. Gazing up at The Beast of a man-made mountain, I'd often question whether it was worth it.

It's cold outside. It's dark outside.
Everyone I know is sound asleep in their warm beds.
Why am I doing this again?
What is all of this for?

Then I'd gather my thoughts and remind myself that it was about so much more than gaining speed. It was about showing myself the lengths I was willing to go to, to make my dreams come true.

Josh and I push each other relentlessly, urging each other to go harder, to do more. Cones are spread out every ten yards, leading all the way up to the top of the dune. We run suicide drills, starting with a sprint to the first cone, then back down to the bottom. Then we sprint to the second cone, and back down again. We repeat this for each cone, working our way up the dune, one cone at a time, until we finally reach the top.

The sand shifts beneath our feet with each step, sinking us deeper with every stride, adding to the grueling challenge. It's like running through wet cement. More than once, I find myself bent over, hands on my knees, the taste of that morning's breakfast lingering in my mouth as I throw up on the side of the mountain. Josh stands nearby, recovering with his hands on his hips, laughing at me while he fights to catch his breath.

But once we reach the top of the dune, everything else fades away. The view is breathtaking—a panoramic shot of the ocean stretching out before us, the cool morning air mixing with the warmth of the rising sun. Sand Dune Park is just a two-minute walk from Manhattan Beach, and as we stand there, drenched in sweat and covered in sand, we take a moment to soak it all in. We talk about our future, about the next level, fantasizing about the possibilities that lie ahead.

After the workout, we shower and head to school, where we exchange knowing smiles in the hallways. We don't brag about it to our teammates, and most of the time, we don't even talk about it. There's something magical about keeping it just between the two of us, a shared experience that bonds us in ways words never could.

The school year eventually comes to an end, and our 4:15 a.m. run-ins with The Beast end too. Summer football camp is approaching, and it's time to gear up for my junior football season. I've put in the work, pushed my body to new limits, and it's time to see how my commitment to The Beast will pay off.

*   *   *

From the first practice, it's clear something has shifted. My body feels stronger, my movements are sharper, and I'm faster than I've ever been. By the time the season kicks off, I feel more like a senior than a junior. My confidence is through the roof, and on the field, I'm virtually unstoppable.

It's clear I've developed and gotten better. I'm faster, stronger, and smarter on the field. My instincts are sharp, and I'm fearless in my attempts to pull off big, game-changing plays. My mom is no longer worried about how many times I get the ball. That silly arrangement with Coach Cox was so last year. This year, the mantra is: *Give me the fucking ball!*

I'd grown an inch that off-season and put on a whopping five pounds, putting me at 5'5" and 135 pounds. Still small, still light, but unpredictable and elusive. The Rabbit puts on a show all season long. Fairfax fans hold their breath every time the ball is in my hands, knowing I'm just a step away from breaking a long one for a touchdown. I have multiple two- to three-touchdown games, and in one game, I score four touchdowns in the second half alone. I'm finishing my runs and rarely getting caught from behind like the year before. I'm faster than ever and feel like I'm reaping the rewards of my hard work.

The year 2001 is a golden era of high school football in California, with an unmatched depth of talent spread across the state. It's an exciting time to be in the mix, especially as the top two high school teams in the nation, Long Beach Poly and De La Salle, are set to clash in a nationally televised championship game. De La Salle hasn't lost a game in nearly nine years, holding an incredible 116-game winning streak, while Long Beach Poly is known for producing more NFL players than any other school in the state.

With no social media to showcase their talents, access to see these players in action was limited, adding to their legend. Stories about their skills passed through households like a game of telephone—each retelling a little stronger, a little different than the last—only fueling the excitement and mystique surrounding this showdown.

*　　*　　*

My family and I gather around the television to watch the game. Our family friend and mentor, Coach Kevin Bell, is there too. Coach Bell is bald, with a big gap between his front teeth and an energy that fills the room. There's something about the way he moves and speaks that can be intimidating, even when he isn't trying to be. When he speaks, it's from deep within his chest and out the back of his throat. Every sound that comes out is loud, raspy, and intentional, often sounding like he's yelling—sort of like Oscar the Grouch, obnoxious but consistently entertaining.

He's a passionate man dedicated to kids and to being a great dad and a great coach. He'd coached me in basketball as a kid, and we had one of the nation's best fifth-grade teams. As a coach, he didn't coddle us. I remember one practice when I turned the ball over, accidentally passing it to the other team. Coach Bell grabbed my arm, pulling me toward where the ball should have gone. Being a mama's boy and slightly embarrassed, I started to cry right there on the court. Coach Bell made me play through my emotions. There was no babying: I had to wipe my tears with my jersey and suck it up.

But he wasn't demeaning; he set a high standard for me and held me accountable. He'd treated me like one of his sons, fueling me with confidence, and he had always been one of my biggest supporters. Though he coached me hard, he always brought out the best in me.

When the championship game starts, we're all thrown off by a player who resembles Barry Sanders, only shorter. He was slightly taller than me, but he has tree trunks for legs and grown man biceps. His name, Maurice Drew, appears in big bold letters on the TV screen. He's a junior, and a running back just like me. But this kid looks ready for the NFL right now.

Every time he gets the ball, it's magical. Maurice makes play after play, and each time he does, Coach Bell glances my way. I see him in my peripheral vision, but I never give him the satisfaction of knowing I know he's looking at me and what his looks might imply.

When Maurice eludes a defender, bulldozes his way through one of the state's top safeties, and then leaps into the air and hits a full-on front flip as he scores a touchdown, my living room erupts. Coach Bell turns his head, looks straight at me, and yells, "Ferguson, are you watching this shit? This cat is different—he's doing something that you're not doing. Just look at him!"

Suddenly, my work ethic is on trial, and everyone in my living room is the jury. Coach Bell is sitting in a foldable chair that looks like it's struggling to bear his weight. He leans forward with intensity, as he barks in my ear. I'm sitting on the carpet, knees bent, arms wrapped tightly around them, trying desperately to block him out. I can feel the heat of his breath on my cheek, every word hitting me like a jab to the face. The living room all of a sudden feel really small.

Now, every time Maurice touches the ball, Coach Bell tosses out a wild suggestion, making it clear he's trying to light a fire under me.

What are you still doing here, Ferguson? You should be outside right now, running laps around the block.

Haven't you seen enough?

I lock in on the TV, refusing to meet his gaze. But his voice is relentless, almost impossible to ignore.

He leans in closer, still seated, and throws out another challenge. "You should be running home from school in your shoulder pads after practice, after conditioning drills. You don't need a ride home; you should be running."

I keep my expression blank, but inside, I'm thinking, *Is he out of his mind? I live nearly three miles away. What the hell is he talking about?* I try my hardest to block him out, willing myself to stay quiet, hoping that if I don't engage, he'll eventually stop.

But he doesn't. Instead, he starts to get up, his voice rising as he continues, "You should be waking up in the morning at 4 a.m. before school, running sand dunes. I don't care if it's the middle of the season—are you really gonna let this kid out-dawg you?"

Oh, hell no. I literally did that all off-season, and now he's using it against me?

At this point, he's fully out of his seat, playing to the room, and with a dramatic, comedic tone, he looks at D-Weez and says, "Danny, get ya boy, he should be out in the middle of the street right now, pushing a tire down the street with his forehead!"

Behind me, I can hear my brothers laughing, their muffled giggles slicing through my concentration. I can't see them, but I know they're getting a kick out of this, which only makes it worse. The life drains from my face as I try to hide the effect this ambush is having on me, but it's useless.

I can't help but feel irritated. This was supposed to be a fun afternoon with the fam, and now somehow the attention is all on me. It's the back end of my junior football season, and I'm one of the most electrifying players in the city. Coach Bell doesn't give a damn about any of that. He's determined to make his point.

* * *

As I lay my head on my pillow that night, I can't get Coach Bell's voice out of my head. I start to question my work ethic, second-guessing everything.

Is Coach Bell right?

What is this kid doing that I'm not?

I start replaying the season in my mind. I haven't realized how content I've become. I've worked hard—there's no doubt about that—but maybe I'm not pushing myself as much as I could be. The success of the season somehow made me feel like I am doing enough.

I didn't consciously decide to stop putting in the extra work. The wear and tear of the season took its toll, and I didn't even realize I'd let my foot off the gas. All of a sudden, I'm questioning my mindset—coming to grips with the reality that I've gotten far too comfortable with my success. The truth is a real pain in the ass. Somehow, deep down in your soul, you always know the truth when you hear it. You can fight it or mask it with positive self-talk, but the truth just sits there, waiting to be acknowledged.

I've always known that even though I've pushed myself hard, there's a kid out there who's working harder. While other kids talk about the work they're putting in, that kid is grinding. While other kids feel entitled and plead for what they think they deserve, that kid is grinding. While other kids complain about anything that doesn't go their way, that kid is grinding. And today, it felt like got to witness "that kid" in action.

I toss and turn all night, obsessing over Maurice's workouts. What is this guy doing? Whatever it was, I was simply gonna have to do more. It wasn't complicated. I was gonna have to empty the tank. I spend half the night planning to do this, just to show other people that I'm made from the same stuff Maurice is. But by morning, I realize I'm gonna have to do it for myself. I'm gonna have to do it for my future.

Some of what Coach Bell had suggested was ridiculous. Pushing a tire down the street with my forehead? The image actually cracks me up. But the other two suggestions are great ideas. So the next day, after practice and conditioning drills, my teammates head to the locker room, but I don't. I keep my shoulder pads on, strap my backpack over my pads, and run the three miles home.

Halfway home, a random car honks at me. Startled, I turn to see if I'm in the way, only to find the driver clapping, cheering me on. That honk feels like a sign from the football gods, saying, "Yes, young man. Now you're on to something. Now you're thinking big. Now you get it. Keep going."

I'm big on signs and nonverbal cues. I believe that when you truly pay attention, the universe will send gentle nudges of confirmation your way. Reminders to continue on the path you're on. Well, I don't miss this one. That guy honking his horn fuels me. It invigorates me to double down on what I'm doing. The rest of the run home, I don't think about anything but Maurice Drew. I don't care how crazy I look or how tired I am; I just run. One foot in front of the other, and eventually, I make it home, where I drop to the ground.

I lay there in my shoulder pads like I'm making a snow angel. Too tired to move a muscle. I live in my head for 30 minutes, focusing solely on my future. Exhausted, breathing heavily, with sweat dripping down my face, I see the stadium. I see myself running onto the field. I hear the crowd roar for me. I know without a doubt that's my future.

The next morning, I wake at 4:00 a.m. and am back at the sand dune, back to battling The Beast. This time, I'm by myself. All in on Coach Bell's workout plan of doing something different. Knowing that while deploying this level of grind will make my body stronger, the true benefits will be in my mindset.

Oh, and "that kid" Maurice Jones-Drew went on to be an All-Pro running back, playing in the NFL for nine seasons and setting multiple records for the Jacksonville Jaguars.

*   *   *

Watching Maurice that day inspired me to find another gear. Between his dominance on the field and Coach Bell's ability to strike a nerve and light a fire, something inside me shifted.

I went on to finish my junior season with 24 touchdowns and over 3,000 all-purpose yards, marking me as an undeniable force on the field. The sheer number of touchdowns highlighted my knack for making crucial plays and consistently adding to the scoreboard. Meanwhile, racking up over 3,000 yards in various roles showcased my versatility and constant threat in multiple areas of the game.

My achievements didn't go unnoticed. I was named First-Team All-League and Offensive Player of the Year in my conference, cementing my status as one of the top players in the area. On top of that, I earned First-Team All-City honors as a running back, wide receiver, and return man, proving I could dominate against the best talent L.A. had to offer.

The results of all my hard work were tangible, not just on tape but also in the most important way possible. I started getting recruited by several big-time college football programs: Nebraska, UCLA, and Washington, to name a few. But my dream school was still USC. I was determined to make them notice me.

By then, I had learned the formula for success, and it was simple: Be obsessed, or be average. That obsession, however, wasn't just about stacking stats or impressing scouts. Those goals lit the fire, but they weren't the endgame. Pushing myself to the limit became a way to transform, to build a stronger and more resilient version of myself. Every yard I gained and every touchdown I scored wasn't just proof of my talent; it was evidence that obsession, when paired with purpose, could fuel something extraordinary.

Looking back, I realize this lesson wasn't just about football. It was about life. It was about understanding that *the line between extraordinary and average is razor-thin,* and crossing it requires a level of commitment most people shy away from.

Being obsessed isn't just about working harder. It's about pouring your whole self into the things that matter most. It's about having a vision so clear that it pushes you to grind when others rest, to keep going when most would quit.

And that's what obsession really is: a relentless commitment to your vision, your purpose, and your future. It's what separates those who dream from those who achieve.

If you hold onto anything from this chapter, let it be this:

Obsession, when channeled with purpose, is your greatest weapon. It allows you to break through barriers and unlock levels of performance you didn't know were possible.

Without direction, obsession can burn you out or pull you away from what truly matters. To make it your weapon, you need clarity, a vision that guides your effort and keeps you aligned with your values.

Commit fully, not halfway. Leave no room for excuses, hesitation, or mediocrity.

Being obsessed isn't just a choice; it's a mindset. When you embrace it with purpose, it becomes the fuel that drives you to levels you never thought possible. The question isn't whether you can be unstoppable; it's whether you're willing to commit to the vision that demands you to be.

7

You Want to Make God Laugh?

College recruiting is different in 2002. Colleges mail out letters, selling you on why their school is the right decision for you and encouraging you through generic messages they send to every single player they are considering. But the special ones show up as handwritten notes. They are personalized. Someone has taken time to sit down and write something just for you.

It's incredible when these letters start showing up. They do so much for my confidence, serving as a reminder to keep pushing, keep believing, keep reaching for my dream.

The first letter I ever receive marks the beginning of it all. Coach Cox is in his usual spot at the front of the locker room, cracking jokes with every player who walks in. In his right hand, he's holding a stack of envelopes, the kind I've seen him hand out to seniors being recruited.

I nod "What's up," then try to slip by him, but he stops me and hands me an envelope. I take it, a bit surprised, and flip it over to see who it is from. There it is, a big purple *W*. It is a letter from the University of Washington. Suddenly, it all feels real; the process has begun, and I am officially a part of it.

I dash into the locker room and tear open the envelope like a six-year-old tearing into a long-awaited birthday gift. The letter is generic, clearly, but that doesn't matter. I am on their radar now, one crucial step closer to the next level.

Over time, I start getting 15 to 20 letters a day from college programs all over the country. I keep them in a shoebox, and the feeling I get from peering into that box is insane. Oregon State, UCLA, Nebraska, San Diego State, Nevada. I've spent my childhood fantasizing about being recruited, and now here I am, looking through hundreds of letters from schools all around the country. Something is happening. I can feel it. Man, it's exciting!

Before I know it, coaches start randomly showing up on campus. One day I'm sitting in class, my face buried in my hands, fighting desperately to stay awake. I'm tucked in the back corner of the room, which usually offers some cover if I doze off or zone out. Today, though, the dimly lit room and the monotonous tone of my teacher's lecture are slowly wearing me down, pulling me into a nap I'm fighting hard to resist.

Suddenly, a movement by the door catches my eye. I turn and notice Coach Cox peeking through the classroom door. I quickly straighten up, frantically trying to look alert. I can see my classmate subtly swiping at me, trying to catch my attention, unaware that I have already seen Coach. I have no clue why Coach is here, and a rush of anxiety hits me as I hope I'm not in trouble.

Coach Cox scans the room, his gaze locking with mine before he signals me over. I rise slowly from my desk, stalling just enough to compose myself. As I make my way over, I notice someone else is at the foot of the door with him. He inches his way into the classroom, and I immediately recognize the mascot on his polo. It's the wide receiver coach from San Jose State.

He stopped by to evaluate "the guy" he'd seen on the highlight tape, dominating games from multiple positions. I go from fearing I might be in trouble to feeling a flood of excitement and pride. In front of the entire class, this coach is pulling me into the hallway to chat. It's epic. I feel like a rock star.

The first thing these coaches do is give you the eye test, sizing you up. I usually fail this part miserably. Seeing my size in person is always underwhelming. I once had a coach from Oregon State tell me to my face that I look more like a middle school soccer player than a football player. He said it with the tonality and timing of a comedian, so I laughed, but he wasn't trying to be funny. He was being serious.

Although these schools are impressed with my on-field play, they are concerned with my size. While they seem to be heavily recruiting me with letters, school visits, and phone calls, they aren't offering scholarships. Not surprisingly, I struggle to understand the logic. If you watch my highlight tape, it's clear that I'm the best player on the field.

I learn quickly that other players around the city are already receiving scholarship offers. Not to sound like a hater, but their tapes aren't half as good as mine, nor are their stats. This teaches me just how subjective and emotionally taxing the recruiting process can be. I work hard to not be a victim or feel entitled, but it gets more and more difficult the longer it goes on.

I somehow think that as soon as one school makes me an offer, the rest will come flowing in. But it doesn't happen like that.

One day after practice, Coach Cox hands me an envelope with a Nike swoosh on it. Inside is an invitation to a Nike Camp reserved for the state's top football players. It's held at USC, and major coaches from across the country will be in attendance. This is exactly the opportunity I need, the chance to show them what I can do and finally get their eyes on me.

These camps are perfectly set up for a player like me to thrive. My on-field play is great, but guarding me in a one-on-one setting, with no pads, no helmet, just me and a defender?

Good luck! I'm a real pain in the ass.

As I arrive at the camp, the air is charged with a competitive energy that you feel instantly. Rival school athletes, the best of the best, usually kept apart by schedules and geography, now face off on common ground. You can see the tension crackle between them as familiar faces turn into immediate rivals. The shit-talking starts the moment we step on the field—each player asserting their dominance, their words sharp, their taunts unleashed like a whip, snapping through the air with biting precision.

Even with all the noise, I can feel all of the eyeballs on me. Granted, I'm the shortest person there, sporting a huge curly afro that bounces around when I run and bright red receiver gloves that catch the light. Everyone is eager to prove themselves, not just as individuals but as representatives of their schools, and here I am, impossible to miss, ready to stake my claim.

This initial chaos is just the warm-up. As the intensity on the field builds, we transition into the day's structured series of drills. The first event is the 40-yard dash, where they gauge our speed in a straight sprint. Following that, we break into skill position groups—running backs with running backs, receivers with receivers, and so on.

We drill our footwork and run passing routes with the quarterbacks, each move scrutinized by the trained eyes of coaches and scouts. Then the real fun begins: the one-on-ones. This is where I truly shine. Running routes against the state's best defensive players becomes a mental game, where strategy intertwines with physical ability.

My height, often seen as a disadvantage, actually gives me an edge here. Being quick means defenders usually struggle to lay a hand on me, and my itty-bitty frame slips through their grasp, making me virtually unguardable.

Despite my anticipation, I wind up running an underwhelming 40-yard dash, but I shine in the individual drills. By the time the one-on-ones begin, I'm locked in, shaking off defenders left and right, some twice my size, without a single finger touching me. With each play, I hear the crowd erupting in "oohs" and "ahhs," their voices rising with every move I put on these guys. I struggle to keep a straight face, the urge to smile tugging at me, but D-Weez's voice echoes in my head: "Act like you've been here before, son."

The crowd fuels my creativity. I stick my foot in the ground, cutting as hard as I can in an attempt to destroy the poor guy in front of me.

While I'm putting on a show, I notice a kid on defense wearing bright yellow shorts who's putting on one of his own. His energy is magnetic. His confidence is through the roof. He's the best defensive player, hands down. It's not even close.

Yellow Shorts is dominating, shutting down receivers with ease. He gives them no room to breathe, no separation to even think about catching the ball. Play after play, he swats passes out of the air or forces receivers to quit mid-route. At the line of scrimmage, he muscles them up the moment the QB yells hike, jamming them so hard they can't take a step. He's not a big guy, barely 5'8", but his strength and technique make him a nightmare for anyone across from him.

Yellow Shorts is a baller, but he doesn't intimidate me. I want all the smoke. Instead of avoiding him, I cut the line, determined to match up with him on the next round. This is my chance to show him that I am cut from a different cloth and unlike anyone he has faced before.

We're up next, and you can practically feel the excitement surging from the crowd. Just as we line up, the whistle blows to signal the end of the camp.

Bruh, are you kidding me!?

I can't believe camp is ending like this, right before the main event. I'm certain I'm going to see this guy again, and when I do, it'll be the showdown everyone's been waiting for.

Despite the abrupt ending, my performance clearly leaves a mark. Nike Camp is a total success. I'm mentioned in nearly every write-up, article, and recap of the event, and I end up being the talk of the camp, along with Yellow Shorts, of course. Newspapers and sports columns are highlighting my cut-on-a-dime style of play. My reputation explodes, all from this one camp, and exposure is the name of the game. In these days without social media, getting noticed by more coaches and more programs comes down to moments like this.

Coach Cox and I devise a new plan. We're going to hit every in-person camp around the state. We're gonna give every coach who's hesitant to offer me a scholarship a chance to see just what I can do in person.

The first camp on our list is USC, my dream school. A place filled with deep tradition and rich football history. Any player would feel privileged to be mentioned in the same breath as USC, and this is my shot to show head coach Pete Carroll just what I can do. He's in the midst of creating a dominant football program that will be talked about for decades to come.

This camp starts just like the Nike Camp did, with the 40-yard dash. Because my legs are so short, it looks like I'm flying, stretching my legs out as far as they can go to cover as much ground as possible. But it's not enough. Again, my times are not impressive.

When we get to one-on-ones, though, I put on another show, electrifying the crowd. Part way through, Coach Carroll walks straight up to me.

"What a move, Fairfax," he says, ferociously chomping on a piece of gum with the left side of his mouth. "You caught the ball with your chest though, man. You gotta catch the ball with your hands, then tuck it right away."

Incredible! The head coach from USC is literally coaching me up right now.

But then, his words hit me in a way I don't expect. "USC is in a good spot right now," he says. "We've got a strong group of guys already in the pipeline. We're looking for specific pieces to round it out." On the surface, those words could mean anything, I could even be one of those pieces. But it's not just what he says; it's how he says it. His tone is blunt, almost dismissive, and his voice carries none of the excitement or encouragement I'd hoped for. His body language is relaxed, his gaze steady but detached, like he's already made up his mind. It stings more than I thought words could.

He tells me I'm a great player and a fierce competitor, but underneath it all, I hear what he's really saying. He doesn't come out and say it directly, but what he's signaling is clear: I'm not the type of receiver they're looking for this year. I'm not part of their plan.

My brain starts to spin:

Am I reading this wrong?

Is he telling me to keep working, to prove I belong, or is this his way of saying I don't stand a chance?

Why say this in the middle of camp, when there's still over an hour left?

I'll never know why Coach Carroll chose that moment to plant that mental land mine, but I know exactly how I respond. I don't sulk. I don't cry, even though I want to. Instead, I shake his hand, thank him, and head back out, determined to make my presence undeniable.

For the rest of the day, I destroy every defender I come up against, step by step, play by play, letting my performance speak louder than anything I could say.

With every rep, a voice in my head fuels my fire:

Keep it together, Filly.

Just breathe.

Don't you fucking crack.

When I get home, I climb onto my top bunk and stare at the pictures taped above my bed. These pictures of USC have been fueling my drive and imagination for so many years. I'm crushed. For so long, there has never been a doubt in my mind that USC was the school I'd be attending. And now, suddenly, that plan is gone.

I lay my head on my pillow, my heart heavy with grief. Suddenly, I hear my mom's voice in my head:

"You want to make God laugh, Sweet Pea? Tell him your plans."

*   *   *

Her words lingered, sinking deeper with each passing second as I lay there, staring at the pictures. The plan I had clung to for so long was gone, and I didn't know how to process the loss. But the more I thought about her words, the more I realized she was right.

Life doesn't follow the scripts we write for it. No matter how much effort or hope we pour into the picture we've painted for ourselves, things can still fall apart.

Along the path to greatness, we often craft perfect narratives about how we think things should go, a perfect story, with the ultimate happy ending. But life doesn't work like that.

There will always be twists, setbacks, and unforeseen detours. And that's okay, because the truth is, it's not about the plan. It's about how you adapt when the plan changes.

When life laughs at your plans, laugh back. Then recalibrate, refocus, and keep moving forward.

Because no matter how many twists and turns your path takes, *the outcome will always be determined the things you can control,* and here's what I know I can control in this moment:

- My mindset
- My attitude
- My effort
- My ability to remain grateful and not entitled
- And my belief that this rejection is just a redirection

The truth is, life doesn't owe you anything. If you want something, you have to go out and earn it. Nobody cares what you think you deserve.

I reminded myself that scholarships aren't given away; they're earned. And it was time for me to earn a fucking scholarship.

8
Yellow Shorts

Now that USC was off the table, I needed to be more open-minded about other college programs. The next camp on our list was UCLA, led by head coach Bob Toledo. UCLA had been recruiting me heavily, and it felt like I was on the verge of getting an offer. This was a chance to solidify my spot and show the Bruins coaching staff that I was exactly what they were looking for.

Excited about the camp, I have a hard time sleeping the night before. I spend all week working on the 40-yard dash, perfecting my start. Coach Cox picks me up as usual, but I'm late coming out the door because I can't find my signature red gloves. The panic sets in.

Let me take a moment to explain the relationship between a receiver and his gloves. It's like Thor without his hammer or Captain America without his shield. These gloves aren't just equipment; they're a part of me when I'm on the field. They're my comfort zone. Without them, I feel naked and exposed, as if I've lost a part of my armor.

Did I mention that I'm also extraordinarily superstitious? And these are my good luck gloves. I mean, come on, I'm the kid who cut up the Barry Sanders hat and wore it in his socks for an entire season, remember?

As I make my rounds, from camp to camp, I've become known as the little shifty receiver with the curly 'fro and the red gloves. It's a signature look that feels as much a part of my game as my quick cuts. But today, something feels off. I'm on edge, struggling to snap myself into the competitive headspace I need, with so much on the line.

Already running late, I plead with Coach Cox to swing by the school so I can check the locker room. The gloves aren't there. They're nowhere. I'll be going gloveless today, and it leaves a strange feeling in my gut, as if part of me is missing. A nervous energy creeps in, the kind I haven't felt all spring, but I try to push it aside. I've got one job today: shine in the one-on-ones.

As I walk onto the field, I hear someone shout, "Ay yo, Fairfax," and I turn to see none other than Yellow Shorts smirking at me. I've been so focused on my glove drama that I haven't given him any thought. I knew I'd run into him again at some point, and here he is, standing right in front of me, saying, "Me and you, bro. All camp. Let's go." I don't say a word in response; I just flash a smile that says:

Really? In front of the entire camp?

You got me fucked up, bro; let's run it.

Wow. With no hesitation, he calls me out in front of everyone—players and coaches alike. Yellow Shorts is definitely the toughest opponent I face all spring. He's a worthy competitor for sure. But in my mind, not even he can fuck with me. With all the extra work I've been putting in, I truly believe there isn't a high school defender on the planet who can guard me.

A crowd gathers to watch us go head-to-head. There's an electric buzz in the air. Coach Cox paces on the sidelines like a manager ready for his prizefighter to duke it out in front of the world.

Also on the sidelines is Ricky Manning Jr., UCLA's best player and soon to be a third-round draft pick by the Carolina Panthers. Right now, Ricky is a campus legend. He is from Fresno, CA, just like Yellow Shorts, and he graduated from the same high school where Yellow Shorts is now the star. Ricky is more than just a familiar face; he's like a big brother and mentor to Yellow Shorts.

Ricky is currently standing on the sideline with a humongous pit bull attached to a chain-link leash. The dog is practically the same size as me. And yet, no one bats an eye, like it's completely normal to see a giant dog, restrained by a massive chain, all on the sidelines of a high school football camp. It's wild, but in a strange way, it fits. Nothing about this process feels predictable.

I take my stance on the line of scrimmage. Inside foot in front of me and on the line. My other foot behind me, bent to give me some leverage. My body is relaxed, loose even. My arms dangle at my sides, swaying slowly, back and forth.

Yellow Shorts lines up inches in front of me, squatting in an almost seated position. His eyes are glued to my waist. The scent of fresh cut grass combined with the soft whispers from restless spectators fill the air, heightening the anticipation.

I turn my head slightly to the left and glance at my QB with a confident look, signaling, "I'm ready."

"Set hut," yells the QB, and I explode into action.

I pump my arms and stutter my feet, flowing naturally into the rhythm of my move. My gloveless hands are now balled in fists, slicing through the air with each precise motion. I give a quick head-and-shoulders fake outside, then back inside, channeling every ounce of energy I have into each step. The move I put on him leaves me with a clean outside release, untouched. I shake him so bad it's disrespectful, yelling out, "Oops!" while I blow past him.

Here I am, up against one of the best defenders in the country, and my little ass can't help but talk smack to him. The crowd goes nuts as I sprint toward the end zone. Yellow Shorts recovers well, and he's trailing me on my inside hip. I've got a step and a half on him, and after 20 yards or so, I look back for the ball. I track it through the air, focusing on its descent. Touchdown. A 50-yard bomb that I cradle in my arms in the end zone.

"Okay, Okay. Good shit," says Yellow Shorts as we make our way back to the line. I smile, and it takes an extreme level of discipline not to start mouthing off.

When it's our turn again, even more people gather to watch. Yellow Shorts takes the same seated stance right in front of me, then begins to back away slowly. Just as I hear "Hike," he dashes toward me with sudden intensity, timing his move perfectly and startling me, catching me off guard. The crowd leans in, captivated by the unexpected move.

He tricks me. First he acts like he is going to get physical, then as if he is backing off, only to surge forward and muscle me up, jamming me on the line of scrimmage, ending the play immediately.

I never even have the chance to get into my route. He dominates me that round. This time, the crowd goes crazy for him. I can't believe it. Nothing like this has ever happened to me at camp before. I have been dominant in every round of every one-on-one drill. And now, I have officially just taken my first *L*.

Yellow Shorts came prepared, ready to engage in mental warfare. This battle is going to be about much more than just football ability. It is a thinking match, a contest of wits, and I'm all in. I've dedicated myself fully to the game as a student, and now is the time to exercise my strategic intellect. He's digging deep into his bag of tricks, but now I'm on to him.

The rest of the drill goes on just like the first two. I make a play. He makes a play. I make a play. He makes a play. Until finally, we're down to the final round of the drill. I've been saving my favorite route just for this moment.

It's called a "post-corner."

It becomes my signature move during these camps. No defender can guard it. And it usually ends with the defender getting turned in a complete circle, while the crowd loses it.

For those of you not familiar with the route, first, you run straight ahead at full speed. After about 12 yards, you stick your outside foot in the ground and take a slight angle toward the middle of the field. Then you take three very convincing steps, selling the defender in "this" direction, before immediately sticking your inside foot in the ground and heading in the opposite direction.

The built-in double move and change of direction usually give you enough separation that the defender ends up looking silly. When done crisply, it's a true work of art. It's important not to rush any phase of the route. There is a rhythm, a cadence to these moves, that's only found through consistent practice and patience.

As I line up for this final play, a calm certainty washes over me. The pressure is immense, like being tied two to two going into the fifth and final round of a UFC fight. We're in championship rounds now, where legends are made. It is too close to call who is winning—it can go either way—but my confidence doesn't waver. I'm relaxed, completely sure of myself and the play ahead.

When the quarterback says, "Hike!" I sprint full-speed directly at Yellow Shorts. I stick my foot in the ground at the

12-yard mark. I force my way inside of him, so now he's trailing me on my outside hip exactly as planned.

First step.

Second step.

Just before my third step, I see him out of my peripheral vision. He bails. He turns his hips like he's running the route for me.

Fuck! He knows what's coming!

My alignment at the line of scrimmage must have given away my route. I was usually really careful with my alignment, mindful not to accidentally tip my hand before the play began.

If you line up too far inside or too far outside, it can tip off the defender, giving him a clue as to what you might be doing. This time I messed up. Yellow Shorts had watched me run this route at Nike Camp. He'd studied me. He'd gone the extra mile and paid attention to the fine details like no other player had. He knew exactly what was coming.

Damn. Checkmate!

I take my third step and stick my foot in the ground as hard as I can in an attempt to oversell what I'm doing.

POW!

A loud, explosive pop rings through my ears as I'm launched off my feet. My body twists in midair, contorting awkwardly before I crash hard onto the ground. I grip fistfuls of grass, struggling to regain my senses, to digest what the hell just happened.

It feels like my kneecap was hit point-blank range by a shotgun, like a blast just tore my right leg off from the knee down.

I grab my knee with both hands, seesawing from my back to my right side while adrenaline surges through my body.

Oh fuck!

Oh fuck!

OH FUCK!

The explosive pop was followed by a chorus of shocked "Ohhs," the kind that hits hard, like they've just witnessed something gruesome, catching them off guard. I'm freaking out, not from the pain but from the explosion that erupted from my leg. I can still hear it, rattling around in my head.

The pain hasn't actually set in yet, but the internal explosion spooks me. The popping sound didn't just ring; it traveled through my entire body, which shakes me to my core.

All the onlookers stare, eyes wide, mouths nearly on the floor, partly shock and partly horror. The coaches who are closest to the play rush around me, followed by a flurry of whispers.

I've dealt plenty with injuries before. I'd broken my elbow and my foot twice, cracked my shin—needed 14 stitches from that one—fractured my rib, and fractured my finger. But this is different. I know immediately that this is like nothing I've ever experienced. This is bad.

Coach Cox runs my way with some medical staff. Yellow Shorts is already on the ground consoling me.

Had he heard the pop too?

The look in his eyes suggests he had. He's shaken, and I can tell he feels horrible.

Coach Cox whispers in my ear, "Ferg, I know you're in pain, but you've got to stop cursing." He's right, of course. I've been cursing like a sailor.

I'm carried off the grass to the bleachers and handed an ice pack. There are no doctors on hand to assess how bad the injury is, but it's clear something is seriously wrong. Within 20 minutes, my knee balloons to the size of a softball, the swelling thick and angry. The adrenaline drains from my body, leaving only raw, searing pain in its place.

As I sit on the sidelines, waves of pain pull me in and out of focus. I'm terrified about what has just happened, but I force myself to stay optimistic. Best-case scenario, it's just a sprain, and I'll be back on the field in no time.

*　　*　　*

The next day, my mom takes me to the doctor. As we drive, she reaches over and squeezes my hand, offering a reassuring smile. "You know, everything's going to be just fine, Sweet Pea," she says, her voice warm and steady.

When we arrive at the clinic, she walks beside me as I lean on my crutches, her presence steady and reassuring. Even in the waiting room, she chats with me about anything but the injury, her tone light and optimistic, as if we're just on another routine errand. Her calm confidence keeps my nerves at bay.

I'm finally called into the patient room, and my anticipation tightens like there's a vise around my chest. The doctor performs a manual test, wrapping one arm under my knee and the other over it, pulling and pushing to stress-test for something specific.

His poker face is sharp, so I can't gauge his initial thoughts. Inside, I'm praying for it to be nothing more than a sprain. I'm trying to will it into existence, but the anticipation is almost too much to bear. I force myself to keep a brave face, even as my mind races, with fear and hope playing a cruel game of tug-of-war with my emotions.

Next comes the X-ray, and then the MRI. We sit in silence waiting to hear the results. Seconds feel like minutes. Minutes feel like hours. It's pure torture.

So much is riding on this. My childhood dream of playing Division I football. My goal of making it to the NFL and being able to financially support my mom. Everything I've ever dreamed of is on the line.

The door swings open, and the doctor walks in holding a big yellow envelope. He takes out some pictures, holds them up to the light, and says, "Yep, just as I suspected. You tore your ACL."

I look at my mom. She looks at me. The doctor has delivered this news in such a matter-of-fact fashion, it's almost distasteful. There is zero empathy in his tone. I feel like I've been stepped on by an elephant.

"What does that mean?" my mom asks.

"He's going to need surgery immediately. It's a six- to eight-month road to recovery that's going to include a lot of physical therapy."

I immediately start doing the math in my head. Okay, it's April, and my senior season starts in late August. Then it sinks in.

"Oh my God, I'm going to miss my senior season?" I say, more as a statement than a question.

"Most likely, yes," he says.

I let out a scream and bury my face in my mom's chest. I can't believe this.

How is this happening?

Why is this happening?

I've given so much. I've fully committed to this process. This is how the universe responds?

I break down in my mom's arms as she holds me close. Finally, she pulls back, gently holding my face in both hands, her eyes locking onto mine with a look that goes straight to my soul.

"Sweet Pea," she says softly, but with strength in her voice, "we will get through this. I don't know why this has happened, and I don't know what's waiting for you on the other side of this, but we will get through it. Your journey isn't over. It's just beginning. We'll figure this out. One day at a time."

I stare into her eyes. I can tell she truly believes every word she just said.

So I do too. I believe every word. I have to. I have to believe that everything is going to be okay.

*   *   *

As it turns out, I've really done a number on my knee. I've completely torn my ACL, and to make matters worse, I've done serious damage to my medial and lateral meniscus. Partial meniscus tears are common, but not with me. In true Ferguson fashion, when I go big, I go all the way. My knee is obliterated, and my senior season of football is no longer an option.

Blowing up my knee is just the tip of the iceberg for me and my family. People don't realize what comes after an injury like this. The phone calls start immediately, countless calls to find the right surgeon. We're not leaving anything to chance. My parents pore over recommendations, researching every option. It's a team effort, with my family rallying around me, determined to make sure I get the highest quality care possible.

But as we search for the right surgeon, I can't shake the thought of what's really in store for me. The grueling weekly rehab sessions, the pain, the physical endurance I'll need to push through. It feels like a marathon before the race even starts.

Then there's the mental battle: finding a way to stomach standing on the sidelines, watching my brothers, my team, play without me. The thought pains me, knowing I won't be out there with them. It's all looming ahead, but I can't let it slow me down. I plan to beat the timeline given by the doctors. If they say eight months, I'm going to do it in six. I'm over the shock of my injury and laser-focused on recovery.

I'm fortunate that we have excellent insurance, which allows us to secure top-notch treatment. That's how we land on Dr. Clarence Shields, aka Mr. Sports Medicine 2006, who now serves as a neutral physician (used when there are conflicting opinions or interests) for the NFL. Dr. Shields has operated on some of the biggest names in sports, and knowing that some of the best athletes in the world have trusted him is comforting. It's as if being treated by him places me in an elite group, reinforcing the feeling that I'm not just another patient but someone worth investing in.

And if I'm honest, I love the fact that he is Black. Growing up in Los Angeles, you don't see a lot of Black doctors. Seeing a Black man stand out in a highly competitive field like this is incredibly inspiring to me. It sets the tone before I even meet him, filling me with hope that I'm in the right hands.

At the consultation, he is everything I need him to be, confident and reassuring. He knows just how important this is to me and fuels my optimism rather than dousing it. He sets proper expectations with an eight- to twelve-month timeline and reinforces the amount of work and commitment I'll need to put into my rehab.

I remember him saying: "I'm going to do my job and do it well. I'm going to need you to meet me halfway and commit to your part." I love this. I know how to work with this, like working with a coach. He puts the ball in my court.

If I stay truly committed, my knee will recover, and I will come back stronger than ever. Dr. Shields is everything the first doctor wasn't. He is confident, reassuring, and fully invested in my success. He makes me believe that my dream is not just alive; it is still within reach.

9

Hurricane Henry

On the day of my surgery, not surprisingly, I'm anxious. I mean, really nervous. I've never been under the knife before, and the fear of the unknown keeps gnawing at me.

What if something goes wrong?

What if the surgery doesn't work?

My mom, unfortunately, has had many surgeries, so she coaches me through what to expect, reassuring me repeatedly on the ride to the hospital that everything will be fine. Her calm voice helps, but the nerves are still there, simmering beneath the surface.

When we arrive, I'm brought to a cold room, and my heightened anxiety takes over. I start to shiver almost uncontrollably in my hospital gown, and my mom stays by my side, trying to keep me warm.

A nurse appears with something she calls "a cocktail," assuring me it will help me relax. The moment it hits, it's like a slow wave of heat washing over me, seeping into my skin, and loosening every muscle. The harsh, cold vibe of the hospital room fades away, colors bleeding into one another until everything feels softer, more fluid. The fluorescent lights above me begin to dim as if the room itself has been draped in a cozy filter.

My mind, which had been racing with anxious and concerned thoughts, is now floating somewhere above me, detached and unaware of anything beyond this peaceful moment.

It's the first time my body has ever experienced a narcotic like this, and its grip is strong, holding me in this euphoric state that lasts until I'm wheeled into the operating room.

Oh, shit, this is really happening.

The anesthesiologist puts a mask over my face, and I count down: *10, 9, 8, 7 ...*

Blackness. I'm out like a light.

*   *   *

I open my eyes to the sound of the nurse's voice. The surgery is over. It's a success. I'm now officially on the road to recovery.

My regimen is vigorous and takes 100 percent commitment. I'm scheduled for rehab three times a week. Once I'm capable of driving myself, I'm responsible for going from school to watching practice, to rehab, and then home. And I do this religiously for months.

After the surgery, my leg atrophies almost overnight. I've always had strong, muscular legs, but now it looks skinny and frail, as if the surgery drained all the strength from it. It's still short and stocky, which only makes the loss of muscle more glaring. The definition in my quad and calf is completely gone, leaving my leg looking hollow and lifeless. I stare at it, turning it side to side in my hands, as if it doesn't belong to me. It feels like an alien limb, unrecognizable and unfamiliar.

But as the shock fades, one thought takes over: *I've got my work cut out for me.* If I want to rebuild this muscle and get my knee back to where it was, I'm going to have to fight for it.

My physical therapist refuses to take it easy on me. She isolates the muscles needed to regain full range of motion, which includes tearing through the scar tissue that has built up. This process is more agonizing than I ever imagined. My body is prone to developing excessive scar tissue, making each session a test of willpower.

She lays me on my stomach, grabs my ankle, and slowly pushes it toward my butt. The pain is excruciating, like the bone in my knee is pushing against the scar, ready to burst through my skin. And yet we do this every single session, week after week, month after month. It is brutal, but it is the only way forward.

Over time, I notice small but significant improvements. I can bend my knee a little further than the day before. I move from crutches to walking on my own, first with a limp, then without wincing from the lingering tenderness. Slowly, the muscles in my thighs and calves start to reemerge. Each of these victories fuels me, reminding me that I'm getting stronger, bit by bit.

To get through this, it takes a tribe. All of my close friends band together, and surprisingly, Yellow Shorts really steps up and goes out of his way to be there for me. Immediately after my knee injury, we develop a bond that lasts for years to come.

A few months after the injury, he invites me down to Fresno to stay with him, and I end up taking the train out there on two different occasions, staying with his family for several days each trip.

During one of my trips, I get the chance to watch the City All-Star game, where the best high school football players from all around Northern California compete. Yellow Shorts, of course, is the star of the team. As the game winds down, the opposing team punts the ball to Yellow Shorts, who is standing back, waiting to return it. The kick is shanked, nowhere close to being fielded out of the air, so it rolls around, bouncing awkwardly, and almost coming to a complete stop.

Yellow Shorts strolls over to the ball casually, like he is going to let it die out and end the play. The defenders start to relax, thinking he has given up. Just when they are lulled into believing the play is over, he suddenly snatches up the ball, takes off like a rocket, and scores the game-winning touchdown. It is crazy, something straight out of a sports movie, adding to his local legend. And I get to see it all with my own eyes.

Spending time with Yellow Shorts off the field gives me a whole new perspective on what makes him great. I watch him go from a two-hour football practice straight to his school's batting cage, where I feed him balls through a pitching machine. He hits balls for an hour straight. I didn't even know he played baseball.

Afterward, we eat dinner with his mom and sister, and then we play video games for a bit. Just as I think we are winding down, Yellow Shorts abruptly tells me to get my shoes. I have no clue what is in store for us. As I step out the front door, I see him untangling a footwork ladder and setting it up in the middle of the street. It is nearly 9 or 10 p.m., but he doesn't care. I watch him crush the ladder drill with some of the sharpest, quickest feet I have ever seen, besides mine, of course. I join in, doing what I can while being mindful not to mess up my progress.

It dawns on me then that Yellow Shorts and I are made from the same stuff. It is no wonder he is the best at all those camps. His motor is relentless, and he pushes himself beyond limits most people wouldn't even consider.

After those trips, he checks in on me regularly, offering words of encouragement exactly when I need them. He reminds me that I was the "guy" that spring, that nobody could touch me, and that "that guy" is still in there and will be back better than ever.

What starts as a rivalry evolves into something deeper. He is no longer just "Yellow Shorts"; he becomes my friend, my brother, Clifton Smith Jr. The rival who once pushed me on the field now pushes me in life, helping to reshape my mindset and reminding me of the dedication and grit it takes to be great.

(Cliff eventually went on to play for the Tampa Bay Buccaneers in the NFL and was selected for the Pro Bowl, the NFL All-Star Game, in his rookie year.)

*   *   *

My senior year of high school starts, and it's time for the first game of the season. Until now, I'd always felt like there was a chance I'd make it back on the field this season. But when game day arrives, I'm forced to admit it's pretty unlikely. My knee isn't anywhere close to where it needs to be for me to play. It's been four months since my surgery, and I'm still not running yet.

I grapple with all of this in the locker room before the game, trying to keep it all together. I feel like I'm in a state of mourning. My closest friends at Fairfax, Ques and Kareem, have been trying to keep my spirits up all week, making sure I don't feel left out in any way. Those are my guys, my brothers, and we've been joined at the hip, inside and outside of school, since ninth grade. We do everything together. But even these guys don't have the right words for me as the team gets ready in the locker room.

I am filled with heartache. Agony. The thing I love most in the world is right here, and I can't participate. Watching my brothers put on their gear, break through the banners held by the cheerleaders, and run onto the field is torture. I cry my 17-year-old eyes out. Devastated.

And then, I never cry about it again.

I learn to cope, and with each game that passes, I grow more resilient. I focus on the things I can control, like giving my rehab everything I have and staying on top of my grades. Even from the sidelines, I contribute by cheering on my teammates and injecting them with as much positivity as I can.

I've always naturally been an optimist, but now I double down hard, refusing to be negative in the face of a super shitty situation. I believe in my heart and soul that if I focus my mind and energy on the right things, something will happen in my favor. I believe my mind holds the key to evoking a response from the universe, and I am all in.

* * *

As the season progresses, my routine becomes second nature. I show up to practice every day, staying for the first hour before heading to rehab. One afternoon, I'm standing around on the sideline, watching my teammates gear up, when two of my friends walk over with a look that tells me something is up.

"Ferg, bro, you won't believe this. Yesterday after practice, we were on the bus, and this guy saw us wearing our Fairfax football shirts. He asked if we played for Fairfax. At first, we didn't even want to talk to him—he kinda looked homeless. But when we said yeah, we play for Fax, he goes, 'Do you know my son, Jason Ferguson? He plays ball at Fax. I'm his dad.'

"We started dying, bro. Like, come on, man. You're Jason Ferguson's dad? J-Ferg? The Legend? No way!"

I'm caught completely off guard. No clue how to respond.

My relationship with my biological father is extremely complicated. D-Weez is my dad. The power isn't in the title; it's in the actions. And based on D-Weez's actions over the years, he is, without a doubt, my pops. He's shown up for me consistently. He loves my brother Ryan and me unconditionally. He challenges me about everything under the sun, forcing me to think more critically about things. He praises my athletic performances when I deserve praise, and he gives constructive feedback to sharpen my skills.

Raising another man's kids has to be one of the hardest things in the world, and yet, D-Weez has done it at the highest level. He set a precedent for me of what being a real man looks like. So yeah, D-Weez is my pops.

*   *   *

Over the years, my biological father, Henry Ferguson, has come in and out of my life. My brother never wants anything to do with him, but I keep letting him back in. I want to understand him, give him the chance to work on our relationship. But it always ends with him going dark on me for long periods of time.

It had been two years since I last saw him. The last time, he picked me up to take me to church. Respectfully, I had very little interest in going to church. First, I was raised Jewish, and second, spending my Sunday morning sitting through a three-hour service at the Crenshaw Christian Center didn't exactly feel like father-son bonding time. I would have preferred a movie, grabbing a bite to eat, anything but that. But I went anyway. I fidgeted through the entire thing, restless and bored, forcing myself to stay because it was the only way to spend time with him. I hoped he'd see my effort, see how much I wanted this relationship to work.

The truth is, I wrestled with loving him and resenting him at the same time. When he was around, he could light up any room. He was charismatic and funny as hell, and it was clear he loved my brother and me. But as a kid, I was confused by his inconsistency, his disappearing acts, and what I perceived to be a lack of effort. I never excused it, but I fought to see beyond that whenever he did come around, making those rare attempts to hang out.

There was this constant battle inside me. Part of me wanted to scream *fuck off*, to unload on him at the top of my lungs and ask why he couldn't just be there like a real father. But another part of me, the part that still longed for his approval, kept quiet.

I played the middle, avoiding conflict and being obedient. I hoped that maybe this time it would be different. Maybe this time, he'd stick around. It was the complete opposite of my brother Ryan, who had no problem ignoring him when he came around, confidently declining offers to hang out. But I couldn't bring myself to do it. So I sat there in that church, silent and too afraid to rock the boat.

Before the church visits, I hadn't seen him since I was ten or eleven. He randomly came to one of my flag football championship games, popping up on me out of nowhere. I remember being so excited to see him. I balled out that game, scoring five touchdowns, desperately hoping to impress him.

But that was a long time ago. Hearing from my friends that he's still alive feels complicated. Part of me is relieved, but with everything I'm dealing with now, I don't have the emotional bandwidth to think about him, let alone consider letting him back in.

*　　*　　*

My earliest memory of Henry is straight out of a nightmare. Ryan and I are lying in our mom's bed with her between us. We're cuddlers, and my mom has always shown us a ton of affection.

The room feels small and cozy. The dim lighting, the warmth of the blankets, and the sound of *ThunderCats* on the TV make me feel safe. Ryan and I love this show, especially the intro, when we yell, "ThunderCats hooooooo!" at the top of our lungs.

Suddenly, the front door bursts open. The crash is so loud it sounds like someone kicked it in. Papers scatter in the hallway. Then the punches start, hard and sharp against the walls, shaking the apartment like an earthquake.

Henry is home, and something isn't right. He barrels through the house like a hurricane, pummeling everything in his path. Ryan and I sit up, wide-eyed, listening to him get closer and closer to the bedroom.

I don't remember everything about what happens next. The memory jumps forward, and suddenly, Ryan and I are standing at the bedroom door, staring in. Mom is still lying on the bed, but now Henry is on top of her.

His left arm pins her down while his right arm swings wildly, throwing punch after punch at her face. Ryan and I are frozen, unable to move. Henry straddles our mom, his fists crashing into her like he's pounding on his drum kit.

Her eyes are filled with fear. Her voice is panicked as she begs him to stop, her words desperate and trembling. Somehow, she manages to tell Ryan to take us upstairs to her best friend Susie's. Ryan grabs my hand, and we bolt for the door.

Our footsteps ricochet off the stairwell walls as we climb. Each step feels heavier than the last, like we're carrying the weight of everything happening below us. Ryan's grip on my tiny three-year-old hand tightens with every floor we climb. He's holding on to me like his life depends on it.

But my thoughts are only on Mom.

How is she?

What's happening to her?

Will I ever see her again?

Is she alive?

No wonder Ryan wants nothing to do with Henry. He was five when it happened, old enough to remember everything in vivid detail. My memories are blurry, fractured by time, but even knowing what I do, I still tried to give Henry a chance.

I would think to myself:

Man, he hit the jackpot with me.

I'm a good-looking kid, smart, well-behaved, and an athlete.

Most parents would kill to have me as their son.

So how can he be so effortlessly uninterested in being my dad?

*   *   *

Two days after my friends tell me about seeing Henry on the bus, I'm standing on the sideline watching my team play, and I hear, "Yo, J-Dog!" I know instantly who it is. I'd recognize his voice anywhere. It's loud, enthusiastic, and raspy like mine. My heart sinks in my chest. I see him in the top corner of the stands, smiling ear to ear, no clue I'm out all season.

His smile slowly fades, morphing into confusion as he spots me from across the field. He gestures with his hands, a questioning look in his eyes, wondering from afar why I'm fully clothed on the sidelines instead of suited up. The noise of the game, the shouts of players, and the roars of the crowd fade into the background. All I can focus on is the look he's giving me. The weight of his unspoken question, planted between us, presses down on me.

I glance away, my throat tightening as I fight to keep my emotions in check. I take a quick peek toward the stands, where my mom and D-Weez are sitting, watching this silent exchange unfold. I know they can see the struggle on my face, but I try my hardest to maintain my composure, swallowing the lump in my throat as I turn back toward the field, pretending to focus on the action happening right in front of me.

After the game, I take the long way off the field, slipping through a side gate that leads around the school to the far end of the parking lot. I know he'll be waiting for me by the locker room, so I go out of my way to avoid him.

Right now, there is just too much at stake for me. I know I need to focus my energy on myself. I can't let this man be a distraction. He is, in fact, a hurricane who pops up every few years to shake things up and then bounce. I'm already in the biggest battle of my life, fighting for my dream. I need to avoid him at all costs.

As I've gotten older, I've started to understand more about Henry's story. He ran away from Louisiana, leaving behind something I'll never fully comprehend.

What could have prompted a teenager to run away with just the clothes on his back to an unknown place like Hollywood, CA?

When he landed in L.A., he had nowhere to go, didn't know anybody, and spent his nights sleeping in a laundromat. I guess the warmth from the dryers, the well-lit space, and access to running water offered him the basic elements he needed to survive in an unfamiliar city. Eventually, a woman who frequented the laundromat noticed him, took him in, and became a mother figure to him until she passed away many years later.

In L.A., he found drumming and quickly became one hell of a musician. He dreamed of making it big and formed a band, where he met my mom. She was the lead singer of the band Allison Gail and The Finishing Touch, and Henry was the lead drummer and songwriter.

For a while, it probably felt like life was finally coming together for him. But the music scene came with its own traps—the partying and the drugs—and he got caught up in it. He became a heavy user, and it changed him, warping his personality, his decisions, and ultimately, his relationship with us. The violence he showed my mom wasn't just anger; it was driven by addiction, trauma, and probably a lifetime of scars.

What he did was messed up, and that hurt doesn't just disappear. But as an adult, I see that everyone has a story, and understanding his helps me make sense of it all. Today, he's turned his life around. He's a pastor now, leading a church he founded in Louisiana. He walked a hard road and made some terrible choices, but he found his way back.

This understanding has reshaped how I view our relationship. The scars remain, and we don't talk much, but I see the transformation in him and respect it. I have a sense of empathy for the struggles he's faced, struggles that shaped both who he was and who he is now. *I've learned that people are more than just their mistakes.*

While I may never fully reconcile the father he was with the man he is today, I can respect his journey and the work he's done to become a better person. We're all shaped by our stories, and his, like mine, is one of survival and finding a way forward.

10
The Pathological Optimist

My senior year football season ends almost as fast as it starts. I spend the entire season on the sidelines, doing my best to cheer my team on. The problem is, my recruitment starts to dwindle, and it is really hard on me.

A few coaches seem to hold out hope that I'd make a miraculous return midseason, but once it's clear I'm not even running yet, their interest disappears. What once felt like a real possibility with UCLA is now nonexistent. After tearing my ACL at their camp, the only thing I got from them was a handwritten letter expressing their condolences and wishing me luck. Not a peep after that.

The days of Division I coaches calling me and pulling me out of class gradually slip away, replaced by the occasional interest from Division 2 schools or junior colleges. The shift is jarring, a cold splash of reality. Still, I am not ready to let go of my dream. D2 is not the path I have envisioned for myself.

One evening, I'm lying on the bed with my mom. D-Weez is out of town on a work trip, so it's just the two of us. Hanging out in her room is my comfort zone, a place where everything feels a little easier.

The phone rings, and she answers it. It's the offensive coordinator from Mt. San Antonio College, one of the top junior college football programs in Southern California. His voice is full of excitement and enthusiasm as he tells me he's seen my highlight tape and is blown away by what I can do on the field.

He addresses the elephant in the room, pointing out how signing day, the day when high school athletes with verbal offers make their scholarships official by signing their National Letter of Intent, is approaching fast. He counters that by insisting I don't have to settle for a D2 or D3 school. He sells me hard on the idea of going to his junior college (JUCO), promising he can get me into a Division I program in a year, two years max.

He rattles off a list of JUCO players he's coached; some I recognize, others I don't. But their schools are all legit—SEC, Big 12, Pac-10—the kinds of conferences where football is more than just a game. There's tradition, talent, and community.

He acknowledges that for a player of my caliber, having to go the JUCO route might be a tough pill to swallow, and it's not hard to see why. I've spent my entire high school career preparing to compete at the highest level—Division I. Settling for anything less feels like giving up on that dream.

The JUCO route isn't just a step down; it's a detour from the path I've always envisioned for myself. But he frames it as a stepping stone, not a setback. He assures me that my journey isn't over and that this could be the path to something even greater. He's got a spot for me in his high-powered passing offense if I want it. I express my gratitude and do my best to stay engaged and interested in the conversation, even though my heart isn't in it. When we hang up, it all hits me at once.

Is this really what it's come to?

Am I really going to have to go the JUCO route?

More and more calls like this one begin to flood in, and even though time continues to escape me, I refuse to let go of my dream. I don't give any of them an immediate answer, choosing to hold on to the hope that something will happen.

I've spent hundreds of hours feverishly imagining myself playing in front of 80,000 screaming fans. The parties. The girls. The fun. The whole experience. I mean, come on. Yes, I am likely the most obsessed student athlete in the country, but I am also just a teenage boy!

So even with the odds stacked against me, with time working negatively in my favor, I insist on remaining optimistic. When doubts creep into my thoughts, I catch them, course correct, and refocus my energy.

I do my best to resist the urge to question God or the universe, trusting that everything is unfolding just as it needs to. I hold onto that belief, knowing that optimism breeds hope, and hope drives perseverance.

*   *   *

As the days fly by, the pressure intensifies, and holding onto that belief gets harder. I try to stay positive, but the reality is hard to ignore. Time is running out, and signing day is closing in fast.

For me, the thought of signing day has become a source of anxiety. A day that once represented the culmination of years of hard work now looms as a reminder of my uncertain future. As it approaches, the reality of what might not happen takes an emotional toll on my 17-year-old heart. It's devastating for me and for my family.

But I can't afford to dwell on what I can't control. I've got to focus on what's in front of me, crushing my rehab, keeping my grades up, staying sharp. The controllables.

Every time a coach reaches out, even if it's not the caliber of school I've always envisioned, I remind myself to be respectful, to be interested, and to be grateful.

I tell myself: *You can't control what happens, but you can control how you respond.*

Optimism alone won't create opportunities; I have to keep grinding. I lean into the controllables, knowing that staying ready is the only way I'll be able to take advantage when my moment comes.

Meanwhile, one my best friends and teammate, Ques, is getting heavily recruited by a lot of big West Coast schools. Ques stands 6'1" and weighs 190 pounds. For a high school cornerback, he is everything most colleges are looking for.

One afternoon, I'm sitting in Coach Cox's classroom during a free period. We'd set up a PlayStation in the classroom, so you'd often find a group of us in there gaming and talking smack to one another.

On this particular day, the head coach from Fresno State shows up and pulls Ques outside for a chat. I keep playing the game until I notice someone else has walked in.

It's a tall, fairly skinny man with salt-and-pepper hair. He's clean-shaven with sunglasses on. When he removes his shades, I get a good look at him, and then his University of Hawaii shirt gives him away: *Oh, shit! That's June Jones.*

June Jones is the head coach from the University of Hawaii, a school I've been interested in ever since letting go of my USC dream. Their team is known for their dynamic passing offense, so as a receiver, I would be a perfect fit.

June is looking for Ques. When he doesn't see him, he looks disappointed. Coach Cox explains Ques will be back shortly, and he invites June to hang out for a few minutes.

So here I am, sitting in an empty classroom with Coach Cox and June Jones beside me. My eyes are locked on the whiteboard in front of the room, almost too nervous to acknowledge the man sitting across the room.

Is this it? Is this my shot?

Say something, anything!

Those thoughts storm into my mind, urgent and insistent, recognizing this as a moment that could change everything. The room feels cool, but the AC is no match for my nerves that bubble beneath the surface, making my armpits sweat through my deodorant.

And then, the doubt creeps in.

He's not here for you.

He doesn't even know who you are.

Don't do anything stupid.

It's like an angel is perched on my right shoulder, urging me forward, while a devil clings to my left, feeding me doubt. Their conflicting whispers clash and spiral, filling my mind with doubt and urgency, making it impossible to settle on my next move.

I glance down and notice my leg bouncing up and down like a piston.

Go talk to him. You gotta say something. Say anything!

Then something snaps.

Fuck it. He's just a guy.

I push myself up and walk toward him, determined to make eye contact. For a brief moment, it seems like he actually might recognize me. But even if he doesn't, there's something inviting in his gaze, urging me to keep moving forward.

I hope I'm not doing something stupid.

I pray I'm not about to make a fool of myself.

And then I'm face-to-face with him. Well, more like my face to his stomach, as he peers down at me from his 6'4" frame. I feel really small. I slowly extend my hand out and introduce myself.

Right on time, Coach Cox joins us, and suddenly, I have no idea what to say. Ironic, right? The little fella who normally can't shut up is speechless. Lucky for me, Coach Cox knows exactly what to do.

He starts telling June all about me, the person:

"June, Jason isn't just special on the field—he's also impressive off it, from who he is as a student to who he is in his community. He's always looking to improve, always asking the right questions. He's a glue guy, the type of guy that holds the locker room together. There isn't a harder-working kid in this program. He's like a son to me, and not because of what he's done on the field, but because of who he is as a person."

Coach Cox turns and beams at me with admiration and pride, then looks back at June.

"Well, maybe a little because of what he can do on the field," he says, laughing as a portion of the truth slips out with impeccable timing.

Eventually, talk turns to football. Coach Cox rattles off the CliffsNotes version of my short but successful high school career. And that's when the TV on the other side of the room catches my attention. There's a VCR sitting on top of it. And on top of that is my highlight tape.

Yes, I know I'm dating myself with that one, but back in those days, the highlight reels with all of our best plays were shared on video tapes. Mine has plays from my sophomore and junior years. Twenty-six touchdowns and nearly six thousand total yards. Seeing it sitting there, I know exactly what I need to do. I look June directly in the eyes and ask if he has two minutes to watch my highlight reel while he waits for Ques.

"Sure, I'll check it out," he replies, walking toward the TV.

The first play shows me taking a kick return 90 yards for a touchdown. I burst through a tiny crease, make a quick cut, then outrun all the defenders while they chase me down the field.

No reaction from June. His poker face is stellar.

My first thoughts are, *Damn, what a cut. That was sick.* Even though I've seen that play a zillion times, it gets me every time.

But then my thoughts turn to *What is he thinking right now? Is he not impressed?*

I try my best to put on a poker face too. I'm very aware of how real and important this moment is. I'm desperate for him to be impressed, but I don't want to appear too eager. Sometimes, he who cares the least wins, so I find myself fighting for middle ground—mindful not to come across as disinterested, instead opting for calm, cool, and collected, and fighting hard to maintain my composure.

After watching a few more plays that are similar to the first, June walks over to the VCR and pushes the stop button himself, still giving me no indication of what he thinks of me.

Finally, he says, "You've got great 30-yard speed, and your cuts are phenomenal. How's your knee?"

"Stronger and stronger," I reply. "I'm almost running. Everything's going exactly as planned."

"Great, I want you. I think I'd like to gray-shirt you. You'd sit out this fall and won't enroll in school or be a part of the team until the spring. That'll give you almost a full extra year to get that thing strong and back to where it was. How does that sound to you?"

He phrases it like I have 20 other offers lined up to consider. But honestly, I hadn't really heard much after he said, "I want you."

My instinct is to say:

Hell, yes!

That sounds great.

Where do I sign?

But I keep my cool, and reply with, "That sounds amazing, Coach. I won't let you down. My knee will be back 100 percent. I'll be ready."

My eyes well up. The urge to let the tears flow is almost unbearable, but I fight it, refusing to let a single tear break free. I want to pour out my heart out, to express my gratitude and reassure him that taking a chance on me is the right call, but the words are stuck behind my tonsils.

I'm frozen, caught between disbelief and awe, trying to process the weight of what just happened. That morning, I woke up to just another day, unsure about my future and trying desperately to stay optimistic. Still waiting for that "something" I'm sure is going to happen in my favor one day. But I guess we can never really be prepared for when that day actually comes.

But here we are. June Jones has just offered me a full scholarship, and he's even structured it in a way that buys me more time to heal.

He tells me another coach will be in touch to schedule my official player visit to Hawaii *that weekend*. Signing day is only a couple of weeks away, so it has to happen immediately.

As June Jones walks out the door, I hug Coach Cox with a grip so tight it feels like I'm holding on for dear life. He's never given up on me. He's fought for me, like an agent or manager, pitching me to everyone he could. I mean, the man kept my highlight tape on top of his VCR, for Christ's sake!

So many athletes get treated like disposable property. The minute they can no longer contribute or serve a purpose on the team, all of their hard work and sacrifice is forgotten.

There's a motto that players often use to describe the player/coach relationship:

What have you done for me lately?

Coach Cox never once treated me that way. He loved me like a son, and his actions reflected just that.

And now, here we stand, having accomplished what seemed impossible. Me. A 5'5" receiver who runs a mediocre 40-yard dash and has missed his entire senior season due to an ACL injury, just got offered a full football scholarship to the University of Hawaii.

Aloha, mothafucka!

I take out my cell phone to call my mom. I can't dial her number fast enough. Nothing feels real. I keep expecting to wake up from a dream.

"Hello?" My mom answers in a concerned tone. I'm calling during school hours, so she's probably expecting bad news.

"Mom, oh my God, Mama, you won't believe what just happened," I say frantically.

"What's wrong?" she asks. "Is everything okay?"

At last, I get the words out. "I'm going to the University of Hawaii. *I'm* going to the University of Hawaii. They offered me a scholarship. They want me, Mom. They want me!"

Once those words leave my lips, it's like a lever's been pulled, offering me release. And I release everything. All the devastation, frustration, anxiety, worry, jealousy, fear, and doubt. All the emotions I've tried so hard for so long to keep in check. Everything comes flowing out of me.

And I do nothing to stop it. These are tears of triumph. Tears of perseverance. I've earned these tears. And my mom joins in.

This is just as much a victory for her as it is for me. She's been by my side every step of the way. My pain is her pain. But my joy is her joy too.

And now I'm headed to the University of Hawaii, feeling like I've just been granted a new lease on life.

*   *   *

Looking back on that difficult time, I realize that overcoming it took more than simply trying to "be positive." Forcing positivity often feels hollow or inauthentic, especially in the face of real adversity. But there was another way: optimism. After my injury, that meant becoming pathologically optimistic, deliberately focusing on what could go right instead of what could go wrong. This wasn't about denying reality; it was about choosing to see the possibility for good.

Optimism, I've learned, isn't a fleeting feeling. It is a discipline, a skill that can be trained like a muscle. Challenges have a way of feeding negativity, creating a cycle of doubt that holds us back. Research from the National Science Foundation reveals something startling: humans have between 12,000 and 60,000 thoughts per day, and a staggering 80 percent of them are negative. Even more surprising, 95 percent of these thoughts are repetitive.[1] This overwhelming reinforcement for pessimism underscores just how deliberate we must be to break free from its grip.

For me, optimism bred hope, and hope became the resilience I needed to keep moving forward. It sharpened my focus and tuned me in to opportunities. When June Jones walked

---

[1] Brownstein, Barry, "Why Positive Thinking Doesn't Work," *Intellectual Takeout* (Online February 21, 2019). https://intellectualtakeout. org/2019/02/why-positive-thinking-doesnt-work/

into the room, I was ready to act. Had I been consumed by negativity or doubt, I might have missed my shot entirely. It would have been easy to be a hater, bitter that Coach Jones was there to recruit Ques and not me, but I wasn't. Instead, I stayed focused, waiting for my moment. I didn't know how it would come, but I held on to the belief that it would.

Hope isn't just an abstract idea; it's a lifeline. Viktor Frankl, a Holocaust survivor, observed that those who clung to hope in the most horrific circumstances were often the ones who endured.[2] In my own life, hope didn't just help me survive setbacks. It fueled the resilience I needed to move forward, even when progress felt impossible.

Resilience, I've come to understand, isn't built on toxic positivity. It is forged through metacognition, the act of thinking about your thinking. By examining and challenging negative thoughts, metacognition allows you to reframe your perspective and replace doubt with possibility. Gratitude takes this even further by shifting your focus to what you have rather than what you lack. Together, they create a powerful foundation for optimism.

These insights reveal an important truth: *Within every challenge lies a hidden window of opportunity.* Without the right mindset, those windows remain invisible. Recognizing these opportunities requires cultivating the qualities that make us adaptable and strong. Gratitude and metacognition don't just build resilience. They are the driving forces behind a pathologically optimistic mindset. This mindset transforms setbacks into stepping stones, proving that a small shift in perspective

---

2   Frankl, Viktor, *Man's Search for Meaning,* (Beacon Press, 1st edition June 1, 2006).

is not just a change. It is the spark that can ignite growth and transform your life forever.

* *Master your thoughts and transform your mindset. Download the free Metacognition Playbook at JFinspires.com/TheBlueprint and start creating the mental foundation for success.*

11
Goodbye

The plan Coach Jones has to gray-shirt me turns out to be the biggest blessing I could ask for. Instead of starting college in the fall with other incoming freshmen, I get to stay home and rehab my knee. During this time, I'm finally cleared to participate in full-speed agility drills.

I've spent nearly seven months focused on strengthening my muscles and regaining full range of motion. Now it is finally time to get my feet back in sync with my mind, focus on my footwork, and polish my routes. I've been off the field for months, and it's critical that I recapture the rhythm and level of performance I'd reached before getting hurt. To get there, I hit the field daily, focusing on wide receiver drills, and I head right back to that sand dune for more torture.

The problem is that I'm in agonizing pain. It's sharp and relentless, like a screwdriver twisting deep into my kneecap. The pain shoots up my leg, radiating through every nerve ending. No matter how hard I try, I can't fully extend my leg; it feels locked, like it's been welded into place.

No amount of stretching, Icy Hot, or BENGAY dulls the ache or soothes the tightness gripping my muscles. I grit my teeth and try to power through, convincing myself I can endure it.

But eventually, I'm back at the doctor's office, blindsided by the diagnosis: my body is prone to developing more scar tissue than most, and it's the scar tissue buildup that's restricting my range of motion and causing the searing pain when I cut.

Shit, just my luck.

So back under the knife I go for a second surgery to "clean up" the scar tissue. At first, I panic. I can't afford a setback now; I need to be 100 percent by January to start training with the team.

But the surgery is a success. After six weeks of rehab, I'm back.

I'm running, cutting, and jumping with no pain. My legs are getting stronger. And I start to feel more and more like the athlete I once was.

My knee never quite feels like it did before the injury, but I tell myself: *I can totally work with this.*

Over the years, I've learned a lot about my mental endurance by embracing the "be obsessed" mindset. I discovered how to push my body beyond its perceived limits, realizing it was more mental than physical. I also gained a deeper insight than most when it comes to fear and the brain's response by experiencing that "get hit" moment.

I knew my mind was likely amplifying the doubts, the hesitation, and the whispers that said I couldn't do it. The work I had done leading up to this moment said otherwise.

Even though my knee doesn't feel quite as strong as it once did, it feels good enough. In fact, it feels more than enough for what I need to excel at the next level. I decide to believe in it, to trust it. Rather than making excuses or fixating on how different it feels now, I get to work. I familiarize myself with this new leg, testing it, polishing it, and learning how to work with what I have. This is my controllable. This is my path forward.

*   *   *

I count down the days until January, marking them off my calendar one by one, until finally, it's time for my big move to Hawaii.

I'm feeling all the feels: I'm excited, anxious, and even a little sad. Leaving my family is hitting me harder than I thought it would.

The night before I leave, we eat dinner together at the dining room table, like we always do. My mom makes my favorite: meatloaf and mashed potatoes. The table is loud and vibrant, filled with the usual back-and-forth banter about the state of the Lakers, debating whether Shaq and Kobe can keep it together long enough for another title. Everyone has an opinion. As we all fight to validate our take on the topic, our voices overlap and fill the room with energy.

I look around the table at my brothers, Donovan, Dominic, and Ryan, then at D-Weez, and finally at my mom. I take a moment and breathe it all in, this beautiful, chaotic mix that is my family. I'm struck by how amazing this moment is, how lucky I am to have it. Still, there is a tug in my chest, a quiet ache that reminds me things are changing. I'm leaving the state for college, Dominic will be next, and Ryan is already out on his own. We are growing up, all moving in different directions. I know I'm stepping into something new, but it feels like I'm leaving something just as precious behind.

After dinner, my brother Ryan and I drive around L.A. blasting "Hot Damn" by The Neptunes on repeat. We're singing and rapping our asses off to Pharrell's smooth, airy vocals and the gritty flow of Pusha T and Malice. We're reminiscing, doing everything we can to stretch the night out as long as possible.

The next morning, the drive to the airport feels surreal. I'm thrilled to be taking this massive step closer to my dream, but a sense of melancholy lingers.

As we drive, I notice everything. Kids walk to school with their backs slightly hunched under the weight of their backpacks, their laughter lighting up the morning air as they create their own childhood memories. For a moment, I feel a hint of longing, almost jealous of how simple and grounded their lives seem.

As we continue our drive, I notice a shop owner pulling open his metal shutters with a sharp clatter, a sound that pierces the quiet and announces the start of his day. There is something about the ritual, its predictability and rhythm, that makes him feel so connected to this place. He is rooted here, tied to the pulse of the city in a way that stirs something deep inside me. It is a reminder of how much L.A. has shaped me, those same rhythms woven into the fabric of who I am.

I am heading to Hawaii, a place most people dream of, but I cannot shake the quiet pull of my city. It feels as if L.A. is whispering, asking me not to go, holding on to me just a little longer.

That tug grows stronger as we reach the airport. My mom, Ryan, and D-Weez all come inside to see me off. As I stand at the escalator that leads up to security, I realize the moment has finally arrived to say goodbye.

Goodbye to D-Weez.

My father, my role model. The man who made me a better man. I give him the biggest loving hug to thank him for raising me as his own.

Goodbye to Ryan.

Who never missed a single game of mine. Who was never jealous of my success. Who beams at me through tears as we grasp each other tight.

He doesn't say a word, but his smile says it all.

You little motherfucker! You did it, bro, you actually pulled it off!

He's never doubted me for a second. And now we're here. It's happening, just as we dreamed it up as kids. I kiss him on the cheek and force myself to continue down the line.

Goodbye to Mom.

My rock, my biggest fan. The person who helped me truly buy into these massive dreams I had. Dreams we pursued together.

When other people gave up on me, this woman didn't flinch. She continuously poured into me, fueling me with love and confidence. She conditioned me to believe I could do anything I put my mind to.

I go in to hug my mom, and she bursts into tears. Then I burst into tears. Our journey together has been filled with love, violence, hope, and resilience. And now it's culminating in this beautiful and bittersweet moment.

As I step onto the escalator, I turn back for one last look. My mom is still wiping her tears, flanked by Ryan and D-Weez. I wave as the escalator slowly pulls me away. My family waves back. One last goodbye.

The clock is no longer ticking. I'm now officially clocked in. I've spent years asking the universe for this. It's time for me to go live out my dream.

12
Aloha

Coach Miano, Hawaii's defensive backs coach, scoops me up at Honolulu International Airport. On our way to the dorm, we detour to a public storage space to snag the boxes my parents have shipped over.

My parents really outdid themselves, packing way more than just the essentials. Boxes full of new clothes, undies, and tank tops. A brand-new desktop computer, not a laptop, because there was no way they were trusting me to keep track of that thing outside of my dorm. They even went as far as making sure I had a TV from day one, and it was waiting for me in the storage unit.

Looking at everything they put together, I couldn't help but feel the love and effort behind it. Since they didn't have to pay a dime for school, they had gone all out to make sure I had everything I needed, and then some.

But as much as they set me up for success, there were still things outside of their control. Starting midyear meant there was no room for me in the freshman dorms, which are only five minutes from our practice field, and from what I've heard, "full of girls." I can't believe I'm not staying where the action is. Instant FOMO.

Instead, I'm in a dorm in the upper campus area, isolated all the way at the back end of the college. This means a 25-minute walk to and from practice each day. There's no vibe in my building; however, there is an all-girls dorm right next door, which slightly improves my feelings about the situation.

Another plus to living farther away from the action is that I'll be able to focus on school and football, putting me in a prime position to stand out amongst the other freshman talent. I've heard horror stories of freshman players not making it through a single semester after falling victim to the college party life.

Coach Miano pulls up to my dorm and hands me my new roommate's phone number, assuring me he'll come down to help with my boxes. Then he drives off.

I call the number. No answer. I try again. No answer.

Damn.

I've only been on the island for an hour, and here I am stuck in the lobby with all my stuff: two big suitcases, three big-ass boxes, and a backpack. There's nobody at the front desk, I can't get ahold of my roommate, and I don't even have a key to my room yet. At first, all I can do is laugh. But that's followed by a sad longing that creeps into the pit of my stomach.

Am I homesick?

I've never felt quite like this before, so I start questioning why I feel this way now.

Do I miss my mom—the comfort she brings?

Is it my friends—the familiar bond that feels like home?

Or is it my city?

L.A. has a certain energy, a rhythm that gets into your bones. It's magnetic, shaping you and pulling you in until you feel like you're part of something electric. Like you're in a bubble, and it's the only city in the world that exists.

My thoughts spiral, pulling me deeper into this strange, unfamiliar feeling.

What's happening to me?

I should be happy, but all I want to do is cry. I sit here like this for almost two hours. Alone. Until finally, my roommate, Ryan Santos, shows up, apologizing, saying he lost track of time at the beach.

I try my best to seem grateful and excited to meet him, but I'm annoyed as fuck. Annoyed at him, and at Coach Miano for dumping me in the lobby and bailing.

When Ryan walks in, I make an effort to mask my irritation, but it's hard to shake completely. My first thought is how massive he is, towering at 6'5" and easily over 300 pounds. He carries himself with a quiet confidence, friendly but not outgoing like me. There's something about the way he moves, calm and comfortable, that tells me this is his home, which it is. He's a local boy, with his entire family living on the island.

Ryan helps me carry my stuff to our room. As soon as we step inside, the heat presses against me, thick and unrelenting. The air clings to my skin, heavy with humidity, and there's no AC to offer any relief.

I glance over at my side of the room, which is bone dry. There's a twin-size bed shoved against the wall, and the mattress is bare and exposed. A desk is tightly wedged at the foot of the bed, and an armoire-type closet is crammed at the head. Everything feels cramped and tight, positioned perfectly to fit, like a game of Tetris.

I look over at his side, and it is in complete disarray. Clothes are scattered everywhere, forming a messy border that separates my side from his. His bed is unmade, sheets tangled, and yesterday's lunch sits on the desk, half-eaten. Beside it is a stack of DVDs towering precariously, and I notice that at least two dozen of them are Steven Seagal movies. It catches me by surprise. It is such a random thing to see. It is not every day you meet a big Steven Seagal fan. I laugh a little in my mind, and the annoyance I feel starts to fade. I almost like him a little more because of it.

He casually tells me to help myself to the DVDs, hangs around for a few minutes, then heads out.

And just like that, I'm alone again. That feeling I wrestled with in the lobby starts resurfacing. I pull out my phone and call my big bro, praying that Ryan will answer. When he does, I start rambling. "Big broooooo, just wanted to hit you up, man. Let you know that I made it safe. I'm in the dorm as we speak. Getting unpacked and settled in."

I try to sound happy, charismatic. I even smile while I'm talking in an attempt to mask my emotions, along with the knot in my throat.

But Ryan knows me. He hears it in my voice right away; something is off, and he goes straight to work, snapping me out of whatever moment I'm having. Usually when we talk, Ryan is all jokes. He's hardly ever serious, and you never know what's going to come out of his mouth. He loves the word fuck, and he uses it a lot, just like me. He has a sick, twisted, hilarious sense of humor, which is exactly what I think I need right now.

But today, on this call, that's not the version I get. He knows exactly what I need. He's in full-on big brother mode, committed to pulling me out of this funk I'm doing my best to downplay.

His voice shifts, steady and deliberate, and he starts talking about the journey we've been on. He brings up the dreams we had as kids playing football in the yard and everything I've fought through to get to this very moment. Then he reminds me, "You're a Ferguson, and Fergusons aren't soft. We don't quit when things get uncomfortable. We don't run from pressure or discomfort. We run toward it, then we run through that shit."

It's exactly what I need to hear. I've never been more grateful to my brother for answering his phone. It's the pep talk I desperately need, a reality check, and a necessary reminder of who I am and how I got here.

After the call, I sit at my new desk, peering out the window at what looks like a mini jungle. It's the most tropical backyard I've ever seen, with humongous trees packed together and all kinds of vegetation covering the ground. There's even a creek running along the back of the building, filling my dorm room with the calming sound of running water.

I stare out the window and reflect on my brother's words, on what I've been through to get here. Not just my ACL tear and recovery, but my childhood.

*   *   *

In many ways, I feel like Ryan and I had the best childhood any kid could ask for. It was filled with sports, adventure, and amazing friendships that still hold strong to this day. But it wasn't without adversity. I don't care who you are; nobody escapes adversity. It's part of life.

After the brutal beating my biological father put on my mom, she wound up in the hospital for weeks. My grandfather and uncle showed up in town, pistols in hand, ready to kill Henry. And they were both cowboys. Horse-riding, land-loving, pistol-packing cowboys, through and through.

Their protective instincts were matched only by their deep love for family. They taught us the value of standing up for those you love and being there when it matters most.

I'll never forget visiting her in the hospital. She looked nothing like the mom I knew, the bruising on her face a stark reminder of what she endured. No kid should ever have to see their mom like that.

But my mom was a fighter. She didn't allow Henry's violence to break her. She wouldn't dare give him the satisfaction. Once she fully recovered, she moved Ryan and me into a small two-bedroom apartment in Hollywood. Financially broke and spiritually battered, she still found a way to keep our family tight.

She used our naivete as an opportunity to get creative, to make things fun. No money? No problem. We spent hours on end in our living room, playing board games. We had dance parties, just the three of us, alongside Luther Vandross, Bell Biv DeVoe, Celine Dion, and C+C Music Factory. We'd go to Sizzler and share a big plate of food from the salad bar. All the fruit, salad, and chicken strips you could eat. Being broke forced her to be innovative, and it made the three of us extremely close. A trio with an unbreakable bond. The Tripod, as we liked to think of ourselves.

That apartment in Hollywood wound up being an amazing playground for Ryan and me. This was a time when kids took pride in their neighborhood blocks, spending endless hours playing outside together. We'd play everything under the sun, depending on the season. Street hockey, basketball, roller-blading. Ryan and I would have to be practically dragged in by our collars at the end of the night because we never wanted to stop playing.

This is also where I learned the art of shit-talking and getting under people's skin. I learned how to fight, even if that meant taking an ass whooping.

It all started in our backyard, where Ryan and I would go head-to-head in some of the most epic, fierce one-on-one basketball games two brothers could have. As the games intensified, Ryan would crank up the physicality, using his older, stronger frame to his advantage. He played like it was game 7 of the NBA Finals, bodying me up with that nineties-style of basketball that was all about brute force. I was 10, he was 12, and I wasn't nearly as strong, so I leaned on my shit-talking to even the playing field.

I'd hit him with a Tim Hardaway crossover, then mock him with, "You ain't quick enough, dog." He'd usually double down on the rough style of play, hitting me with a spinning elbow or knocking me to the ground as I tried to make a layup.

I'd respond with another move out of my arsenal of tricks I'd learned by mimicking some of my favorite players, then throw a verbal elbow of my own that usually sounded something like, "You suck, ain't no way you can guard me, bitch."

Calling him a bitch while hitting a game-winner would lead to a fistfight ten out of ten times, and while our one-on-one games were pretty even in terms of who would win, he'd always kick the crap out of me whenever we fought.

The better I got, the quicker I was to launch into my trash talk, often unprovoked. These moments toughened me up, made me resilient, and sharpened my skills for when I competed against kids my own age. Those backyard battles didn't just build my game; they also strengthened my character.

Ryan was by far the best athlete on the block. He was faster, quicker, and more naturally confident than all the other kids. There wasn't anything he didn't think he could do, and I was always there cheering him on, encouraging him to go for it.

Half the stuff he tried, none of the other kids would even consider. Like the time he rode down a ramp on rollerblades and cleared five trash bins. We all watched with our mouths wide open in amazement as he flew through the air like an X

Games champion. Moments like this made him a neighborhood legend. He was running the block in no time.

He was my role model and my protector. He'd kick my ass, then hug me affectionately right after. I followed him around like his shadow, mimicking his every move. Getting the opportunity to compete against him on a daily basis grew the competitive beast inside me. I'd be sitting in class, plotting out ways to dominate him the minute we got home. Thinking through some new move I could try on him. Every year I'd get a little better, a little stronger, and a lot more mentally tough.

Together we were known as the Ferguson Brothers, often mistaken for twins at Pan Pacific Park, where we were total park rats. We rotated sports with the seasons, spending most of our weekdays after school and entire weekends shaping our identities and building friendships.

It was there that Ryan and I finally had the chance to connect with strong Black father figures who left a lasting mark on us. Some coached us. Others coached against us. Over time, a few went out of their way to train and mentor me as my athletic career began to take off, shaping not just my game but also the man I was becoming.

We were a community. A big family of park rats using sports as a tool to help kids develop into strong human beings.

Apart from my blended family, the Fergusons and the Whites, who came together at the park, there's one other family that stands out: the Walkers.

The Walkers consist of Devin, Donnie, and D'Andre, along with their mom, Stacy, and their dad, Dave. (And yes, it's not lost on me how many of the people closest to me have names that start with *D*!)

The Walker boys were also mixed, Black and White, like Ryan and I. When all of us were together, we looked like one big-ass blended family with White mamas, Black daddies, and Beige babies.

Devin and I were the same age, and we instantly became inseparable. Even though we went to different schools, our families spent so much time at the park that we saw each other nearly every day.

When we were 12, we ended up on the same basketball team at the park, with his older brother, D'Andre, as our coach. Before our first game, D'Andre and Dev got their hands on the jerseys and decided to pull a little prank. On game day, D'Andre handed them out with a grin, and I immediately noticed something off about Dev's jersey. In pink glitter glue, they'd written "D Willy 'The Deal'" across the back.

I spun mine around to check, and sure enough, mine read, "J Filly 'The Real Deal.'" They thought it was hilarious, and honestly, it was. What started as a joke ended up sticking.

Before long, everyone was calling me J Filly, or just Filly, whether at the park, at school, or even at home. The nickname followed me all the way to college, where I met some of my closest friends, who still call me Filly to this day.

The Walker boys were so much more than friends; they were like brothers. Nearly every memory I have of growing up is deeply rooted in time spent with Dev and Donnie. When I tore my ACL and was stuck in the house, bedridden for weeks, Donnie came over almost every day. My leg was strapped into this bending machine that forced my knee to slowly move at a 90-degree angle to regain range of motion, so I couldn't leave my room. Donnie continuously went out of his way to keep me company when I needed it most. We wound up playing a ton of Halo, and we eventually beat the game.

From the moment I met Dev and Donnie, I felt an instant connection—a magnetic pull, an undeniable bond. It was like finding my soulmates. Being with them felt perfect. And the parties their dad, Dave, would throw were some of the best times of my young life. Whether it was a Mike Tyson mega fight or the Super Bowl, we always found ourselves at Dave's.

The adults would be inside turning up, and the kids would be in the back alley going at it. There were endless, epic games of two-on-two basketball we called "backyard balling." These were some of the most competitive, disrespectful games you could imagine. Being part of this group meant competing constantly and talking a ton of shit, which I know helped shape my spirited personality. It also taught me a lot about loyalty, and what it's like to really feel supported by people you can trust.

Dave became an important father figure to me early on. When I started to shine on the flag football field, Dave would go into the end zone in the middle of a game and stand there with a five-dollar bill tucked into his hat and a confident look on his face. Whenever I scored a touchdown, I would race over to grab the money and dap him up really fast before running back to my teammates. Somewhere along the way, he gave himself the nickname "8ball," and I've never called him Dave since. To me, he was Uncle 8ball.

The Walkers. The Whites. My mom and Ryan. As I sit in my dorm, battling this uneasy feeling in the pit of my stomach, reflecting on my childhood, these are the people who come to mind.

They shaped me, believed in me, and never let me settle. They're a part of my journey, woven into the fabric of who I've become. I'm grateful for them, not because I owe it to them, but because they've been alongside me every step of the way, helping to build the person I am today.

College is the beginning of a glorious new chapter. I take a deep breath, and let it out slowly.

Gratitude is one hell of a drug.

*   *   *

These memories and experiences weren't just part of my child-hood; they were my training grounds. The battles with Ryan in the backyard forged resilience in me, crafting a competitive armor that I still wear into every battle today. I can almost always tell when someone hasn't had a sibling pushing, poking, challenging, and sometimes whooping their ass. But mine did, all out of love, and yes, most of the time due to my own instigations. But because of it, I'm battle tested.

That same resilience showed itself differently in my mom. Watching her turn scarcity into creativity made me deeply aware of the opportunities hidden in every challenging moment. We found joy, even when the odds were stacked against us, and that was all her doing. It took being an adult to even realize just how broke we were, which is crazy. My mom chose to focus on what we had rather than what we lacked, and because of that, it felt like we had everything in the world.

And just as my mom taught me how to thrive in tough circumstances, the Walkers and the Whites showed me the strength that comes from community. Doing life with them rooted me in the power of having a tribe that stands strong together. They say you're an aggregate of the people you spend the most time with, and I'd like to think I've adopted their best qualities, shaping me into a stronger, more resilient human being.

*   *   *

As I step into this new chapter of my life, I carry those lessons with me. Before I know it, I've moved into my dorm, I've started my classes, and I've settled into a routine. I'm living the life of a student athlete at the Division I college level.

Sounds glorious, right? But let me take you through my first day of team workouts, my rude awakening to what my days will look like for the next few months.

I report to the weight room every morning by 6:00 a.m., and since my dorm is a 25-minute walk away, I'm up by 5:00 a.m. The weight room is buzzing with energy. As soon as I step inside, I'm greeted by the sight of massive Polynesian linemen, their sheer size and athleticism impossible to ignore. Tribal tattoos snake down their legs and arms, a blend of cultural pride and intimidation.

The diversity in the room is striking. While the linemen dominate with their presence, the skilled players bring a different kind of intensity. Some are local, others from the mainland, each contributing their own unique energy. A few look like bodybuilders, huge and ripped, their muscles bulging as they move through their workout.

The weight room itself is a beast, far larger than the cramped space I was used to in high school. It's a sprawling, open area filled with rows of state-of-the-art equipment, including benches, racks, and machines, all gleaming under the bright lights. The walls and equipment are adorned with the University of Hawaii Warriors logo, a fierce, stylized *H* in dark green and black, edged with traditional Hawaiian patterns.

As I take it all in, the clanking of iron plates echoes through the room. With each sound, I feel a mix of intimidation and excitement, as well as a rush of adrenaline that wakes me up more than any alarm clock ever could.

The energy carries over as we lift weights as a team for an hour before heading to the gym for speed and quickness drills. The gym is small and suffocating, and the air is thick with the pungent mix of body odor and alcohol seeping out of someone's pores. Whoever it is, they must be feeling like shit.

We start with ladder drills, our feet moving rapidly through each square, the sound of sneakers squeaking on the slick hardwood floor. The intensity ramps up as we move to line sprints, where each burst of speed is a test of quickness and endurance.

Our morning workouts end with a quick round of conditioning drills, leaving just enough time to shower, grab breakfast, and rush off to class. The pace is relentless, but I'm confident I'll settle into the grind.

After class, I head to the field with the other skill players for seven-on-seven drills. This is my first time competing against college players, and the speed of the game is a wake-up call. Seven-on-seven is football stripped down to its essentials; no linemen, just skill players perfecting the passing game. My head spins, not from trying to fit in, but from my determination to stand out. I feel confident. My knee feels great. All I need is time to adjust to this new, action-packed daily routine.

As you know by now, I'm no stranger to hard work. I've always embraced the grind. But college quickly forces me to take inventory of my blind spots. Not only do I need to cover these blind spots, but I also need to find a way to do more!

*   *   *

When I first step into the weight room with my new team, I can feel how far behind I am. In strength and size, I'm outmatched, and it's obvious I have a lot of work to do. Back in high school, I avoided the weight room altogether, too insecure to face how weak I really was. I told myself I didn't need to be strong if I could just master the art of avoiding hits, but now that excuse feels hollow.

I knew I had to change. High school thinking wasn't going to cut it anymore. I needed to get stronger, so I committed myself fully to the weight room, especially after I met Chad Owens.

Chad was already a star offensive player, an All-American with a real shot at the NFL as he headed into his senior year. People often compared my style of play to his, and I was eager to see him up close.

The first thing I noticed was that Chad was bigger than me. His dedication in the weight room was obvious, and it showed in his build. Watching him lift made it clear I had to step up my game, but it was seeing him on the field that truly opened my eyes.

Chad moved with a sharpness and quickness that mirrored my own, something I wasn't used to seeing. His cuts were precise, exploding with a burst that felt familiar yet elevated. At 185 pounds, he carried his size with the kind of strength and control I aspired to. Even though he was considered a "little guy" like me, earning him the nickname "Mighty Mouse," his muscle-packed frame made him seem anything but small.

Watching Chad dominate on the field made one thing clear: He was someone worth emulating. His work ethic, intensity, and attention to detail set the standard for the entire team. Over time, he took me under his wing, almost like a mentor. I didn't just admire Chad; I studied him, determined to model my game after his, both on and off the field.

13
Those Four Words

After three months in Hawaii, I'm itching to reconnect with family and friends. I book a flight home for spring break, and during the flight, I meticulously plan out every minute of my vacation.

On the drive home from the airport, I fill D-Weez in on college life. With every passing mile, my anticipation to be home grows stronger. As we pull into the driveway, I barely have time to unbuckle before the front door swings open.

My mom bursts out the door with her arms wide open. She wraps me in an extended squeeze, and I can feel her warmth, her love, and a wave of relief in her embrace. When she steps back, her eyes scan me from head to toe, taking in my frame. Months of hard work in the weight room have paid off. My once atrophied leg is now solid as a rock, and I've grown bigger, stronger, and more sculpted overall. Her exhale says everything: it's filled with unspoken pride.

Inside, the house is alive with chatter and energy as we catch up. There's a comfort in being home that I haven't felt in months. As the warmth of the evening settles in, my mind drifts to reconnecting with friends I haven't seen in a while.

An hour later, just as I'm about to walk out the door, my phone rings. The number seems familiar, but I can't place it. I rarely answer unknown callers, but in my excitement to be home, I decide to pick up.

"Jason," the voice on the other end says. It's a voice I know well but haven't heard in years. It's Nicky's voice. We went to junior high together. Her tone is startling, cutting through my excitement and stopping me cold. There's panic, hysteria, something dark and terrible threading through her words.

"Jason. Domo is dead."

For a second, the world stops. I freeze, the phone pressed to my ear, caught in a moment that feels unreal. My eyes drift to the corner of the room. The lights are off, and the only illumination comes from the flickering glow of SportsCenter on the TV. Its reflection dances on the wall, casting erratic shadows that seem to echo my anxiety in this moment.

On the phone, there's a tense pause. A moment where we both hang in the balance, waiting for the other to take the lead or break the silence.

Then she says it again, and the words shatter the silence like glass. "Jason. Domo is dead. He's dead. Oh my God. He's fucking dead!"

*   *   *

I can still hear her voice as if this happened yesterday. The burn of her words as they sear into my brain. The sharp pain that lingers. This is a "forever" kind of scar, marking me in a place no one else can see.

Those four words, "Jason. Domo is dead," change me forever.
This can't be real.

I pace around my room like a madman, my breath quickening as if the walls are closing in. My mind races, grasping at straws. Losing a best friend doesn't happen in real life; it's the kind of nightmare you see in movies.

My heart pounds, and I'm praying, begging, hoping this news is wrong.

I grab my phone and call Javon.

My voice cracks with desperation as I beg him, "Tell me it's not real, bro. *Tell me it's not real!*"

The weight of my words seems to drag through the airwaves, heavy and distorted, traveling slowly from me to him, giving Javon a chance to respond. But there's nothing.

Just silence. Thick, suffocating silence.

We sit on opposite ends of the phone, suspended in that unbearable quiet.

I strain to hear something, anything—tears, a sniffle, some small sound that can confirm the unthinkable.

The waiting stretches on, each second feels like a lifetime.

Then I hear it.

Javon's voice cracks, fracturing the silence, and in that moment, I know. I know before he even gets the words out.

"They got him, Ferg. They got him."

I can't really process what follows. I hear the words *fight* and *shot*. My mind scrambles to make sense of it all as I try to regain my composure and focus on what to do next. Although it's 11 p.m., I head for the door, ready to meet Javon at Domo's house.

But then I stop. My legs give out beneath me, and instead of the door, I find myself in my parents' bedroom. I fall to my knees and bury my face in my hands, choking through my sobs.

A party. A fight. Gunshots. Domo.

My mom drops down beside me, her hand gently rubbing my shoulders as the full weight of the situation crashes over me.

D-Weez is also on the floor, sitting on the opposite side of me. The three of us sit there in complete silence. There are no words, no attempts to rationalize. Just the sound of our tears and complete devastation.

That night, I don't get any sleep. All I can think of is Domo, gasping for air, trying to catch his breath. I torture myself with questions.

Did it hurt?

Was he scared?

Was there a point when he thought to himself, "Oh no! I'm about to die?"

The thought that someone I know so well, someone I loved like a brother, is truly gone feels impossible to comprehend.

The next morning, I pull up to Domo's house, where there's a small crowd gathered on the front porch. My focus locks on Sheryl, his mom, sitting on the steps. She spots me immediately and throws her arms around me, crying, "Jason, oh my God, where have you been?!" I haven't seen her in almost three years.

As she holds me, I'm reminded of all the time we spent together. Years of memories and experiences that make up a significant chunk of my childhood. Domo and I became best friends in middle school, a bond that grew into a brotherhood. His family became my family, and standing here now, it's impossible to reconcile those years with this moment.

*   *   *

I'll never forget my first day of middle school. We were all standing around super awkwardly, avoiding eye contact if at all possible. Then, in walked this Black kid with a fresh flat-top fade and a part on the side. He was good-looking, with chubby cheeks and a mischievous smile. Energy radiated off this kid like he was a celebrity. Even his outfit was fresh, rocking the LL Cool J look with one pant leg down and one pant leg rolled up.

When we ended up in desks next to each other, I looked over and said, "Hi, I'm Jason," like a complete dork. He grinned and said, "I know who you are, foo', we played basketball against each other this summer, remember?" So that's why he seemed so familiar.

"Oh yeah, Dominique, right?" I said.

"Yeah, Domo," he replied. And that's how Domo and I became best friends.

Our first sleepover at his house turned into a four-day extravaganza. His mom gave us a much longer leash than my mom normally would, and we took full advantage of it. In those four days, we ran around our West L.A. streets, linking up with the other neighborhood kids. We played tag until the wee hours of the night and two-hand touch football in the middle of the street.

We played video games in his bedroom, bumping Tupac's *Me Against the World* album until the sun came up. That was the least amount of sleep I'd ever gotten, experiencing for the first time what it felt like to be running on fumes.

We stayed up talking about everything under the sun a 12-year-old might be into back then: sports, rap, girls, and more girls. We went through his shoebox of phone numbers, calling every single girl he knew. He was fearless when it came to talking to girls. He had the charm and charisma of a superstar.

On the last day, while his parents were out, we snuck into their room and jumped up and down on their bed, blasting their stereo while memorizing the lyrics to Eazy-E's "Real Muthaphuckkin G's," dissing Dr. Dre. That third verse hit different—it was gritty, unapologetic, and unlike anything I'd ever heard before. We played that third verse over and over again so we could spit it back perfectly, mastering every pause, every punchline, nailing the cadence and delivery to Eazy's flow.

Picturing two 12-year-old kids jumping up and down on the bed, rapping every explicit word of an Eazy-E verse, cracks me the hell up. We were happy and carefree. That was us.

Domo and I eventually added a middle man to our bestie group: Javon. Javon was the perfect addition. He was funny as hell, with an amazing sense of humor. He was by far the freshest out the group. He was always rocking the flyest gear that was hot back then: FUBU, Enyce, Tommy Hilfiger, you name it. And he didn't just have the clothes; he always had the new Jordans the day they dropped. His shoe collection was something serious.

The three of us were inseparable. We decided to start a rap group called JDJ and would spend hours in Domo's room, rapping our asses off, mimicking the cadences of Jay-Z, Snoop Dogg, Kurupt, or Eminem. Those sessions were legendary.

Javon lived right across the street from Domo, and I was just a quick ten-minute walk away. We walked to and from school together every day. On weekends, we always found something to get into. If I wasn't with the Walkers (Dev or Donnie), I was with Domo and Javon. No question about it.

Domo's garage became the 24/7 hangout spot. It was a detached garage that we turned into our middle school man cave. The walls were plastered with posters of our favorite rappers and some of the hottest girls of our day: Tyra Banks, Halle Berry, Lil' Kim, and Foxy Brown, all staring down at us like we were kings of our little kingdom.

It wasn't just about the posters. Every inch of that garage felt like ours. Two foldout mattresses stretched across the floor, their sheets hiding years of food stains, drool, and whatever other nastiness we'd added over time. A big boom box sat proudly on a desk against the wall, always ready to blast whatever song or album we were obsessed with that week. This wasn't just a space; it was our refuge, our little slice of freedom.

We used that garage for everything: writing rhymes, having late-night talks, and sneaking girls over. We were badass little kids, planning it out all week and executing our plans to perfection. As soon as Domo's parents went to sleep, we'd sneak the girls in, pull an all-nighter, and then head inside with bags under our eyes but happy as could be.

One night, we snuck out to a girl's house instead, praying that Domo's parents wouldn't wake up and notice we were gone. We were eighth graders, little kids with no business being on the streets that late. Plus, there were several gangs right there in our backyard. We knew we had to keep our heads on a swivel for police and for other kids looking to stir up trouble.

We ran across the street, where Javon grabbed his stepdad's gun and tucked it under his shirt; then we headed out. We didn't ever walk around with a gun like that, but it was late, so it somehow felt appropriate. Almost responsible?

After hanging at the girl's house for a couple of hours, we headed home. That's when we saw a car full of high school kids notice us. We could feel their eyes on us. Growing up in this part of L.A., you learned to trust your "spidey sense." A lot of kids gangbanged. You could find yourself in serious trouble in seconds if you weren't careful.

We turned to walk the other way just as three police cars pulled up, shining their lights on us, demanding that we "Stop right there!"

The high school kids took off in their car. Domo, without hesitation, bolted in one direction, while Javon and I ran in the opposite.

Javon tossed the gun in some bushes as we ran full speed back to Domo's, taking all side streets. Every time we stopped to catch our breath, we looked around for Domo, hopeful that he'd pop up out of nowhere, right behind us. But he was nowhere in sight.

The closer we got to his house, the more we began to freak out.

What if the cops got him? What if the kids in the car got him?

We got to his house but couldn't bring ourselves to go inside without him. What if his mom woke up and saw he wasn't with us? We'd have to explain what happened. It'd look like we left him.

Instead, we went to Javon's house across the street. His parents weren't home, so we sat for hours in front of the living room window, waiting, watching, praying that Domo would show up.

The longer we waited, the more we started to lose our shit, picturing worst-case scenarios. Domo tied up in the back seat of that car. Or worse. Each passing minute felt like an eternity, and the images in my mind grew darker. I couldn't shake the feeling that we had left him, abandoned him in the worst possible situation. I knew we hadn't, but that didn't stop the guilt from creeping in.

The L.A. streets were unforgiving.

We decided we had to go back to look for him. And we definitely had to get the gun. We couldn't just leave it there.

Just as we were heading out the door, we saw him—Domo. Sprinting down the street. His chest arched up, his head leaning back. His arms pumping up and down, firing away like an Olympian. He was in an all-out sprint with a massive smile on his face. Like this was fun to him. I'd never been more relieved to see that beautiful smile of his.

We ran outside and launched into one another, celebrating Domo's return like we had just won the lottery. He was fine.

When Javon and I had run one way and Domo the other, he'd ended up back at the girl's house. He waited there for a while before making a mad dash home. By the time we saw him, he was in a full-blown sprint, so close to home, anxiously trying to get back to us.

After middle school, Domo and I went to different high schools. All of my time was focused on sports, and we were both finding our own identities, so we drifted a bit.

*   *   *

Now, standing outside his house on this awful day, I can feel his mom's pain as we hug. It seeps out of her pores, washing over me like a tidal wave. I have to work to avoid eye contact with her, terrified of what I might feel if I look into her eyes. The devastation, the trauma, the overwhelming reality of what has happened.

In a scene where everyone was hysterical, not just crying but wailing with immense pain and heartache, I was desperately trying to keep it together. I needed to stay strong, and I knew that one look into her eyes would shatter me completely.

I head inside and find Mo, Domo's dad, sitting on the floor in the corner of the room. His head is down, and he has a drink in his hand, but he jumps up as soon as he sees me. "Son," he says softly, with tears streaming down his face. We hug in silence. As he takes a step back, he extends his cup and motions for me to take a sip. I stare deep into the bottom of the glass, swish it around, then take a big, slow gulp of warm bourbon.

From the back of the living room, I stare at the door, watching people come and go. My mind starts to play tricks on me. I'm taken back to that night when we ran from the police. When Javon and I had spent all those hours looking out of the living room window, waiting for Domo.

I remember the thrill that came when we finally saw him running down the block, smiling ear to ear. The exhilaration. I'm desperate for this scene to play out again. Every time the front door opens, I hold my breath, hoping it'll be him, praying that this has all just been one big misunderstanding. I peek out the window again and again, searching for that big, bright, beautiful smile sprinting down the street toward me. But no matter how many times I look, it doesn't come. It never comes.

*   *   *

I'd just spoken to Domo a week before spring break. He called to check in, asking when I'd be coming back to L.A. He wanted to know everything about Hawaii and pressed me for details about football. He knew how much it meant to me. Domo had always been one of my biggest supporters, someone who truly understood the sacrifices I'd made to get here. He'd seen it all and respected that football was my priority. He knew firsthand just how easy it was to get caught up in the chaos of gang activity and the endless distractions the city threw at you. But he always insisted I keep my main thing the main thing. I loved him for that.

I wondered how I could have been a better influence on him. What more I could have done as a friend. It made me feel selfish about my goals, like I should have done more.

Losing Domo wasn't just a tragedy; it was a brutal reminder of how fleeting life can be. We hear the saying "Live every day like it's your last" so often that it feels hollow, like just any other phrase we repeat without meaning. But now, for the first time, it struck me deeply.

There were things I wanted to say to Domo, conversations I thought we had time for. Moments I imagined we'd still get to share. Even as life pulled us in different directions, he was still my brother. I believed we had more time. Time to reconnect, to laugh, to grow old together with our families by our sides. But that time was stolen, and I'll never get the chance to tell him what he meant to me.

Domo was killed four days before his 19th birthday.

I served as one of his pallbearers. And then I returned to Hawaii, physically exhausted and emotionally depleted.

14

One Snap, and Clear

Back in Hawaii, I feel like I'm being followed by a dark cloud, and no matter what I do, I can't shake it. And to make matters worse, almost immediately upon my return, I get hit with a random drug test.

I'm sitting in team meetings when I hear my name called, telling me to report to the training room at 8 a.m. the next morning. I can't believe it. A drug test, of all things.

Here's the problem: After tearing my ACL and then losing Domo, the adversities were compounding, and I was desperate for some kind of release. During spring break, while dealing with Domo's death and preparing for his funeral, I turned to marijuana.

Marijuana wasn't new to me; L.A. has a huge weed culture. Hardly anyone I knew drank alcohol in high school, which I later realized was unusual. Most of the kids on campus at UH had been drinking most weekends during their high school years. The kids in my circle didn't drink; they smoked.

The first time I ever tried weed was in sixth grade with Domo. He'd swiped some from a neighbor, and we decided to give it a go. We got high out of our minds. Laughing hysterically and snacking all night long. So now, it felt like the right thing to do, a familiar escape in a week that felt like hell.

Instead of seeking therapy or counseling, I coped that week by working out during the day and smoking at night with friends. We pulled together, united by his memory, and smoking seemed to be the only thing that helped me get through that painful stretch of days.

But now, I can't believe it. *You've got to be kidding me. I didn't smoke at all before this trip, and the one time I do, I end up on a drug test list.*

The night before the test, I chug a gallon of water, determined to do whatever it takes to beat it. A teammate hooks me up with several niacin pills, swearing they'll flush any trace of drugs from my system.

Niacin is supposed to be a quick fix, a way to cleanse your body in record time. But those pills come with a brutal price—they make your blood itch and burn like it's on fire. I scratch myself raw, desperate for relief, clawing at my skin in sheer agony all night. I'm supposed to take the full dose, but after that first one, I'm done. "Fuck that." Instead, I find myself praying for a miracle, though deep down, I already know how this is going to end.

Walking into the training room feels like marching down the green mile to my execution. I feel so stupid for putting myself in this situation. It feels like I've let Coach Jones down after he gave me a once-in-a-lifetime shot that no other coach would even consider. I'm concerned about how this will alter my reputation. How will I be viewed among the coaching staff? I can already hear the whispers behind closed doors:

"That Ferguson kid is a great player, but he's an off-the-field liability."

The thought of being labeled like that eats at me.

This can't be the reputation I adopt; no way. I've worked too hard, sacrificed too much to be seen as anything other than a dedicated athlete.

When the results come back, I'm forced to face what I already know deep down. Just as I feared, I fail the test.

Now comes the hardest part. Walking to Coach Jones's office feels like dragging a big rig by a harness strapped to my waist. Each step is heavier than the last, weighed down by the dread of what's waiting for me. I'm not sure what the punishment will be, but the thought of seeing the disappointment in Coach Jones's eyes is what I'm bracing for most.

I walk in and take a seat, and Coach Jones doesn't waste any time. He gets right to it. He brings up the failed test and asks if I have a drug problem or if I need help. I explain what happened during my trip, how I'd been coping with the death of a brother by smoking with friends.

Surprisingly, he's very understanding. He had no clue I was going through this, but he has to be firm. This is a warning, a slap on the wrist. No more free passes after this. Moving forward, I'm subject to random tests, and if I fail another, I'll be suspended. It's a brutal way to start my freshman year, pulling me deeper into this pit of self-loathing and despair.

This dark cloud looms over me like a curse, a constant reminder of everything that has gone wrong. It makes me feel like I'm permanently jinxed, with bad luck shadowing my every move.

Back on campus, everything feels different. I think about death all the time. I walk past strangers on campus and think how, with the snap of a finger, they could be wiped off the face of the earth. Life feels fragile to me for the first time ever.

I should probably seek out a therapist. I should leverage some of the resources I have access to on campus. But I don't.

Instead, I do all I can to simply bury my pain, to ignore the trauma that's compounding inside me. I figure if I just keep my focus on football, it will keep my mind off Domo.

*   *   *

Now that we're knee-deep in spring training, everyone's out on the field, working their butts off and pushing themselves to the limit. Bear in mind, I haven't actually played college ball yet, since I only started school in January. I've been training daily in the weight room and on the field, so I'm feeling pretty good physically about my level of play. But I need to get my mind right. I need to shake off the emotions that have kept me in a trance. On the outside, I fight to appear normal, but inside, I'm battling.

It's around this time that my grades start to slip. I've always been a solid student. But I know I'm capable of much better work than I usually put out. School has always come easily to me, so I've developed bad habits over the years doing just enough to get by. But now, with everything I'm dealing with, even that minimal effort is starting to falter.

In college, I don't have the same freedom to screw around. As an athlete, they give you a very short leash in terms of classroom attendance. As a freshman, that leash is even shorter. Our coaches do class checks every day to make sure our butts are exactly where they're supposed to be. If they notice you aren't there, you have to report to dawn patrol, a special kind of punishment at 4 a.m., running flights of stairs for two hours straight. You also get penciled in on the coach's shit list.

I'm so distraught after losing Domo that I find it really hard to sit in class and focus on anything my professors say. So, I stop going. Or rather, I show up, and as soon as our coach leaves after completing class checks, I wait five minutes and then walk right out, not really giving a damn about the optics or what my professors think.

My roommate's massive DVD collection only makes it easier for me to skip class. I pop in a movie and chill out, biding my time and counting down the days until the semester finally ends.

By the end of my first semester, the consequences of my actions hit hard. My grades slip so badly that I finish with a 1.8 GPA. You need a 2.0 to be eligible, and I'm immediately put on academic probation. Never in my academic career have I been anywhere near academic ineligibility. I've always been pretty good about maintaining a 3.0 GPA without even trying. But now, here I am, only a few months on campus, and I've already failed a drug test and landed myself on academic probation.

The severity of my situation is crystal clear. If I don't get my shit together, I won't last, and I'll have no one to blame but myself. I'm fully aware of the spiral I'm in, and I know I need to do something about it—fast. I can't afford to let this slip any further. I have to turn things around, not just for my academic standing but for my future, both on and off the field.

*   *   *

With that weight hanging over me, spring training comes and goes with me barely keeping it together. But just as summer approaches, there's a new challenge on the horizon: my first Division I college football camp.

Allow me to explain what a Division I college football camp is like. First, the entire team bunks together for the duration of camp. For us, that means we all sleep on rollaway cots for three weeks in an empty dance hall located just above our locker room. Wheeling my bed into the room and positioning it in an area of my choosing makes it feel like sleepaway camp for grown-ass men.

Practice kicks off first thing in the morning, and the tone is set immediately. Tons of fans show up to watch, hoping to catch a sneak peek at next year's team. The sidelines are full of camera crews and journalists studying the day's practice in search of their next story.

As for the players, everyone is fighting for their spot on the team. Returning players battle to earn a starting spot, while guys trying out for the team hope for a walk-on spot or even just to make the practice squad. Everyone has their own personal goals, and everyone is giving 110 percent effort. This is our shot.

I've been rigorously studying our playbook to ensure that I know enough of the complex offense to be able to showcase my skills. This will be my first time on a football field with pads on in nearly three years.

*　　*　　*

The night before camp, my stomach is in a knot, filled with excited nerves, the good kind. This is it. Everything I've worked for, all of the sacrifices my family has made, all of the torture I've put my body through. It all boils down to this.

Determined to make a strong first impression, I'm up before dawn. As the sun starts to peek over the horizon, I'm already at the field, ready to prove myself.

We start the morning off with individual drills, then it's straight into one-on-ones. This is my shot to stand out.

When it's my turn, I take my stance at the line of scrimmage, positioning myself low, intentionally making myself even smaller than I already am. Shoulder pads are an easy target for defenders to grab, push, and pull on, so I want to make myself as small as possible, which for me is easy.

The QB says "hike," and I pause for a split second, waiting to see the defender's first move. He freezes too, waiting to see what I'm going to do. Perfect. I take a soft first step outside, followed by a quick head-and-shoulders fake inside. The defender spins in a complete circle. I hear cheers from the sidelines, followed by a "Damn, Ferg," but I stay focused on the play.

I push upfield to the five-yard mark, break to the outside, and whip my head around to find the ball already on its way. Extending my arms wide, I watch it all the way into my hands to complete the catch.

As I jog back in line for the drill, I hear someone charging at me. Before I can completely turn around, I'm confronted by a tall 6'2" dude who's already committed to giving me a chest bump and nearly knocks me over. "God damn, bro!" he shouts, grinning ear to ear. I have no idea who he is, but I love his energy.

His name is Desmond Thomas, but everyone calls him Dez. He's a wide receiver from Vallejo, CA, and I can tell right away he has that same fire I did.

Dez and I didn't know it at the time, but we'd be glued at the hip all freshman year. Whether we were playing Madden for hours with Brewster, an older running back who took us under his wing, or hitting the Hawaii nightlife with Jason Rivers, a teammate who became more like a brother to me, Dez and I did everything together. We were locked in.

Dez had this old Mazda 929 that changed everything for us. It was poppin'. We'd drive around the entire island, admiring the beautiful ladies and exploring every beach, back road, and hidden spot we could find. The Mazda may have been old and a bit beat-up, but to us, it was a passport to the kind of freedom and adventure you dream about. Football kept us sharp; we were both hungry and clear on why we were there. And finding each other early on, in this new place we called home, felt like a game-changer.

But now, nothing is bigger than this moment. Back in line after the play, I peek over at Coach Jones, not sure what I'm looking for. Maybe to see if he's impressed. Maybe just to see if he's watching me. But I can't tell a thing. He stands there, arms crossed, giving me nothing.

Later that day, we meet to watch the film of the day's practice. This is where you really get better. Every day you watch yourself on film, and you get a chance to see all the good and all the bad you've done. Nothing slips through the cracks. The coaches see everything, and it's their job to teach you. This is where most of the coaching gets done.

Coach Jones is both our head coach and our offensive coordinator, so he runs the film sessions. Today, we start by looking at one-on-ones from that morning, and the first couple of plays go by without much comment.

Then Coach Jones says, "Oh yeah, watch this move." He uses the laser pointer to bring everyone's attention to a particular corner of the screen. I squint my eyes, trying to focus clearly on what he's pointing at. Then I realize it's me. It's the play from the one-on-ones, where I'd spun the defender in a circle.

On film, the play looks just like it felt. I shook the shit out of that defender and finished the catch perfectly.

I take a second to collect myself, tilting my head to the ceiling as the play ends. The ceiling is dirty, with small holes poked into each of the tiles that cover it. I stare at those holes fiercely, trying to process the whirlwind of emotions rushing through me.

Relief. Gratitude. A sense of accomplishment that's been eluding me for so long.

Thank God—finally, a much-needed win.

I'm really doing it. I knew I could if I was given the chance, but here I am, at the most competitive level, fresh off an ACL tear, and I still "got it."

A small smile tugs at the corners of my mouth as the realization sets in. This is just a fraction of what I can do. I feel the hunger deep inside—a fire igniting to show out even more, to prove that this is just the beginning.

I'd always wondered what this moment would feel like. While running sand dunes at 4 a.m., I'd block out the pain by projecting vivid visions of myself sitting in a film room, studying the look of excitement on my coach's face after he'd watched a film of me make an electric play. I'd wonder what the room would look like, who would be in it. I'd daydream in class about what it would feel like in the exact moment I'd won over my coaches.

My journey to this moment has been riddled with adversities and setbacks. But now, something feels different, like the storms I've weathered are finally starting to clear. This is my moment. It's as if the universe itself is leaning in, shifting everything into place for me.

*   *   *

With each practice, I can feel myself improving, getting better and better. As I sharpen my skills on the field, I notice that progress spilling over into my life off the field too. Things are beginning to feel a little lighter, and I'm grateful to be immersed in football. It's the distraction I desperately need.

A big part of that progress comes from Coach Jones. I respond well to his coaching style. It's different from what I'm used to, but it's undeniably effective. Jones isn't the type to show excitement in his communication; he's not the rah-rah motivator like some of my previous coaches. His style is much calmer, more measured. He's a teacher, and his approach, while new to me, is refreshing. With his experience as a head coach at the NFL level, he treats us like professionals, communicating with respect but always holding us to the highest expectations.

He isn't afraid to challenge you publicly, but he never goes out of his way to humiliate his players. His sense of timing is impeccable. Just when you least expect it, he'll show you love on a catch or a route, yelling out, "Nice move, 21."

When you screw up on one of his perfectly drawn-up plays, though, he'll call you out without hesitation: "Hey, 21, where are you supposed to go when you see the safety drop?" he'll ask in front of everyone. Yet somehow, in those moments, it feels like it's just you and him on the field. Teaching, not belittling.

One practice during camp, I run a killer route, leaving the defender looking silly, only to drop the pass. Frustration overwhelms me, and I start throwing a mini tantrum, ripping my helmet off and nearly launching it toward the sidelines before I regain my composure. Coach Jones calls me over to where he's standing. He can tell I'm pissed and doesn't want it messing with the rest of my practice.

As I make my way over, he says, "Jason, one snap, and clear."

I look at him, confused. "Huh?"

He repeats himself, "One snap, and clear." Then he expands, "It doesn't matter if you drop a pass or catch a touchdown. Focus on the next play. One snap, and clear."

Brilliant.

A snap is how the play starts, a fresh beginning. With the QB yelling "hike" and the center snapping the ball to him, it's the moment everything resets. The moment you leave the last play behind and focus on what's in front of you. What he's telling me is not to get too high or too low, but to keep my focus on what's next, the play in front of us. Because the next play is the best play.

Those words resonate far beyond football. At this moment, I'm dealing with so much off the field: Domo's death, academic challenges, and a failed drug test. Here's Coach Jones, dropping a gem that hits home. His advice isn't just about football; it's about life.

The bad plays, the good plays, they're all temporary. Life moves forward, whether we're ready or not. "One snap, and clear" is a call to let go of what weighs you down, to reset with every setback, and to avoid clinging to success as if it defines you. It's about focusing on what's next, staying present, and refusing to let the highs or the lows derail you.

In that moment, I realized how much I needed this lesson. I couldn't change the past, what had happened with Domo, my knee, or that drug test. But I could control how I would choose to respond moving forward. One snap, one moment, one choice at a time.

*   *   *

That mindset carries me into the fall semester and my first season playing Division I college football. My performance in camp this summer earns me a second-string wide receiver spot behind Chad Owens. That first game is everything I've dreamed it would be, minus not being a starter on the team—yet.

As the team files into the locker room at Aloha Stadium on game day, my eyes lock onto my jersey hanging neatly in my locker. The black-and-green color combination is bold, almost daring. It stares back at me like it's waiting for me to step into it and bring it to life, like it's incomplete without me. Next to it, my all-black helmet sits polished to perfection, its surface catching the light in a way that makes it dance, almost like sparks flickering off a firework.

I walk up and take it all in.

This is real. I'm really here, and it's all happening. This is what I've worked for, what I've dreamed about. Now it's time to make it count.

Running out of the tunnel on game day feels like stepping straight into a classic football movie, the kind you grew up watching, like *Rudy* or *The Program*.

As I stand at the exit, waiting for the signal to run out on the field, the roar of the crowd earthquakes through the concrete walls, sending goosebumps up and down my body. I'm not nervous; I'm anxious.

Then the signal comes, and we burst out of the tunnel, the noise of the crowd washing over Aloha Stadium like a tidal wave. It's deafening. I can feel the energy coursing through me as I take it all in.

Midway through the first half, I'm standing on the sidelines, helmet in my hands, watching the game intensely as both teams battle back and forth.

Suddenly, Chad Owens gets tackled and comes up limping. As he limp-skips his way over to the sidelines, I hear, "Jason Ferguson ... Jason Ferguson," and for a second, I'm frozen.

Oh shit, that's me—I'm up.

I look over and see Coach Jones screaming my name, snapping me out of the trance I'm in. I pop my helmet on, heart racing, and sprint out on the field.

As I jog over to the huddle, Timmy Chang, our QB, catches my eye, gives me a smile, and says, "Let's go, Ferg, you ready?" While I'm only out there for two or three plays, I'm out there. My first official game back, and I touch the field.

While I want to play more, I'm proud to be that high up on the depth chart, especially as a freshman. Most true freshmen redshirt, meaning they practice with the team but sit out the season to preserve a year of eligibility. But here I am, playing second string to an All-American, with only one person between me and a starting spot. I find myself on the field at critical moments during several games this season.

I also win the starting kick returner position, where I have a chance to shine. I don't score any touchdowns, which is new to me, but I make over a dozen breakaway kick returns that electrify the crowd and inject the team with energy. Even on plays where I'm not able to break for a long run, my cut-back-heavy, refuse-to-run-into-a-wall style of play makes for great entertainment. The fans love it.

I'm named Special Teams Player of the Week against LA Tech, earning a game ball for my performance. Not only did I break for a 50-yard return, setting up a crucial touchdown, but I'd also left the crowd on the edge of their seats with several other electrifying returns.

Sending that ball home to my mom feels like sending physical proof of my perseverance. It confirms that I'm good enough to play at this level, that I've battled adversity like a warrior, and that it's finally paying off.

I see it this way: if I continue to fully commit, I'll have three years to start and claim the spotlight as Hawaii's next big star.

That spotlight means something different here. Living on the island isn't like living on the mainland. It's small, closely connected, with no pro team. University of Hawaii sports are the pro teams. So when your name blows up, you wind up being recognized everywhere, like a celebrity.

I've seen it happen with some of my teammates, and I desperately want it for myself. I want everything that comes with being a star player. The notoriety, the attention, the leadership responsibilities. And of course, the girls. I want it all, and as far as I'm concerned, I'm on a clear path to claiming it.

*   *   *

During practice one day, I notice this guy hanging out on the sidelines. He stands out like a disco ball in a library.

Growing up in L.A., you see every type of athlete. Baseball players, basketball players, football players, you name it. We see them all. Each one has their own look. If you play the sport long enough, you develop a skill for sizing players up, a way of measuring talent just by looking someone over long before they set foot on the field or the court.

At first, I stare at this guy because he has a big puffer jacket on. While it is only 7 a.m., it's still Hawaii, so his jacket looks crazy.

What I notice next are his dreads, long with bleached-blond tips that hang past his ears and frame his face, leaving just enough room for his eyes to peek through. There's an intensity in his gaze. He isn't just watching our practice; he's studying our practice.

All I know is, he looks like a baller.

By the time practice is over, he's gone. But something about him lingers in my mind. Maybe it's the way he carried himself or the quiet hunger in his eyes. I can't put my finger on it, but I know one thing for sure: whoever this dude is, he's not here to play around. And somehow, I have a feeling that my path and his are about to cross in a way that will change everything.

15
Danza

From my apartment window on the twelfth floor, I find myself staring down at our practice field more often than I'd like to admit. Its quiet stretch of green feels empty, almost haunted without the sound of pads cracking or the commotion of coaches barking out drills. It's off-season, the calm before the storm of another grueling football camp.

I'm not just looking at the field. I'm lost in it, letting my mind wander to all the touchdowns I'm going to score, the records I'll break, and the games I'll help the team win. I can see it so clearly, almost like a highlight reel playing out in my head. Me juking defenders, the roar of the crowd, the scoreboard lighting up with my name. In these moments, I'm not just dreaming. I'm already there, living it, the future so vivid I can almost reach out and touch it.

But today, the moment I look out my window, something catches my attention.

On the field, there's a guy, shirtless, wearing only compression tights as shorts, running wide receiver routes by himself. There's no quarterback throwing him the ball, and nobody else out there with him. He's just running routes at full speed, with a purpose.

I narrow my eyes, leaning closer to the window, drawn to his movement. There's something magnetic about the way he carries himself, the precision in his steps, the intensity in his pace. He's sharp, quick, and polished. It takes a moment to register and then it hits me. It's him, the guy with the dreads.

Curiosity takes over. I can't help myself. Before I know it, I'm out the door, heading down to the field. By the time I catch up to him in the locker room, he's slipping off his cleats, with his expression guarded.

His name is Davone Bess, and he's joining our team midyear, just like I did the year before. Right away, I can sense his hesitation, the skepticism in his eyes. And I get it. Davone's story is the kind that stops you in your tracks: wild, heartbreaking, and almost impossible to believe.

Davone is from East Oakland, a city where violence and drugs often cast long shadows, but it's also a place rich with spirit and resilience, where the community's strength shines through. Davone is a beast on the field, and he had earned a full scholarship to Oregon State. That was the dream, and his ticket out.

But one day, after school, he picked up some friends who had just pulled a home invasion, stealing bags full of stuff. While driving, he was pulled over, and all of them were arrested. Davone, being the oldest and the driver, was made an example of by the judge. He was handed a one-year sentence, and just like that, his scholarship to Oregon State was gone.

His coach and community pleaded with the judge, bombarding him with calls and letters, expressing how much was at stake for this young man who was simply in the wrong place at the wrong time. But the judge was determined to make an example out of him. Davone was sent to an all-boys camp, a euphemism for a detention center.

While there, he participated in a seven-on-seven football passing league, where his team would compete against other camps.

This is where fate stepped in. The head coach at Davone's high school, legendary Northern California football coach John Beam, reached out to a graduate assistant (GA) at the University of Hawaii, who had also attended that same high school as Davone had, years before. The GA heard about Davone's story and decided to go check him out. He went down to the detention center to catch a game, video camera in hand, and what he saw was nothing short of remarkable.

Davone was balling, like a diamond in the rough, shining bright in the unlikeliest of places.

The graduate assistant took that jailhouse footage of Davone running routes on a patchy, dusty field in sneakers straight to Coach Jones, who instantly saw the raw talent and his untapped potential. Coach Jones flew Davone out to Hawaii the day after he got out of jail, which is when I first saw Davone standing on the sidelines. Not long after, he was offered a full scholarship.

In-fucking-credible.

Coach Jones was the ultimate risk taker, the guru of second chances. And now, here I am, standing face-to-face with Davone, cautiously working through the shield he's put up to protect himself. And who could blame him? The kid literally just got out of jail.

But it doesn't take long before he realizes my intentions are good, and that I'm here to grind just like him. Eventually, we start working out together, making it part of our regular routine. The workouts become our shared language, breaking down any walls that were there at the start.

All through spring training, we get after it, pushing each other hard, coaching, critiquing, and polishing every aspect of our game. We do everything in our power to ensure we'll be two of the four starting receivers on the team.

Coach Jones has other plans, though. He shocks us both by putting Davone right behind me as the second-string receiver, forcing us to spend the summer competing for the same position.

This decision baffles me, forcing me to question everything. *Have I been delirious thinking I was up next as the star here?*

Is my emotional intelligence really that far off to have assumed I'd be the guy this season?

But rather than let this become a jealous rivalry, we push each other to the deepest of waters, pulling the best out of each other. His moves are creative. He's got the best hands any of us have ever seen. The kid catches everything thrown his way. Each catch is accompanied by a distinct pop, like the sound of a perfectly sealed jar being opened. His hands grip the ball with a force and precision that make every reception look effortless.

It's impossible to watch without feeling challenged. Each time he makes a play, I push myself to make an even better one.

The paranoia of Davone outshining me makes me dig deep, and what emerges is magical. I once heard the phrase "Only the paranoid survive." I am now living this reality. Paranoia is my fuel: how I watch film, how I take care of my body, how early I arrive for practice. That constant edge of fear and vigilance keeps me on my toes, always pushing me to be better. I stay sharp, anticipating challenges before they hit.

It's this mindset that drives me to work harder, to stay focused, and to innovate. Complacency isn't an option; it's the kiss of death. My success hinges on never letting my guard down, always being ready for the next obstacle. Davone brings out the animal in me. You can either run from competition or embrace it. I choose to *embrace it.*

When summer training kicks off, it's as if we're at the starting line of a track meet. Head down, hands on the ground, butt in the air, feet pressing into the starting blocks, waiting for the sound of the gun. Bang! The grind begins.

Every day feels like an all-out sprint, with Davone by my side. We're in the weight room at 6 a.m., pushing through early-morning grinds. After lifting, we head straight to summer school, the offensive players moving across campus as a unit. A herd of football players, easily identifiable by our size (except for me), swagger, and the collective energy that seems to pulse around us.

In the afternoons, Davone, Dez, and I hit the field for a second workout, driving each other further. Then it's off to the box manufacturing warehouse, where Davone and I spend our nights on an assembly line gluing boxes together until midnight. Living in Hawaii during the summer isn't cheap, and that one scholarship check you get doesn't go far. But through the exhaustion, we keep pushing. This level of grind bonds us in a way nothing else can.

Legendary trainer Tim Grover once said, "Winning is a full-blown sprint with no finish line." Well, Davone and I are determined to win.

*   *   *

Around this time, our team is joined by a new QB, Colt Brennan. Colt is a handsome, intelligent, and insanely talented 6'3", 215-pound QB out of Orange County, California. He arrives on the island that summer as a nobody, just another guy looking for his big break.

But right out of the gate, he proves to be a fierce competitor. He is athletic, has pinpoint accuracy, and throws the ball with a half-cocked sidearm fling that most coaches would frown upon. But it's a thing of beauty. There's an undeniable swagger to his style that makes it instantly lovable. It's unorthodox, but man, is it effective.

He isn't handed the starting job; he'll have to earn it, just like the rest of us. But from the moment he steps on the field, you can feel the energy shift. His presence alone kicks the competition up a notch. He's got the goods, and everyone knows it. This guy is special.

Not only does he raise the level of competition, but Colt and I also hit it off right away. He's one of the most unselfish and thoughtful guys I've ever known. Our friendship is rooted in mutual respect and a shared love for the competitive nature of the game. Colt becomes my guy, more than just a teammate; a lifelong friend.

As Colt settles in, the competition across the team only intensifies. With no starter officially named, every one of us on offense competes like our lives are on the line, constantly asking ourselves, "Am I doing enough?"

Summer camp officially starts, and it's brutal. Long and physically demanding, but it only fuels my rivalry with Davone. All camp long, neither of us backs down. I make a play, catching a ten-yard pass, juking defenders, and breaking out for a big gain.

Just when I think I have the upper hand, Davone answers with one of the most acrobatic, one-handed catches anyone has ever seen. He's quick, with moves that mirror mine, but his larger, more solid frame makes him durable, more like the prototypical receiver. But that doesn't faze me. We go back and forth all camp, both driven by an almost obsessive determination to come out as the top receiver.

This rivalry with Davone isn't just competition. It's a crucible that pushes us to new heights. It brings out that "dog" in me, revealing what I'm truly capable of and restoring the confidence I desperately needed after a knee injury that nearly ended my career.

As fate would have it, our first game of my sophomore season is against USC, right on our home turf in Hawaii.

When I hear the news, all I can think about is that moment four years ago when USC's head coach made it clear he wouldn't be recruiting me. I remember the feeling that followed that conversation, how it set me on a warpath, determined to make him regret it.

Getting to play against USC now feels like a gift from the football gods, an offering on a platter. I'm faster, stronger, and smarter. I don't know if we'll win the game, but I know this is my opportunity for revenge. To embarrass anyone who tries to guard me.

The beauty of college ball is that everything gets put on film. Not a single play is missed. Even if I don't get the ball, I can make someone look silly and force them to relive it over and over on tape.

I want USC film sessions filled with comments like, "Look at what this little dude does right here," and "Damn! Watch this release off the ball." My goal is to terrorize the school that had ignited and then dashed my young dreams.

This will be one of the biggest home games ever played in Aloha Stadium. It's completely sold out. Some 50,000 fans will fill every seat in the house.

*   *   *

The game is a week away when Coach Jones calls me into his office. He never asks to speak with me one-on-one like this, so I'm nervous. I brace myself for worst-case scenarios as I walk in, sweating so much my feet slide around in my sandals.

As I step inside, Coach Jones looks up from his desk, calm and collected, completely at ease. "How's it going?" he asks in his usual steady tone.

"It's going great, Coach. Big week, right?" I babble back.

He continues, "Well, I'll get right to it. I'm gonna move you to the right side this week to prep for USC. Davone will stay on the left. You'll both be number ones."

Wait.

Did I just hear that correctly?

Did he say Davone and I would be starting together?

Coach's mouth continues to move, but I'm barely able to make out the words. What he appears to be saying is that I've shown great leadership during this camp, that I've been here longer than Davone, so I'm more comfortable with our complex offense, and that he trusts I can handle the position change.

I mean, it's not really a position change; it's the same offense, just on the opposite side of the ball. Nothing drastic.

As his words sink in, I feel a rush of relief and excitement. All the hard work, the refusal to quit, the almost delusional belief in myself, and it's all finally paying off. I'd clung to the conviction that I'd get my shot on the biggest stage, even when everything seemed to be falling apart. And now, somehow, I've done it.

I shake Coach's hand and sprint out the door to find Davone. And man, what a beautiful moment it is when I do. All camp long we'd known this was a possibility, and deep down, I think both of us felt like it was supposed to happen. But the closer we'd gotten to the game without it happening, the more we'd started to doubt that it would.

*   *   *

Reflecting back, I recognize that getting through camp with the uncertainty of where I'd land on the depth chart wasn't easy. I had to find a way to stay grounded, and competition alone wasn't going to cut it. What gave us both an edge was adopting an abundance mindset, a shift in perspective that changed everything.

Hating on Davone would have been easy. Turning this into a bitter rivalry in which I celebrated his failures might have felt like the natural response. But I made a conscious choice to fight that urge. Instead of seeing it as Davone or me, which is a scarcity mindset that assumes there's only room for one person to win, I chose to see it as Davone and me, believing there was enough success to go around for both of us.

This shift in perspective shaped how Davone and I approached our competition. We believed we could both shine on the field, and that belief changed everything. We pushed each other, celebrated each other's wins, and competed fiercely without letting it turn toxic. Our level of play rose beyond the level of our competition, leaving no doubt that we were the two best receivers on the team.

Over time, that abundance mindset became more than just a perspective. It transformed into a way of life for me and some of my closest friends. We even gave it a name: Danza.

Danza stems from the Italian word *abbondanza*, which means "abundance." We took Danza and turned it into our war cry. We screamed it to celebrate each other, to mark big wins, and to push through pivotal moments that seemed like bottlenecks. It became our way of manifesting the best outcomes in our lives with spirit and energy. We are all the main characters in our own movie, and Danza symbolizes the best part of the movie: the middle, where the real action happens, where we grow, struggle, and evolve. It's a mindset, but it's also a reminder to show up and claim our place in the narrative.

In every arena, whether it's the workplace, family dynamics, or friendships, we're often taught to see success as a limited resource. We compete for promotions, vie for attention, and measure ourselves against others, believing there's only so much room at the top.

But Danza flips that thinking on its head. It's a reminder that lifting others up doesn't diminish us. It strengthens us.

When we see success as something we create together, it unlocks a powerful truth. We're not in competition with the world. We're in competition with the version of ourselves that holds back, the one scared to risk connection, scared to trust, or scared to fail. *Danza is about showing up, giving your best, and trusting that your greatness doesn't take away from anyone else's. It amplifies it.*

This philosophy guided me through camp and made the announcement even more meaningful. Danza taught me to celebrate the success of others as if it were my own, to shift my focus from competition to collaboration. Success isn't a zero-sum game. It's something we can all share. Competition is essential. It sharpens us, but should never come at the expense of relationships or collective growth.

That's why, when Coach finally made it official that Davone and I would both be on the field together against USC, the only word that came to mind was Danza. All the hard work and sacrifices had led to this moment.

16
Ready for War

SEPTEMBER 5, 2005. USC VS. HAWAII.

The big day is finally here.

The energy on the bus is mellow as we make our way to the stadium. Everyone has their headphones on, relaxing, focusing. As we approach the stadium parking lot, it's immediately clear that the tailgating is in full swing. I can't help but press my face against the window, eyes wide, eager to take it all in. The scene outside is alive; it's electric, full of life and anticipation.

The parking lot is completely packed, with cars squeezed into every available inch. Families are huddled together in tight-knit groups, gathered behind their trucks. Their laughter sweeps through the crowd, a visible wave of smiles and excitement that creates an inviting atmosphere.

The smoky scent of barbecue drifts through the air, seeping through the windows of our bus, and for a moment, I'm taken back to my first USC game all those years ago. The smells and the sights—everything about this scene closely resembles that unforgettable day.

As we continue toward the team tunnel, I spot a group of kids tossing a football around. One of them is wearing a jersey with the number 2 on it. He catches the ball, spikes it on the ground, and breaks into a goofy touchdown dance. That's when a rush of emotions hits me.

That's my number on his jersey.

* * *

In the locker room, the pregame rituals begin. Music blasting, players getting taped up and stretched by our trainers. Some of us are laughing and joking around, while others are quiet and focused. Beneath it all, there's a mix of tension and excitement for what's to come.

With minutes to go before we hit the field, Coach Jones winds us up for his pregame speech. There's yelling, Hawaii-style "Cheehoos!" and a lot of "Let's fucking GO!" The room is intense, and the energy is bouncing off the walls.

As the noise settles just enough for him to speak, Coach Jones steps forward.

"Today's offensive captain," Coach Jones says, "is Jason Ferguson."

Did I hear that right?

I look around to make sure I'm not trippin'. My mind races as I try to mask my surprise, but Coach Jones looks me dead in the eye, steady and deliberate.

Goosebumps.

This is meant to be.

We're playing USC, my hometown dream school that didn't want me. It's my first year as a starter, in *my* stadium, with *me* as the captain, and my family is here to witness all of it.

How much better could it get?

*   *   *

Moments later, I'm standing on the 50-yard line, ready for the coin toss.

My heart is beating out of my chest.

My pads are strapped tight and perfectly fitted.

My helmet is light as a feather, and my body is loose.

I feel nimble. I feel ready.

The stunning Hawaii skies begin to drizzle, as they do every day around this time. But I know the rain will eventually stop.

I can already see the sun beginning to beam through each cloud, like someone is holding a flashlight up to an empty white pillowcase, shining a spotlight down on Aloha Stadium.

I glance at the USC sidelines, where their players stand tense, eyes locked on us, waiting for the verdict like predators eyeing their prey.

These are the guys that didn't want you, Filly.

This is the coach who didn't think you were good enough. Fuck 'em.

I'm locked in, ready for war.

I've been a die-hard USC fan my whole life. And now, here I am, face-to-face with them in the biggest game of my football career.

I lock eyes with Reggie Bush, USC's captain, standing directly across from me. Reggie is easily the number-one player in the nation. His explosive, make-you-miss style has captivated fans. Without a doubt, he is the most exciting player in college football, and I'm about to go head-to-head with him.

To his right is Matt Leinart, Heisman Trophy winner from the year prior. The guy is a megastar. A tall, White, handsome QB? Hollywood ate it up, and he's risen to meteoric fame. He's the number-one QB in the nation, and his demeanor says it all.

You know how your older brother stands over you right before he's about to beat your ass? Yeah, that's the energy Matt gives as we stand face-to-face on the 50-yard line, moments away from our season opener.

To Reggie's left is Darnell Bing, one of the top defensive players in the country, and a big ol' boy. I mean, huge!

And me? I'm 5'5, 150 pounds. Still the smallest player on the field, and arguably the smallest in all of Division I football. A linebacker from LA Tech University had once told me he took shits bigger than me. Then later, in that same game, he told me his dick was bigger than me. Yes, you read that correctly. He didn't say his dick was bigger than mine; he said his dick was bigger than ... me.

I'm sure Darnell is thinking something very similar as he looks me up and down. As the veins protrude from his biceps, I think to myself, "Oh yeah, you're gonna have to shake the shit out of this big mothafucka. If he gets a clean shot on you, it's over."

After what feels like forever, the referee finally flips the coin. We win the toss and elect to receive the ball.

I head back to the sidelines for the opening kickoff, where the energy is chaotic. A few of my teammates are screaming, "Eddie! Eddie!" Eddie is our starting kick returner, a young freshman receiver playing in his first college football game.

USC is lined up on the field, ready to kick. But our team is still taking the field, with everyone out there but Eddie. The chaos around me intensifies as I watch my teammates run up and down the sideline looking for him. Then, out of nowhere, I feel a sudden rush of energy. My eyes start to water. It feels like someone has just injected me with adrenaline.

I'm so caught up in the moment, my mind racing with thoughts of Eddie and the opportunity in front of me, that I barely notice Coach Jones standing right next to me.

Fuck Eddie, I think. *I should just run out there and take this shit to the house!*

I turn my head slowly and look up at my 6'4" coach, who is already staring down at me. His eyes lock onto mine, intense, like he can read every thought running through my head. I give him a slight smirk, and just like that, we're having a full-blown conversation without saying a word.

USC is the number-one team in the nation. I'm a leader on our football team. And this is going to be a long season. Is me running out there really a good idea? Is it worth it?

I'd been the team's kick returner almost all season last year. As a receiver, I'd worked my ass off and handled my second-string responsibilities with pride and excitement. I'd done my time, and I was confident I'd earned my place this year. This season, I'm "the guy." I'm a starting wide receiver, handling all the punt return duties as well, so kick return isn't my responsibility anymore.

But Eddie still hasn't run onto the field, and Coach Jones has to make a decision. It's the biggest game of Eddie's young career, and he can't find his helmet.

You've got to be kidding me.

Then, just like that, Coach Jones's entire demeanor shifts. His intense gaze softens, and a sly smile spreads across his face, like he's saying, *See you in the end zone.*

Without missing a beat, I pop my helmet on, buckle my chin strap, and sprint onto the field.

Holy shit, this is happening.

As I make my way to the end zone to take my position, I throw my hands up in the air to summon the crowd. With every lift of my arms, the crowd gets louder and louder. I feel like a composer conducting a symphony.

My adrenaline is pumping at an all-time high, and the stage is absolutely perfect. I can hear 50,000 screaming fans, belting their support at the top of their lungs.

I take my position, drawing long, slow breaths to calm my nerves. I focus on the kicker, who is set, one arm in the air, on the brink of motioning to his team and kicking the ball.

Boom.

I can almost feel the impact as his foot powers through the ball. It flips through the air directly toward me in what feels like slow motion.

The noise of the crowd is deafening. The only thing I can truly hear is the sound of my own heavy breathing in my helmet.

*   *   *

I catch the ball, tuck it away, and sprint full speed. I'm completely relaxed, almost on autopilot, as if I've handed the keys over to my instincts.

The field ahead narrows as defenders close in from the left and right. My only option is to run straight, trusting the wedge my blockers have created in front of me.

I cut past two defenders with precision, but a third one comes in hot, ready to dive at my legs. With no time to think, I plant my right foot in the turf as hard as I can, shifting direction in one swift motion. I lower my shoulders, bracing for impact.

CLICK.

I feel a subtle, almost muted pop, like the sound of a seat belt being released, but it comes from the center of my leg. I fall to the ground, and as fast as the play starts, it's over.

I pop up, frantically evaluating myself. Something is off. It's my knee, the same knee, but the sensation is different. When I blew out my knee in high school, it was like an explosion, an eruption. I knew I'd done some serious damage. But this, this is something else. The sensation wasn't nearly as violent.

I huddle up and try to shake it off, bending my knee repeatedly, searching for the pain. My adrenaline is pumping too hard. I don't feel anything, I'm numb, but something is off. Distracted by my knee, I go deaf for a second. I can see our quarterback, Colt, telling everyone the play, but I can't make out his words. His lips are moving, I hear the texture of his voice, but the language doesn't connect.

As we break the huddle and take our positions, the disconnection lingers. I realize I have no clue what play we're running. It feels like I'm in the wrong spot, so I panic and try to swap places with Davone.

The referee blows his whistle, "Delay of game."

Damn.

This is nothing like how I imagined this game would unfold. Thousands of screaming fans, my family in attendance. What I thought would be a dream come true has turned into my worst nightmare.

Keep it together, Filly. Don't lose it.

Back in the huddle, Davone can tell something is off. "You good, bro?" he asks. "Nah, man, it's my knee," I reply, fighting to keep myself from breaking down. I watch the life leave his face, like a punch to the gut, stealing his oxygen.

I manage to hear the next play, and I line up correctly this time. Out of nowhere, a dull ache surfaces in my knee and sharpens by the second, but I tell myself that God himself would have to come down and drag me off this fucking field. If finishing this game means losing my leg, so be it.

The next play called is a passing play, and I know it'll be coming to me. I take a few ragged breaths, determined to ignore the pain. When Colt says, "Hike," I sprint into my route and stick my right leg in the ground to cut into my break. My knee buckles, and my leg gives out completely. I hit the ground but hop up as fast as I can, looking left to find the ball already in the air, heading straight toward me.

Instinctively, I catch it, but I can't run and I can't cut, so I make a valiant attempt to burst upfield, and just before the USC players crush me, I dive to the ground in a forward free-falling motion. A normal person would probably have realized by now that staying in the game would be dangerously foolish and horrible for the team. A normal person would have called it a day and left the field, but not me. I can't bring myself to leave.

Something in me knows my knee is not okay, and if this is gonna be the last game I ever play, I'm determined to squeeze everything I can out of it.

After several more plays, my knee is on fire. There's an intense burning that begins to travel up and down my entire leg. I can no longer straighten it. The adrenaline has worn off. The pain is excruciating. There's nothing more I can do.

My grandfather is the toughest son-of-a-bitch I've ever known. Due to an old football injury that was never properly tended to, he had scar tissue and calcium buildup in his knee that completely deformed it. It was as if an extra bone had grown out, bulging from the side of his knee. It looked crazy, but he never complained, and most of the time, you couldn't even tell he was in pain. He raised my brother and me to be tough little versions of himself. We were taught to fight through pain. If something hurt, he'd tell us to rub some dirt on it or spit in our hands and rub it where it hurt. His biggest pet peeve was watching the whining and flopping around on the field when someone got hurt. People who were obviously overdramatizing their pain, only to reemerge back in the game totally fine.

My pain tolerance was directly impacted by this. I always pushed myself to endure to the absolute limit. I know my grandfather would have been proud of me today. I've held on for as long as I possibly can. But the fact is, I'm severely injured, I've left it all out on the field, and it's time to go.

*   *   *

I limp off the field, flagging down the team doctor to assess the damage. He wraps his arms around my knee to stress-test it.

Oh no. All of this is way too familiar.

He looks me in the eyes and says, "Jason, it feels like it's your ACL."

Not again. How?

It feels like only minutes ago that I'd heard D-Weez's famous whistle, a piercing note that somehow cut through the whole stadium to catch my attention. I'd been standing in the middle of the field with such pride, waving at my parents. Smiles all around. Now it feels like the doctor has just pulled the pin from a verbal grenade and placed it in my hands.

Coach Jones approaches me, arms wide. I bury my face in his shirt as he says, "I just heard. I'm so sorry, Jason."

17
Scar Tissue

The MRI results come back worse than expected. I've torn my ACL and my medial and lateral meniscus again. And I've even managed to put a hairline fracture in my femur. At least it was true to my brand: go big or go home.

Hearing the news doesn't elicit much of a response from me. I'd already prepared myself for the worst. I'd been here before. I feel almost desensitized to the news. My first ACL tear. My first surgery. My second surgery for scar tissue. Domo dying. Now this.

Something in me is starting to change, starting to harden. The compounding effects of all these challenging moments, one after the other, are taking their toll. Each setback chips away at something inside me, dulling the edges of my emotions. It's like a part of me is closing off, shutting down to protect itself. The pain is still there, but it's more distant, more muted. Each heartbreak feels a little less sharp than the last, as if I'm bracing myself for the next blow before it even happens.

*   *   *

The team doctor tells me I have two choices. I can stay in Hawaii, have the surgery, and do rehab with the training staff. Or I can go home and do the surgery and rehab there.

I am, in fact, a mama's boy. The idea of going through all of this for a second time is hard enough as it is. But doing it without my mom there to help me through it is impossible. Besides, I can't handle the thought of being stuck alone in my dorm room while the team finishes the season. Being left behind like that would be unbearable.

*   *   *

The decision is made. The next day, Davone helps D-Weez and me clear out my side of our dorm room. As we empty drawers and pull clothes from the closet, nobody says a word. The silence is painful. The sound of the air conditioner that once hummed softly in the background is now a piercing screech, echoing off the walls.

I watch Davone as he pulls the last of my shirts out of a drawer. His head is down, his dreads hanging past his eyes. When he looks up, directly at me, we both begin to cry.

The camaraderie I've found through sports is unlike anything I've ever known, especially in college. The shared struggle to reach the top has created an unbreakable bond between Davone and me. We've sacrificed everything for football: late nights, missed parties, relentless training. We'd dreamed of the NFL together, imagining our first purchases and what we'd do for our moms.

But standing here, hugging him goodbye while my world crashes down, he feels my pain like it's his own. This moment, more than anything else we've shared, solidifies our bond for life.

*   *   *

Later that evening, 8ball (Dave Walker), who came to see the game with my parents, picks me up to go to the airport. My parents have to get back to L.A., so 8ball goes out of his way to make sure I'm taken care of. It's been years since he last stood in the end zone during my flag football games, with money in his hat, waiting for me to score a touchdown. He was so much more than just Dev and Donnie's dad. He treated me like a son. From flag football to high school football, he's always been there, so it's no surprise he flew out for the biggest game of my career.

At the airport, I'm given a wheelchair since I can barely walk. Uncle 8ball pushes me along, cracking jokes to lighten the mood. He knows just how to make me smile, and in this moment, I'm eternally grateful to him. He sits with me for hours while I wait for my flight, distracting me with his infectious energy, something I desperately need on this sad and pivotal day in my young life.

(Uncle 8ball, David Walker, would pass away in 2012 from a heart attack. He was a father, a mentor, and a friend to many. In nearly 20 years of memories with 8ball, this remains one my most sacred. Uncle 8ball—I love you and miss you dearly.)

*   *   *

The flight home feels surreal, a blur of emotions I can barely process. But once I'm back in L.A., it's time to figure out a game plan to get me back on the field as soon as possible.

My new surgeon, Dr. Ellatrache, is a big-time orthopedic surgeon who works with guys like Tom Brady and Kobe Bryant. If this guy is good enough for Kobe, he's good enough for me.

He explains that I've done some serious damage to my leg, but nothing he can't repair. I look him in the eyes and ask flat out, "Will I ever be able to play again, Doc?"

"I'll do everything I can to make sure you get back out there," he says, "but you have to take care of everything on your end. It won't be easy, but it's possible."

That's all I need to hear. I'm injected with life again, with optimism, with a little bit of hope that one day, I might be back on the field with my brothers again, doing what I love most. If it's all going to come down to me and how I handle rehab, consider it done.

*   *   *

The surgery is a success, but the road to recovery is different this time.

Normally, right after knee surgery, they want you to start bending your knee almost immediately to break through the scar tissue. The first time around, my leg was placed in a bending machine that did the work for me, slowly forcing my knee to bend with the machine's motion.

This time, due to the fracture in my femur, they don't want me bending it at all. Instead, I have to keep my leg straight for several weeks, giving the femur time to heal before I start any bending.

This is absolute torture. The stiffness in my leg is unbearable, combined with the pain of having my knee sliced open and screws added. The wound is fresh and tender, and all I want to do is bend my leg, but I can't. It's locked out straight for weeks.

This is the stuff that nobody talks about when you're a kid dreaming of going pro. You see the cars, the houses, the jewelry, and the glamour that comes with making it to the league. But you never see the athlete laid up in bed after an injury, tears streaming down their face from the physical and emotional pain they have to endure.

You don't hear about the long nights staring at the ceiling, wondering if your body will ever be the same. The loneliness that creeps in when the phone stops ringing and the world moves on without you. You don't hear about dealing with the frustration of feeling trapped in your own body, fighting to keep your spirit from breaking as you push through another day of pain and uncertainty.

*   *   *

One of the most difficult things for me to accept is that the college football season doesn't stop just because I got injured. Life goes on for everyone and everything around me. I try to keep up with the season, with everything that's going on with my brothers on the field. Although they call to check on me now and then, they have a season to focus on, so I have to temper my expectations.

One day, I get a phone call, and as soon as I answer, I hear "FILLYYYYYYYY" being screamed by what sounds like 20 people. It's on speaker, and all my bros are in the dorm, pregaming before heading out to a party. Cassidy's "I'm a Hustla" is blasting in the background, and the bass is piercing through my end of the phone. Davone and Dez are running point, their voices loud and full of life as they yell over each other, fighting to be heard. I'm grateful they called, but damn, the pain cuts deep. Just a month ago, I was right there with them in that same dorm, my whole future ahead of me. Now I'm here, laid up in bed, hooked to a bending machine, while they're out living it up.

The contrast is stark. On their end, the vibe is poppin', full of laughter, music, and the intoxicating thrill of a night packed with possibilities. On my end, it's dark. The room is quiet, and the only sound is the mechanical hum of the bending machine forcing my knee to move up and down. As I hang up the phone, reality hits hard. My mind drifts to football, to the field, and to the players who will be stepping up in my absence.

One of them is Ryan Grice-Mullen, better known as O1 (pronounced Oh-One), who has taken over my spot. He's a former roommate and a really good friend of mine. O1 is an extremely gifted athlete, but if I'm being honest, I'd never really seen much of what he could do at practice. Or maybe, since my ego had been the size of Oahu, I hadn't really paid much attention to him on the field.

That changes when our team faces Boise State in a televised game. It's my first chance to see my brothers in action since my injury, and I can't look away. Sitting there with my eyes glued to the TV, I watch as O1 puts on an absolute clinic. The kid goes crazy, dominating the game with flash and flair, one big play after another.

Not only does he force us to pay attention to him, stealing eyeballs from Davone, but he also shows us that the ceiling for his potential is much higher than we'd expected.

I watch in awe, fighting back my emotions while forcing myself to celebrate for him. I'm torn between cheering for a brother and dying of jealousy as I watch him steal my spot from me, one catch at a time.

Every catch that he reels in is like a knife to my gut. Every big-time play is a swift kick to the nuts. But I force myself to applaud him, refusing to let my envy get in the way. O1 has earned everything coming his way, and I genuinely love the guy.

One thing becomes incredibly clear: I'm going to have some serious work cut out for me when I return. Davone is no longer my biggest competition.

*   *   *

By the time the football season ends and I'm back on campus for the spring semester, that realization still weighs on me, and everything feels different now. The energy has shifted.

Colt, Davone, and O1 have exploded as superstars on the island. When I left, they were nobodies. Now they're glowing with star power. As I walk around campus with them, I see other students pointing them out as we go by. I can feel this new energy in the air, and I desperately want to be part of it.

My career has been like a runaway train I'm constantly chasing. Every time I get to the station, the train is leaving. So I keep sprinting after it, desperate to grab hold of the side handles and pull myself aboard. But I can never seem to run quite fast enough, and I'm not sure how much longer I'll be able to keep up the chase. The train, and everyone else, feels like they're moving on without me.

*   *   *

Right away, I start rehab with Hawaii's best sports medicine team, run by a man named Pat Ariki. I work with Pat three times a week, trying to get my knee back to 100 percent. It's January, and I have until August to find the version of myself I left on the field last fall.

The sessions are grueling, sometimes stretching to three hours, but slowly, the muscles in my leg start to rebuild. At first, it feels like progress. Then, out of nowhere, a sharp pain shoots down the middle of my knee behind the kneecap. No matter what I do, it won't go away. I tell myself to ignore it, to grit my teeth and push through.

Days turn to weeks; weeks turn to months. Before I know it, it's time for summer camp. As rehab with Pat comes to an end, I talk less and less about the pain in my knee, hoping to be cleared to participate in camp. This is my big return. My opportunity to get in the mix and be part of the magic that's brewing.

The muscles in my quad, hamstrings, and calves are all extremely strong again. I pass every stress test they put me through, pushing through the very real pain I'm in. I'm terrified of being honest because I can't afford another surgery, another setback. My career won't withstand it.

Once Pat clears me for camp, I only have a few weeks left to pop on my cleats and start polishing my game.

I head to the field with some of the guys to run routes I haven't run in months. Not surprisingly, I'm rusty. And to make matters worse, every time I push off my right leg, I feel that sharp pain rip through the front of my kneecap. With each cut, it becomes more and more unbearable. I try to keep my cool, running every route at 60 percent and convincing the guys I'm just easing back into it. But deep down, I know something isn't right.

I have no clue how I'm going to pull off camp. A part of me holds out hope that the pain will just miraculously disappear. That I'll wake up one morning to find a miracle has ensued and my knee is in perfect playing condition.

But the first day of camp is an absolute nightmare. There's zero room for minimal effort. Competition is at an all-time high. We're expected to give 110 percent on every route, on every single play. I can't hide behind 60 percent.

Every time I stick my right foot in the ground, the pain is excruciating. I grimace through it, whip my head around to find the ball flying toward me like it's been shot from a cannon, and I drop the pass. Rinse and repeat. Pain in the middle of my route, another dropped pass. A total nightmare.

Since I was young, I've had this awful recurring dream in which I'm fighting somebody, and no matter how hard I swing, my punches seem to have zero effect on the guy. I muster up all of my strength, swinging as hard as I possibly can, and each blow lands like pillows are wrapped around my fists. No matter how hard I work, there's zero effect. Being on the field that day at camp feels just like this dream. No matter how hard I try, I can't catch the ball.

In the end, I remove myself from the field and find the trainers to tell them what's going on. As I walk away, my mind races.

Have I removed myself from practice because I dropped five or six passes in a row and look like complete shit?

Or have I done it because the pain is actually excruciating?

Maybe a little bit of both. But either way, I can't keep putting myself through this. That drill was easily the worst playing experience of my life, and it's clear something is seriously wrong.

*   *   *

The pain finally forces me to see the doctor, and before I know it, I'm back under the knife.

Scar tissue has built up in my knee, causing relentless pain, and there's no other choice but to remove it.

A fourth surgery? Fuck it, why not?

I tell myself this has to be the one. The first time I tore my ACL, a second surgery to clean up scar tissue worked, so why not now?

I hold on to that thought and the reassurance from my surgeon, who is optimistic that this relatively simple procedure will get me back into playing form. I need to believe him. I need to believe that this time, the pain will finally be gone for good.

But as the season progresses, I find myself back on the sidelines, watching from a distance. I keep telling myself, "Take it one day at a time." I cheer for my teammates, doing everything I can to support them. At times, I feel like the team mascot, the little guy going ballistic on the sidelines after every big play.

But deep down, the frustration eats at me.

How many times can I go through this?

How much more of this can I take?

I try to push those thoughts down, burying them beneath the hope that somehow, some way, I'll find my way back.

But unfortunately, I see no improvement. The season marches on, and so does time. The team finishes 11–3, cementing their place as one of the best, most exciting teams in our school's history. Colt emerges as one of the nation's top QBs, leading an offense that's virtually unstoppable. The excitement around campus is electric, a celebration of everything we'd worked for as a program.

And yet, none of it feels real to me. My knee still isn't improving, and while the team basks in their success, I'm stuck on the sidelines, fighting a battle that feels more and more like a losing one.

* * *

A month or so later, Coach Jones calls me into his office and gives it to me straight:

"Jason, you're an amazing player. And to be honest, I've never seen commitment quite like yours. I thought we'd be able to get you back out there, but at this point, I think we've gotta call it quits. I can't let you go on like this. I just can't. You're gonna be a father one day. You're gonna want to be able to play with your kids without limping everywhere. I'll keep you on scholarship and pay for as much school as you want to get done. But as far as your playing career, I'm sorry. I think we're done."

Deep down, I think I'd known this was coming. And as hard as it is to admit, I know it's the right call.

I'm physically exhausted and emotionally drained, and my knee has had enough. But I would never have quit on my own. It had to be Coach Jones who made the final decision, the one who brought this long, painful chapter to a close.

Sitting here in front of him, I feel helpless. It's like watching a car crash in slow motion, knowing there's nothing I can do to stop it. All I can do is wait, brace for the impact, and hope I'm strong enough to withstand it. You never really know when your career will end, but you always hope it's on your terms.

The truth is, every athlete faces this day eventually. But sitting here now, it's a bitter pill to swallow. My mind flashes back to everything I've fought through, the surgeries, the endless rehab, the pain that seemed like it would never end.

I think about the relentless commitment, the early mornings at the sand dunes, and those long runs home from school in my shoulder pads.

How I battled Davone and rose to the occasion when it mattered most.

Every ounce of sweat and sacrifice.

Fuck.

It all comes down to this. Here I am, with nothing left to give, nowhere left to turn, and the dream I've chased for so long has finally reached its end.

Just like that, my playing career is over.

*   *   *

In the end, this journey taught me a truth I couldn't ignore: sometimes, no matter how hard you fight, how much you sacrifice, or how deeply you believe, the outcome is beyond your control. But looking back, I've realized the fight was still worth it. Every drop of sweat, every moment of pain, and every grueling hour of rehab shaped me. They showed me what it means to endure, to push through uncertainty, and to keep going when the path ahead is unclear.

Over time, I came to understand that resilience isn't just about perseverance. *It's about accepting the limits of control, the fragility of dreams, and the unpredictable nature of life.* It's about learning to adapt when things fall apart and finding meaning in the struggle itself. Research tells us that the ability to reframe failure as growth is one of the defining traits of resilient people. That's the lesson I carry with me now. While we can't always dictate the outcome, we can control how we respond. We can choose to rise, to shift our focus to what we can control, and to keep moving forward.

Though the dream I chased ended, the journey gave me something far greater: a deeper understanding of myself. These moments, though painful, revealed strength I didn't know I had. But that strength would soon be tested in ways I couldn't foresee.

18
The Wild Wolf

When the University of Hawaii's 2007 football season gets started, I'm officially a spectator. This would have been my senior season, but now my hopes of ever getting back on the field are gone.

Although I'm no longer playing, I'm still part of the team. Still watching practices. Still going to games. I try to focus my efforts on being an emotional leader.

I can't lie; it's painful standing there on the sidelines. But I deal with it the same way I've handled other hardships over the years. I bury it.

I fight my feelings of jealousy and sadness. Once again, I don't seek out therapy, counseling, or any of the mental health services UH has to offer. I just push forward. I've mastered the art of saying, "Fuck it," and forcing myself to keep going.

But why don't I seek help?

I've done therapy in the past, but that was years ago. I was a kid. Back then, I was forced to confront the chaos around me. But this time, it's different. My mom's not here to micromanage my emotions or help me process what I might be dealing with. I'm 21 years old now. I'm a man, and I'm responsible for me. I'm aware of how I feel, but I don't fully understand the weight of it all. I can't see that what I'm dealing with might be depression. I've built this system, this coping mechanism of pushing forward, one foot in front of the other, without really addressing the pain. It's become second nature to me, a survival skill.

I also don't fully realize what resources I have available to me. It was never made clear to me, and I wasn't in the right headspace to even care.

*   *   *

My teammates do what they can to support me, but they can't truly relate to the pain I'm carrying. I know they empathize, but their dreams are still intact, untouched by the kind of loss I'm facing.

Outside of my UH brothers, the silence is deafening. No coaches call to check on me. Not one coach gets in touch to see how I'm doing or if I need anything. I'm grateful to have been kept on scholarship, but now that I'm not playing, there isn't much need for communication beyond saying "hi" at practice, which I attend faithfully every day. I try not to hold this against them. They, too, have their hands full with the season and their own responsibilities. Coaching is a ruthless profession. You're only as good as your last win, and the pressure to keep winning is intense. The moment you underperform, you're gone.

So I've created this makeshift island to live on in my mind and decide to never speak up. I never ask for help.

*   *   *

Meanwhile, the world around me moves forward, and the buzz about the upcoming season is impossible to ignore. All of the UH stars are back, including our Heisman Trophy candidate

QB, Colt Brennan. The island pulses with excitement, and UH football feels bigger than ever.

Then game day arrives. I'm standing on the sidelines as the team readies itself in the tunnel. The crowd is on the edge of their seats. The stands are a sea of restless fans, their collective anticipation buzzing like a live wire, ready to snap.

I spent the pregame in the parking lot tailgating with friends. I'm not drunk, but I'm definitely not sober either. I've got a solid buzz working for me, something I hoped would take the edge off the pain, at least for a while. As I stand there, my shades are on, not to shield me from the sun, but to hide the gloss in my eyes—a mix of alcohol and turmoil.

Finally, the players get the cue, and they burst out of the tunnel. The crowd erupts, their cheers a deafening roar that shakes the very foundation of the stadium.

I watch my teammates warm up, heartbroken that I can't join them. Sure, I've battled through this before. But back then, I had hope. I just knew I'd get back out on the field eventually, and that fueled my optimistic nature.

This time around, that spark of hope is gone. I feel like a wild wolf chained to a fence while someone dangles a bloody piece of meat directly in front of my face. Antagonizing me. Taunting me to come and get it. It's agony.

I'm close enough to see the sweat trickling down my teammates' faces, but I can't step foot on the field. At least I get to be on the sidelines. That is, until right before the game starts, when an assistant makes her way down the field, asking every player not suited up to head to the stands. No undressed players are allowed on the sidelines. I convince myself there's no possible way this applies to me, but I see her beelining in my direction. When she taps my shoulder, my first thought is:

Do you know who I am? I'm Jason motherfucking Ferguson!

I'm about to plead my case directly to Coach Jones when the assistant whispers to me, "Jason, don't do that. This is the last thing Coach Jones should worry about right now. He's focused on the game."

Of course, she's right. It would be really selfish of me to bother him right now. I hang my head and walk slowly toward the stands.

By the time I get there, everything is fuzzy. The weight of the moment is massive. I clench everything, trying not to move a muscle. My attempt to hold back tears ignites an intense pain in the back of my throat. I'm afraid to swallow for fear of losing my composure. I hold on for a few moments, but then I lose my grip and break down. Everything starts to pour out of me.

It feels like just yesterday that I was flipping through the newspaper, a week before the USC game, and I saw my picture, front and center, in an ad to sell tickets. I remember the shock and amazement that washed over me. It was so exciting, and so surreal to see my image being used to promote UH football's upcoming season.

Before the injury, I'd been doing all the media interviews for the team, visiting local elementary schools, representing the program. There's no question I was being positioned as UH's next rising star. Now, here I am, sitting in the stands, watching the greatest team UH has ever assembled about to kick off. It's all too much for the kid. I leave before the first quarter's over.

*   *   *

I'm pretty despondent for a couple of days after that first game. I don't feel like hanging out or talking to anyone, so I stay in my bedroom and keep to myself. My phone rings, and I ignore it. It feels like I have an emotional hangover. I've never really experienced depression before, but I assume that's what this is.

By the third day, I feel restless but still emotionally drained. When a friend calls again, I finally give in and agree to hang out, hoping it will take my mind off things. As soon as I get in his car, he hands me a beer without a word. Then he pulls out two tiny pills and offers me one.

I know exactly what they are. Because of my surgeries, I'm already familiar with oxycodone. I'd dabbled with painkillers while trying to come back from my injury. But the more my knee refused to get better, the more I wanted to party.

The first time I tried Oxy, the guy who gave it to me said, "It's just a painkiller. They're prescribed by doctors. Try one." And my stupid ass took it. I hated it. The itching drove me insane, and I was miserable the entire time, sleeping half the day away. I swore I'd never touch one again.

But after my meltdown in the stands, after days alone in my room, that promise feels distant, almost meaningless. My mind is heavy, my emotions numb. All I think is, *Fuck it. Give it here.* I pop the pill in my mouth, chew it to mush, and wash it down with my beer.

As we make our way to a bar, the warm Hawaii air strokes my face. It's like medicine for my soul. I feel a slight tingling sensation behind my eyes. Everything looks a little brighter. It's gentle at first, then it starts to intensify. It slithers its way from behind my eyes to my brain, feeling extra warm and fuzzy.

And then ... bang!

A euphoric wave of energy smacks the shit out of me. Suddenly, I'm happy. I'm smiling ear to ear, experiencing the song "Suck It or Not" by Cam'ron and Lil Wayne like never before as it blasts from the speakers.

Everything in this moment feels perfect. I've never experienced this type of high before. Something is different this time. It hits harder, and it's far more intense. It's the therapy I've been missing. It's what I've been longing for, a way to block out the emotions I don't want to feel or even acknowledge. It unlocks the enthusiastic, happy, confident me that's been slipping away, fading. It feels like I've cracked the code to finding "me" again. I've found my "limitless" pill.

*   *   *

The next day, I ask my friend if I can buy a handful of those pills for the coming week. He's hesitant at first. He says something about how "dangerous and addictive" they can be, and that I shouldn't do them regularly.

Seriously, bro? You're the guy who just gave me one!

But I get that he's just trying to look out for me.

I haven't ever thought of myself as someone with an addictive personality. I've always prided myself on having self-control, leaning into my healthy habits. I'd been prescribed Vicodin, Norco, and Percocet for my four knee surgeries, and I'd barely even taken them. And I'd certainly never considered the dangers that could come with playing around with these things. After all, they were *prescribed by doctors.*

I assure my friend that I'll be fine, and I collect my pills, making sure I have one for every day of that week. My plan is to end each night by myself, with a 40-ounce beer and a pill.

What starts as a weeklong bender changes something in me. It shows me how easy it is to hide behind a substance, how quickly a pill and a beer can take the edge off reality. I tell myself it's just a way to survive a rough week, a temporary fix. But when the week ends, the pattern doesn't disappear. It just shifts. Weekends become my escape. Every Friday night with the fellas, I pop a pill to take the buzz to another level, to quiet the noise in my head, to shut everything out. Numbness becomes my new normal.

My roommates are the best players on the team, and we are partying like rockstars. We call ourselves the Mag 7, a brother-hood made up of Davone Bess (Von), Ryan Grice-Mullen (O1), Jason Rivers (J-Rivs), Jazen Anderson, Myron Newberry (Shuy), Gerard Lewis (G-Lew), and me.

These guys are celebrities on the island, and every party is like being in a movie. We get into every club for free, and are, without a doubt, the life of the party.

My pregame ritual is the same every time: 30 mg of Oxy washed down with a 40-ounce Mickey's Malt Liquor. It's a temporary escape. All my worries, stresses, and anxieties get washed away, replaced by a euphoric numbness that feels comforting. Our football team keeps on winning, and the parties keep getting better and better.

But as the partying intensifies, something starts to shift. I start losing interest in going to practice and even in going to school. Physically, I'm running on fumes. My body is exhausted, and my mind is clouded. Mentally, I'm checked out, disconnected from the passion and drive that once fueled me. The more I chase the high, the further I drift from the life I once knew.

*   *   *

With only a few months left until graduation, my days start to blur together, each one a little darker than the last, until one evening, I find myself alone, drinking by myself, which somehow doesn't seem so strange anymore. I want to pick up a few pills, but my friend is all out, waiting for his connect to get back to him.

It dawns on me that I'm tired of going through other people to get pills. I wonder if I might be able to go directly to the source, the main connect. Then I could grab more for cheaper.

What starts as a simple thought quickly spirals into something more. The idea of selling pills myself begins to take root. Growing up in West L.A., I'd been surrounded by a mix of influences. Gang culture was everywhere, woven into the fabric of our neighborhoods. For some of my friends, selling drugs wasn't just about making a quick buck; it was about survival. In an environment where opportunities were scarce, the hustle often felt like the only way out.

I'd seen a few friends sell crack back then, watching from a distance as they navigated that world. I wasn't involved, but I'd learned more than I wanted to admit, how they operated, the risks they took, and the justifications they clung to. Back then, I swore I'd never take that path. But now, in this new chapter of my life, the thought creeps in, seductive and persistent.

I start convincing myself I can do it better. I'll keep it on a super small scale, I tell myself. Just enough to make some money, stay in control, and ensure I always have enough pills to use whenever I want.

But there's a moment where I hesitate, sitting alone in my room, staring at the ceiling. I think about what crossing this line could mean, about the promises I once made to myself to never end up here. For a second, I feel the weight of it all sinking in, heavy and undeniable. But then, like always, I push the doubt aside. It's just pills, I rationalize. I can handle this.

So I start asking around about the main connect, a guy known as Old Man Bob. Everybody's heard about him, but only a few people work with him, and those who do, protect him and their access to him.

Almost all of the Oxy on Oahu comes through Old Man Bob. He has relationships with every crooked doctor on the island. He fills scripts weekly, if not daily, and he has others doing it too. I press my friend relentlessly for an introduction until he finally gives in. The moment I get the green light, I can feel the adrenaline kick in.

*   *   *

I meet Bob for the first time at his house, on a windy road up a steep hill in one of Oahu's many valleys.

The house is old and weathered, with a tarnished exterior. The chipped paint combined with the exposed wood makes it look like a beat-up tree house.

Inside, it's straight out of a zombie movie. Two dudes slouch on a couch, faces covered in sores, scratching relentlessly while they talk gibberish. Another guy leans against a wall, nodding off, practically sleeping standing up. It's unclear if they're waiting to see Bob or if they live there.

The house itself is in complete disarray. There's junk every-where: boxes, clothes, garbage in every corner of every room. For a second, I wonder, *What the hell am I doing here?*

Not sure where to go or what to do, I just stand there until Bob comes around the corner and directs me to a back bedroom.

As I walk down the hallway, loud snoring erupts from a closet, startling the shit out of me. I freeze, waiting for Bob's reaction, but he doesn't flinch. It's as if the noise doesn't even register, like this is just another day in his world.

Bob is exactly what I expect: a White dude in his early 70s, long white hair, a face exhausted and worn from age and addiction. He's missing damn near all his teeth, so he speaks with a lisp.

But he's also an extremely nice guy, giving off a mellow hippie vibe that feels disarming. Despite his appearance, there's something oddly professional about him. When it comes to business, he's soft-spoken and straight to the point, outlining the deal like it's nothing more than a casual transaction.

I sit there for a moment, letting it all sink in: the surreal nature of what I'm doing, the line I've just crossed. Then, almost on autopilot, I take the bag of pills he hands me and walk out the door.

*   *   *

I start small, curious to see how long this first batch will last. But I've grossly underestimated the demand for these things. They're gone in a matter of days, and I'm right back at Bob's for a re-up.

After a month or so, I graduate to being one of the guys who drives Bob around to fill his scripts. I wake up at 5 a.m., get Bob by 6 a.m., and we've picked up hundreds, if not thousands, of pills by lunchtime.

As I drive him around, a storm brews inside of me. I'm painfully aware of how fast I'm changing, how quickly I'm descending into a world I never imagined I'd be a part of. This isn't how I was raised; I know the risks, the danger I'm putting myself in.

Some nights, I sit at alone at my computer, grappling with the widening gap between the kid I used to be and the person I'm becoming. But each time, I just say, "Fuck it."

Saying "Fuck it" has become ridiculously easy.

Over time, I start buying in larger quantities. I get myself a safe and keep a steady supply of pills, with hundreds set aside for selling and personal use. The demand is constant, and the cash flows in fast, giving me a warped sense of power. People need what I have, and that makes me feel untouchable, like I'm running things in my own little empire.

But that power is a facade. My habit escalates fast. I'm using daily now, not just at clubs on the weekend. Chewing half of a 30 mg Oxy doesn't do anything for me anymore. It's not enough. So now, I crush two 30s at a time and snort them in one ridiculously fat line.

When you snort Oxy, the effect kicks in almost immediately. The powder burns as it shoots up your nose, but in a weird way, I actually start looking forward to the burn because you know you're only seconds away from a euphoric high.

Next comes the drip, as the powder moves through your nasal passage toward the back of your throat. The drip means you're almost there; your reality is about to shift. The ritual of getting high is almost as exciting as the high itself.

Before long, I'm doing four to six pills a day, two at a time, every time. And I'm morphing into a person I don't even recognize.

Customers come in and out of my apartment at all hours of the day. I've tried to keep my clientele super small, but these pills are so addictive that when word gets out that I have consistent access, I am hit up left and right by more and more people. It takes literally no effort on my part to deal like this.

*   *   *

By the end of the season, my team has gone undefeated for the first time in UH history, earning a spot in the Sugar Bowl. It is a moment that cements the team as legends and puts Hawaii on one of college football's biggest stages. Meanwhile, I've completely stopped going to practice, but I make sure to show up for every game.

Using Oxy like I do makes me want to sleep anytime I'm not high. I struggle to wake up in the morning, so I stop going to class as well. I show my face just enough to keep my professors off my ass, hitting them with every excuse in the book to explain my absences.

On the rare occasions I do go to class, I get high just before walking in, convincing myself that will make it "somewhat bearable." But there's no question that my brain is turning to mush.

What the hell is going on? This isn't me!

I'm the enthusiastic, vocal presence in class, not the guy nodding off under his hoodie. I'm in the final stretch of college and know I need to pull my shit together to finish, but the deeper I get into my habit, the harder it becomes to prioritize anything else.

I want to be high all the time. Anytime I'm bored, it's the perfect time to bust down another pill. Anytime I'm sad, it's the perfect time to bust down another pill. Anytime I'm really excited or happy about something, you guessed it—it's the perfect time to bust down another pill.

The more I use, the more reckless I become. At first, I'm careful about keeping a low profile, making sure only a select few know where to find me. But soon, that caution fades, and the traffic in and out of my apartment becomes ridiculous. People are showing up at all hours, heading straight to my bedroom for a sale.

Clearly, I'm giving no thought to the danger I'm putting my teammates and roommates in by doing this. These guys are some of the biggest stars on the UH team, the best team in UH history. And here I am, putting their livelihoods in jeopardy by selling pills from our apartment. Yet somehow, it doesn't seem like a big deal to me at the time.

When the season ends, our historic undefeated run comes to a crushing halt with a loss in the Sugar Bowl. In the weeks that follow, my roommates, the Mag 7, pack up and head off to their NFL training camps. Watching them go stirs up a storm of emotions. I'm genuinely excited for them, my brothers, my teammates. Their dreams are now within arm's reach, and I truly hope they go to camp and kill it.

But there's another side of me that's harder to face, the side that's overcome with bitterness and sorrow. Deep down, I know I should be right there with them, competing for a spot on an NFL roster.

This is also the closing of a chapter, and I feel the sting that comes with parting ways. The Mag 7, our brotherhood, the parties, our camaraderie. Another moment that's etched into my life's highlight reel is coming to an end. And while they're all gone, I'm left here, stuck with no clear path forward.

Even Coach Jones takes a new job at SMU. My connection to the UH football program is now almost nonexistent. I have no idea what I'm going to do next.

It's the perfect time to bust down another pill.

(Davone Bess went on to break UH records in receptions and receiving touchdowns, finishing third all-time in receiving yards. Despite going undrafted, he signed with the Miami Dolphins and, in true Davone fashion, not only made the team but became a starting receiver. In his rookie year, he caught

54 passes—the second-most in NFL history for an undrafted rookie wideout. Davone played six successful years in the NFL and remains my brother to this day.)

19

What Quitting Actually Looks Like

I wind up graduating by the skin of my teeth because of one person. The girl I'm spending almost all my time with, Apryle. The university lets me walk the stage after the spring semester, but there's a catch: I still need credits from one class to officially earn my BA in sociology. The challenge is that I've lost control over my ability to function without Oxy, leaving me with zero motivation to attend class regularly. I'm on the verge of failing. Everything comes down to this final report and presentation on how the Holocaust impacted Judaism.

Boy, do I have my work cut out for me.

Apryle and I dive in headfirst. For nearly 48 hours, we live in a bubble of research, writing, and caffeine-fueled editing marathons. My tiny apartment morphs into a war room of crumpled notes and glowing laptop screens. When it's all said and done, we have a PowerPoint polished to perfection and a 20-page report ready to go.

The grind is grueling, but it transforms into something deeper, something that sharpens our focus and strengthens our bond. We find a rhythm in the shared drive to leave no detail unchecked, no flaw uncorrected. She laughs at my hopeless attempts with PowerPoint, her patience grounding me in ways I didn't even realize I needed. I can't help but smile when she insists on rereading every paragraph, even when we just finished it. Somewhere in the long hours, the pursuit of perfection becomes something more, a connection that pulls us closer and tighter than we had ever been before.

Without her, there's zero chance I graduate from college. Zero chance.

She is a breath of fresh air, a ton of fun, and pretty naive about everything going on with me. I do everything I can to keep it that way. I hide my growing addiction from her any way I can.

When she asks about the bags under my eyes or why they're bloodshot, I tell her I struggle with sleeping. It's not a complete lie, I tell myself, but it's enough to keep her off my trail. She doesn't know what's happening when I disappear into the bathroom for what must feel like the hundredth time. I brush it off as a bladder problem, but behind that locked door, it's a different story. I roll up a dollar bill, crush the pill into fine powder, and snort it off the side of the sink. The loud, deep sniff would be a dead giveaway, but I've perfected the timing of the flush to mask it completely. Every time, I glance at my reflection in the mirror and wonder how much longer I can keep this up.

I'll never forget the first time I saw Apryle. I was riding around on my moped my freshman year when I passed this really short, mixed-race chick bursting with energy. She was hella cute.

Being the L.A. kid that I am, of course, I tried to holler at her. Every chance I got, I was in her friends' ears, asking them to hook me up. I sought her out on the dance floor at the clubs, and we'd dance all night. But no matter what I did, she was never interested in me as anything more than a friend.

I think she saw me as a bad boy, and she wasn't wrong. I was a football player with "L.A. swag" and all the baggage that came with it. She was smart to keep her distance, but I couldn't stay away. There was something about her spark, her energy. It felt like a magnet pulling me closer.

Over the years, I continued to pursue her. I like to think I was tastefully aggressive. And eventually, it worked.

We started dating right before our senior year, right around the time I got into Oxy. It's ironic, almost cruel, how the two things in my life started growing at the same time. While my habit worsened, my relationship with Apryle deepened. I tried so hard to shield her from everything I was doing, but in the end, I couldn't.

*　　*　　*

My apartment, once home to six, now houses only three of us: me and two budding superstars on the UH football team. While they're knee-deep in camp, preparing for the upcoming season, I party and sleep 'til late.

Early one morning, my bedroom door bursts open, and my roommates rush in, looking visibly shaken. They're breathing hard, like they've been running, and they're both screaming my name frantically.

"Ferg! Ferg, bro! They're coming for you! For real, bro, they're coming for you!"

The panic in their voice was jarring. It turns out that a high-ranking, credible source within the police force, who happened to be a huge UH fan, had tipped off the new head coach that investigators were eyeing the apartment. There had been complaints about unusual activity at our place, and a raid was imminent. Since my two roommates were stars on the team, their coach had given them a heads-up so they wouldn't get caught up in my mess.

My mind races. Fear grips my chest, tightening with each question I throw at them.

"Are you sure? Who told you? When's it happening?"

My voice cracks as I demand answers, but their responses stay the same, unwavering. It's not a dream. And for a moment, all I can do is stare at them.

Every instinct screams at me to run, to get as far away from this mess as possible. My heart is contracting and expanding so rapidly it feels like it might explode. Adrenaline tears through my veins, sending a rush of heat to my face and stopping at the tips of my ears. They burn, sharp and disorienting, distracting me from the crucial details my roommates are trying to share.

My mind is clouded as I wrestle with my next move, but one thought crystallizes with alarming clarity:

I gotta get the hell out of here.

I decide on the spot that my time in Hawaii is up.

*   *   *

I call Apryle, frantically begging her to come over. She doesn't ask any questions; she just comes. When she gets here, she helps me calm down, her presence grounding me as we methodically pack up all my things. It feels robotic, like I'm watching someone else's hands stuff clothes into bags. We drive to her house in silence. I'm too ashamed to call my mom. Instead, I book a one-way ticket to L.A., telling myself I'll figure out what to say to her when I get there.

Right now, I have an even bigger problem. I have $20K in cash that I have to figure out how to get back to L.A. with me. I can't deposit it at the bank because it'll be flagged by the IRS, and I can't just put it in my backpack and walk into the airport.

We spend all night talking through every possible way to deal with the money. In the morning, I ask Apryle to grab some plastic wrap. She looks at me like I'm crazy, and maybe I am, but it's all I can think of.

She watches as I wrap $10K to each of my thighs as tightly as I can. I tape that money so snug it doesn't budge when I walk around, and when I put on my biggest pair of basketball shorts, it looks totally normal. Apryle sits in silence, her face tense, her fingers tapping the edge of the table as if she wants to say something but doesn't.

Then she drives me to the airport, and we say our goodbyes. It's so tough. She's crying, really upset. Meanwhile, I'm trying to keep it together, paranoid out of my mind, convinced a black car is about to pull up any second to drag me away. I'm not in the right headspace for an emotional goodbye like this, but Lord knows this one cuts deep.

I walk directly to security. Inside, I'm a mess, but outside, I'm calm and collected. Sweat starts building up under the plastic wrap, making my legs itch, and I can feel the money growing soft and damp.

You're almost there, Filly. Just get to the runway.

Let's be clear: I'm no Pablo Escobar. But in my head, I'm public enemy number one. I have no idea how long someone has been watching me, or if my phone is tapped. My imagination runs wild. I assume anyone at the airport who looks at me for more than a second is a Fed.

At security, I send my carry-on through the X-ray machine and head for the metal detector. It's 2008, so they don't have the giant scanner that can see what's in my pockets or on my body yet. Once I'm through the metal detector, I'll be in the clear.

I walk through as casually as possible, slowly releasing the breath I've been holding as I reach for my bag on the other side.

Just then, a TSA agent waves me over, directing me to an area where someone is being patted down.

I nearly shit my pants. This is it.

I'm so fucked.

I want to cry. I want to run. But all I can do is walk to where he's pointing. My brain is racing, trying to think of what I can possibly say when they find the money. I don't even know if what I'm doing is a crime, but it sure doesn't look good.

A TSA agent holds up my backpack, instructing me to open the side pocket. When I do, I find a small pocketknife I must have tossed in there when I was packing in a hurry.

This can't be what gets me caught.

All because of a pocketknife?!

I can see the headlines already: "Ex-UH football player busted at Honolulu International Airport with $20K taped to his thigh and hundreds of Oxys."

The agent sighs, then asks if I'm okay throwing it away.

Wait. What?

"Hell yeah," I say. "I didn't even realize it was in there. Sorry about that."

He shrugs, hands me my backpack, and sends me on my way. The relief I feel cannot truly be put into words. I've seen people get a pat-down for so much less.

In the bathroom, I move the money to my backpack. Then I take three pills out of my fanny pack, crush them on top of the metal plate above the toilet paper dispenser, and snort what feels like the fattest, most well-deserved line of my life.

On the plane, as I wait for my flight to take off, I stare out the window at the tarmac, and my mind drifts back to the bright young star who had once touched down in Honolulu. Back when the world was wide open and full of promise, when the dream of having an extraordinary college career and a shot at going pro was a real possibility.

But now, as the plane's engines roar in preparation for takeoff, a deep sense of disgrace washes over me. I'm ashamed of who I've become. Tucking my tail between my legs, barely escaping this beautiful island I've called home for almost five years. Some $20K stashed in my backpack. A $120-a-day habit. I'm leaving behind not just the island, but also a version of myself I know I'll never get back.

*　　*　　*

In the years since, I've replayed those moments countless times, and two lessons have stayed with me.

First: Perception is reality.

How you perceive a situation shapes the way you experience it. It becomes your truth, for better or worse, and it forms the foundation of the world you create for yourself to exist in.

When my football career ended, I saw it as my entire world crashing down, and that is exactly what happened. My identity was so tied to the game that without it, I was lost. I thought football was what made me "me," the reason people admired me, the reason I mattered. Without it, I convinced myself I was nothing, and that belief became my reality.

Our minds are constantly absorbing the narratives we tell ourselves, feeding our subconscious behavior, and programming the software we run on. It is like coding a computer; every thought and action is a line of code that dictates how we function. This programming shapes our identity, our responses, and our view of the world.

For me, the lines of code I was writing were not just abstract thoughts. They became directives that reinforced my doubts and insecurities. Each negative thought subtly rewired the system, shaping a version of myself that saw the world through a lens of limitation and self-doubt. It was as if my mind was running on autopilot, and I didn't even realize I was programming it that way.

Neuroscience shows us why this happens. Repeated thoughts strengthen neural pathways, turning them into our default settings. This efficiency can be useful, but it is also dangerous. The narratives we tell ourselves can trap us in cycles of negativity or empower us to grow. I did nothing to stop the negative loop. Every day, I became more convinced that without football, I wasn't enough.

I couldn't see it then, but the mindset that kept me trapped in negativity was the same one that could have unlocked my freedom if I had seen things differently. The story I kept telling myself wasn't the whole truth. Opportunities were right in front of me, hidden within the fog of self-doubt. The end of my football career could have been the beginning of something else, something that allowed me to explore parts of my identity I'd ignored. Had I paused to explore, I would've realized I love writing. As a kid, I spent hours rapping, crafting punch lines and metaphors, finding ways to express myself creatively. Writing, even without a beat, was and continues to be a deeply fulfilling outlet for me.

If I'd had the clarity to look beyond my loss, I would have seen more. I would've realized that I am a learner. It turns out, I actually love to learn. School always bored me because I wasn't engaged with the right material. I avoided academic tasks because they didn't capture my interest, but in reality, I have a strong affinity for history, technology, and reading. Man, I love to read. I was just reading the wrong shit.

One of the biggest opportunities I fumbled came straight from Coach Jones. He saw potential in me that I couldn't see in myself. He offered me a graduate assistant role, saying he'd pay for my education as long as I wanted to go to school. I could have earned my master's degree and stepped into coaching, working with the wide receivers and using that as a springboard into a new chapter.

The path was there, waiting for me to take it. But in that moment, I couldn't zoom out. I couldn't widen my lens to see the big picture and all of the possibilities that lay ahead. I couldn't see the new chapters I could write, the parts of myself I could rediscover, or the opportunities that were mine for the taking.

This isn't just my struggle; this is something many athletes face. Psychologists call it "identity foreclosure," when someone commits to a single identity so young that they neglect the rest of who they are. Research confirms that athletes with strong athletic identities often experience crises when their careers end. It is not just the loss of the sport but the loss of who they believed they were.

The second lesson I learned is just as important: What quitting actually looks like.

Quitting isn't a dramatic moment like we see in movies. It isn't a single decision or a sudden crash. It is a gradual erosion of the principles and habits that once drove you. For me, it started with small concessions. I slept in because I wasn't playing. I skipped class because it didn't feel important. I told myself the weight room didn't matter because I wasn't on the field. Slowly, without even realizing it, every good habit that once defined me disappeared.

As those good habits faded, destructive ones took their place. Partying went from occasional to every day. Experimentation with drugs became a free-for-all. Each bad decision made the next one easier. The changes were so incremental that I didn't even notice myself becoming someone I didn't recognize.

Looking back, I can see how easily those destructive patterns became my new normal. It started small, but over time, the routines became automatic, the habits hardwired into my daily life. Habit formation is unforgiving. Research shows that it takes an average of 66 days to form a new habit, but breaking a deeply ingrained one can take even longer. I failed to recognize the cycle I was trapped in, and by the time I did, the habits were so deeply ingrained that they felt impossible to undo.

What I lost in that cycle was everything that once made me who I was. Pathological optimism, the get-hit mentality, and an obsession with pouring myself into the work all became a distant memory. Slowly but surely, I became a shadow of who I once was. One day, I looked around at the wreckage of my choices and wondered how it had all slipped away.

What I've learned is this: *Adversity doesn't just happen "to" you; it happens "for" you.*

Challenges, though difficult, have a way of pushing us to grow in ways we never expect. They force us to adapt, uncover strength we didn't know we had, and redefine what we're capable of. More importantly, they often reveal new opportunities, paths we might never have considered but that could set the stage for our greatest triumphs. Whether we seize those opportunities depends on one crucial factor: how we frame the experience. The way we view our struggles determines whether they become stepping stones to growth or anchors that hold us in place.

Today, I see how these lessons connect. Perception shapes reality, and the reality I created led to a slow erosion of the person I was. Quitting wasn't a single decision; it was the result of losing sight of my values, one moment at a time.

20
The Holy Grail

I ring the doorbell at my parents' house and wait, exhausted. The last 48 hours have taken their toll. When I hear D-Weez's footsteps squeak on the hardwood floor, my nerves spike. I haven't told my parents I'm home. My game plan is to be as honest with them as possible, but my appearance is my biggest concern at the moment. I've always prided myself on my appearance: staying in great shape, always having a fresh cut. But right now, I look terrible.

I have vicious acne on my cheeks, slowly becoming scabs that scar my face. My skin is pale from sleeping by day and partying at night. My eyes are puffy, with purple bags so big they look like mini pillows have been shoved beneath the skin. I look as exhausted as I feel. They say the eyes are the windows to the soul, so I keep my sunglasses on, trying to hide just how far I've fallen.

When the door swings open, the look on D-Weez's face says it all. "Jason," he gasps. "What's up, man? What are you doing here?" My stomach churns as I struggle to keep the shame and embarrassment from overwhelming me as I lean in to give him a hug. The last few days have been an absolute nightmare. It's so nice to see him, but I know what's coming.

I hear my mom's steps as she races down the stairs. Then there she is, smiling ear to ear, arms outstretched. My mom. My comfort zone. The familiar warmth of her presence makes this moment even harder.

But before I can take a breath, they hit me with a barrage of questions, one after another, and I'm in no rush to answer.

"What are you doing here?"

"Is everything okay?"

"Why didn't you call us and let us know you were coming?"

I sit down and take that breath, shades still on. My pulse quickens, knowing that the facade I've been trying to maintain is about to crumble.

D-Weez pulls back from his line of questioning and tells me to take my glasses off.

Damn. Time to come clean.

"Are you okay?" D-Weez asks, his tone softer now, almost inviting. It's the alley-oop I didn't know I needed, and I take it. I tell them everything.

Well, almost everything.

I start to unravel the tangled mess I've found myself in. I tell them about the pills, how they started as fun but quickly spiraled out of control. I explain the sketchy decisions I made along the way, how I sold them out of my apartment. The strangers coming and going at all hours, each transaction pulling me deeper into a world of risk, destruction, and addiction that was far removed from anything I once knew.

Then came the whispers of a raid, the feeling that I was constantly being watched and that it was only a matter of time before everything came crashing down.

They can see the evidence on my face. The dark circles under my eyes, the hollow look in my gaze. I lay it all out, everything but the full extent of my habit. I conveniently leave out the fact that I'm snorting six to eight pills a day and the number is only climbing.

They listen with looks of utter disbelief on their faces. I've always been able to tell them anything, so confiding in them isn't difficult. I'd literally called my mom right after losing my virginity, and her response was, "Did it feel good?"

But I'd never been in trouble with the law before. I'd never sold drugs or done anything that would put my freedom in jeopardy. This is a lot to ask them to take in.

*　　*　　*

All things considered, they handle it really well. I'm already embarrassed, feeling disgraced. And they don't shame me, ridicule me, or make me feel worse than I already do. They just focus on me, on how I'm doing, gauging the state of my mental health.

My mom doesn't say much, but I can see it in her eyes. My appearance has her shaken up. She's a fixer, and I watch her trying to figure out what she can do to make this horrible situation better.

But there isn't anything she can do but listen. So that's what she does. That's what they both do. They listen, and they don't overreact.

After my confession, I go upstairs and collapse into my childhood bed, feeling a strange mix of relief and paranoia. I'm grateful to be home, to have made it out without getting arrested, but the stress of what might still be out there hovers in the back of my mind.

I have no clue what the authorities know, how much information they've gathered, or if they're even still after me. But here, in the familiar comfort of my old room, I find a small sense of peace. I sleep for almost two days straight, only waking long enough to snort a pill to fend off any potential withdrawals before sinking back into the safety of sleep.

Even though I've brought enough pills to last me for a month, it doesn't take long for the fear of running out to start festering, slowly eroding that brief sense of peace that temporarily kept my anxiety at bay.

I've never been in a situation where I couldn't get pills for more than a day or two. I've always bought hundreds, if not thousands, at a time, and I've kept a hefty personal stash. I'm terrified of what will happen if I run out—of the brutal, unforgiving withdrawals I'll have to face. I need a connect in L.A., and I need a job.

*　　*　　*

Lucky for me, I have D-Weez. He owns a maintenance business that performs janitorial services for local apartments, condos, and commercial buildings. It's a no-brainer to start working for him. He needs an extra body, and I need to make money.

I need to stay busy. Sitting around the house getting high all day isn't going to cut it, so I jump right in and start working for D-Weez almost immediately.

The job is bittersweet. On one hand, it's perfect for what I've become. We start early, in the truck by 6:30 a.m., and work until about 3:00 p.m. The buildings we hit each day are scattered across Los Angeles, with long stretches of driving in between. It's enough time to snort a pill first thing in the morning, settle into the van, and disappear into my own world. Headphones on, music blaring, I go through the motions: cleaning laundry rooms, wiping down elevators, vacuuming hallways. It's the perfect setup for staying high, a job that lets me move without ever being fully present. Here, I can drift unnoticed, hiding in plain sight, just another janitor doing his work.

But when a tenant does notice me, even briefly, it shatters that sense of invisibility. On the rare occasion someone makes eye contact or says something, I'm convinced they see me as a loser. They don't see the guy who was a football star his entire life, someone with talent and a bright future ahead of him. All they see are the tattoos on my arm or the mop in my hand, and they assume I'm just a thug, someone beneath them, not worth their respect or even a second glance. Those moments, rare as they are, cut deep and start to mess with my head.

I have no clue what I'm going to do with my life. I'm just taking things day by day. Being run out of Hawaii and finding myself working as a janitor takes a toll on my confidence. Maybe it's all in my head, a narrative I've conjured up, but it feels real. It eats at me, fueling my need to get high. I just want to feel nothing.

*   *   *

Meanwhile, my pill stash is dwindling fast. I'm taking way too many pills each day to stretch what I have left, and paranoia is creeping in. I try my connects in Hawaii to see if someone will FedEx me some, but things there are changing fast. The main doctor Old Man Bob had been working with got busted. With the main source gone, everyone is scrambling for themselves.

Even though almost everyone I know in Hawaii is either dabbling with pills or a full-blown addict, I can't get a single one of them to ship me anything. I know there are pills in L.A., but I have no idea where to find them.

I think about Skid Row, those dark streets where danger and desperation collide. I imagine myself walking those alleys, cash in hand, searching for a connect. But I can't bring myself to do it, not yet.

I have $20,000 in cash, so money isn't an issue. But downtown L.A. feels like a risk I'm not ready to take. Instead, I turn my focus closer to home: my little brother, Donovan. By this point, he's spent a year in college, and I figure I'll start with him.

Still, I know I have to be careful. I don't want him to see how bad things really are. I don't want him to know what I've become.

One day, on the drive home from work, I decide to make the ask. I take a deep breath, trying to frame the question as casually as possible, like it's no big deal. "Lil Bro, you know anyone that sells Oxy out here? I'm looking to turn up this weekend, and those things are a ton of fun." I glance at him out of the corner of my eye, bracing for whatever comes next.

He doesn't respond immediately, which makes my heart thump harder. I grip the steering wheel tighter, replaying the question in my head, wondering if I've said too much. Finally, he looks at me, his tone calm, confident, like he's been holding onto a secret no one else noticed.

"Filly," he says, "your mom has everything you could want in her bedroom, bro!"

My eyes go wide, and my jaw practically hits the floor.
How did I not think of this sooner?
For a second, I'm frozen, caught between shock and elation.
Jackpot.

I've been making frantic calls to people in Hawaii, stressing about running out, when the answer has been right here all along, just a few steps down the hall.

What comes next doesn't even feel like stealing. My mom is my best friend, always has been, and yet, I feel nothing. No guilt. No second thoughts. None of it registers. It's all about me. My priorities have shifted so completely that I can't even consider how crossing this line could hurt her or damage our bond. All I see is an opportunity, a quick fix to my immediate problem.

Nothing else matters.

*   *   *

My mom has been living in pain for as long as I can remember. She has a degenerative disc disorder and has endured at least 20 surgeries in her lifetime. Her prescriptions for opioids have always been legit, never anything shady. Just a necessary response to the endless pain she deals with daily: neck pain, back pain, wrist pain. Despite all that, she's tough as hell. She's spent her life coping with the cards she's been dealt, doing the best she can with the hand she's been given.

But of course, none of this matters to me right now. I'm giddy with nervous excitement, my mind spinning with possibilities. All I can think about is getting a glimpse into her medicine bag to see what kind of options we're talking about.

When we get back to the house, nobody's home.

Perfect.

Donovan leads the way into our parents' room, heading straight for the nightstand on my mom's side of the bed. Without hesitation, he opens the second drawer and pulls out a medium-sized black bag with a zipper on top. It's bigger than I expected, almost like it was designed to house medication, and a lot of it. He sets the bag on the bed with a pause so deliberate it feels theatrical. Then, in dramatic fashion, he slowly unzips it.

It's like stepping into that iconic scene from *Pulp Fiction* where John Travolta opens the briefcase, and a heavenly, golden light spills out. I swear, I can almost hear angels sing. I've uncovered the holy grail. There are 20 to 30 different prescription bottles in that bag. Norco, Xanax, Soma, Vicodin, and Oxy. Each Oxy bottle contains 90 pills, enough to take three a day. I am easily staring at 300 pills. And according to my brother, these are her "reserves." They're brand-new, unopened prescriptions. I've found the mother lode.

All my anxieties are washed away. No more fear of withdrawals. As long as I don't overdo it, I can use my mom's stash to keep me afloat while I find my own local dealer.

*   *   *

Weeks go by, and, as expected, I run out of my personal stash. In fact, I only have one pill left. My plan is to snort that one and then start scheming how to crack into my mom's stash. So that's what I do. I snort the pill, give it a second to kick in, and head downstairs, acting like I'm getting something out of the fridge. I scan the backyard to make sure my parents are still in the garage.

The coast is clear. If I'm gonna do this, the time is now.

I sprint upstairs, laser-focused on the bag in the second drawer. I set it on the bed, my hands shaking uncontrollably. The faster I try to unzip the bag, the harder it is to get open. I need to calm my nerves. I need to slow down.

When I finally get it open, I go straight for the Oxy. I grab four, and then two Xanax, planning to just do one Oxy a day: half in the morning, half at night. Each time, with a quarter of a Xanax. I figure this will last me at least four days.

Over the last few months, I've learned to love the potent effects of snorting Xanax with Oxy in one big line. Together, they deliver a high that's stronger, longer-lasting, and harder to resist. I tell myself that this regular Xanax/Oxy combo will be enough to curb my withdrawals and suppress my opioid appetite.

Even though I've snorted a pill just moments earlier, I go straight into my bathroom to test the plan. With practiced hands, I use my debit card to crack the Oxy in half, break off a quarter of the Xanax, and crush them down, chopping and smushing until the powder is fine and ready. As I snort the line, a familiar mix of relief and disgust washes over me. The drip hits, and I wait, knowing exactly what comes next.

Slowly, I droop down onto the floor of the bathroom, letting the high take over. I'm in heaven, like my brain is wrapped in a cocoon of pure bliss, sealing in every drop of dopamine and smothering every trace of regret and shame. Those feelings aren't just quieted, they're buried deep down, right next to the son I used to be.

*　　*　　*

The pills are supposed to last me at least four days. That's what I tell myself. But with each passing hour, the urge to take just a little more pulls me back into the bathroom.

I'm watching *Entourage* to pass the time, and as soon as the theme song kicks in at the start of a new episode, it feels like the perfect excuse for another. First, it's half a pill. Then a quarter. The night blurs by, episode after episode, until morning comes and all that's left is a single Xanax staring up at me. I didn't even make it through the night.

I brush off the failure almost as quickly as I realize it. There's no reason to panic. There are hundreds more where those came from.

This is gonna be easy.

This cycle goes on for almost a month: fistfuls of Oxy, Xanax, Norco, and even a Soma or two. Mom's pill stash is the gift that keeps on giving. Endless euphoria is just steps away, waiting for me to stroll into her room. I'm stealing at an alarming rate, but I don't care. Nothing else matters.

After a couple of weeks, I notice the bottles feel lighter, the stash visibly shrinking. Still, I can't stop. Every day, I brace myself for the moment my mom bursts into my room, screaming at the top of her lungs. But it never happens. So of course, I keep taking.

The only reason I haven't been caught is that my mom keeps her daily pills separate from her reserves. She hasn't needed to check them yet, but I know my days are numbered. The thought of her discovering the truth makes me sick to my stomach. My secrets laid bare for my parents to see—it feels like the beginning of the end.

Even with that dread creeping in, I manage to shrug it off. The part of me that says "fuck it" is louder than my paranoia. I tell myself I'll deal with it when it happens, convincing myself I'll know exactly what to do when the shit hits the fan.

And of course, just as I let my guard down and stop thinking about it, the moment blindsides me.

One afternoon, after I get home from work, D-Weez calls me into my parents' bedroom. He sounds casual, chipper even. When I walk through the door, he's standing next to my mom, who is holding her unzipped medicine bag in one hand and a bottle of Oxy in the other.

In true D-Weez fashion, he says in a calm tone, "Anything you want to tell us?"

I take a second to weigh my options. My mom looks pissed, but also confused and sad. I need to decide how much to tell them. What can I say that'll be just enough to make this make sense, but not let on that I'm a full-fledged junkie who can't control himself?

I let out a sigh.

This is my chance to come clean. I've been hiding it long enough, and I really don't see any way out. So I tell them everything, truly everything this time. How many pills I was taking per day in Hawaii. How I'd come home with my own supply but had recently run out. How I'm so desperate to feel normal but can't control myself. I lay it all out there. Raw and uncut.

I watch my mom go from angry to understanding, the frustration in her eyes softening into something I can only describe as love. She knows firsthand how brutal opioid withdrawals can be, and without missing a beat, she slips into mom mode, focusing entirely on how to get me through the next few days.

And just like that, the jig is up. The safety net I've been clinging to is gone, and all that's left is the fight ahead. I'm staring down the barrel of a full-blown detox, completely terrified. I know it's going to be hell, but no amount of fear or dread can truly prepare me for what's coming.

*   *   *

That fear becomes reality the very next morning. The withdrawals hit hard and fast, starting with hot and cold sweats that soak my sheets. I'm talking puddles of sweat, enough to wring out cupsful with your bare hands.

Next come the body aches. It's impossible to sit still, impossible to find a comfortable position. It's constant. There's no relief. The aches start in my head, make their way down to my lower back, and end up in my calf muscles, which is the weirdest thing to me. No lie, my calves are sore as shit. And speaking of shit ...

There's the diarrhea, followed by the most intense bout of nausea I've ever experienced. My body pleads with me, begs me for the smallest taste of Oxy. For anything to relieve me from this pain. But there really is no relief. All I can do is lie there, yawning uncontrollably, my eyes streaming like faucets.

For three days, I feel like I'm dying. I feel like dying. Nothing compares to the agony of opioid withdrawal.

Finally, on the fourth day, the physical intensity begins to ease, but the mental anguish takes over. I try watching TV to distract myself, but it doesn't work. Out of nowhere, a memory of Domo surfaces, and the tears come hard and fast. The grief feels fresh, like I'm losing him all over again.

Then the frustration creeps in, frustration over my injuries, over the bad breaks that derailed everything I'd worked for on the football field. It's like a floodgate opens, and I'm drowning in all the unfairness I've tried to ignore.

And then there's Davone. My brother, my teammate, my rival. He's in the NFL now, a starting receiver for the Miami Dolphins, living the dream we used to talk about together. Meanwhile, I'm stuck here, battling withdrawals in my parents' house, light-years away from the life I thought I'd be living.

These thoughts consume me, ripping open wounds I've been burying for years. I don't want to face them. I'm not ready to face them.

*　　*　　*

After about a week, I'm finally able to go back to work. It feels like a relief at first, a way to keep my hands busy and my mind distracted. I've convinced myself that I don't need therapy or rehab, that I'll be fine if I can just take things one day at a time.

But staying busy doesn't stop the pull. It doesn't take long for my thoughts to fixate on finding Mom's pill bag again. Once the thought is in my head, I can't shake it. It starts as a whisper, a faint idea that grows louder by the hour. I know it won't be in the same spot as before; this time, I'll have to really look for it. The unrelenting voice in my head convinces me that not only can I find the bag but also that I'll be able to swipe a few pills unnoticed.

And once that voice takes over, it pulls me further, straight into the memory of what I'm chasing. I want to feel that high again, just one more time. I crave the rush from the drip and the calm that follows. I can already picture myself in my room, lights off, Joe Budden playing in the background, letting it all wash over me. It's a ritual I can't seem to let go of, one that feels both comforting and addictive.

As the idea takes hold, so do the questions, creeping in one by one:

Can I pull it off again without anyone noticing?

What if I get caught?

Shit, what if I don't?

I know I'm playing with fire. My mom had been understanding the first time, letting me off easy. She won't be so understanding if I get caught again. It's been weeks, and the longer I hold off, the stronger the impulse becomes. I tell myself I can resist, but the thought refuses to let go of me. It claws at me until it's impossible to ignore.

The second my parents leave the house to run an errand, I give in. Like a man possessed, I'm scouring their bedroom. In the closet. Under the bathroom sink. Behind the dresser. I search that room high and low. And just before I give up, I drop to my chest and peek beneath the bed. Bingo! There it is, looking right at me.

There's only one bottle of Oxy in the bag, which means it'll be even easier for me to get caught. So I only take two pills, careful not to push my luck. I've just fought my way through withdrawals, so I convince myself I can pace it out, telling myself I don't need to take them daily. But the moment I crush down the first pill, I lose all control. It's impossible to stop.

*　　*　　*

The next few weeks become a strange game of hide-and-seek. I don't know if my mom realizes I'm back in her bag or not, but she moves it to different hiding spots around her room. Each time, I search relentlessly until I find it, violating every ounce of privacy she has. In a twisted way, the search itself becomes part of my ritual. The thrill of the hunt, the risk, the commitment to thoroughly scouring her room in the short window of time when she's gone. It's intoxicating in its own way. I start fiending for more, the excitement feeding into my need like fuel to a fire.

At first, I didn't think twice about what I was doing. But now, it's impossible to ignore. I'm spiraling. The lengths I'm willing to go to feed my addiction keep growing, crossing lines I never thought I would cross. I can't stop. I'm not even sure I want to.

I tell myself I'll rein it in, that I'll stop before it gets worse. But deep down, I know that's a lie. My addiction doesn't care about promises or boundaries. All it cares about is the next high.

And then, one day, the inevitable happens—again.

I hear aggressive footsteps pounding down the hallway toward my room. My mom bursts through the door. She's holding a half-empty bottle of Oxy in her hand, and she's in tears. She's fuming, but she's also in disbelief.

It's been less than a month since she helped me through withdrawals, and here we are again. I can't lie about what I've been doing. All I can do is own it. I apologize profusely, trying to explain that I hadn't realized how big of a dent I'd put in the bottle. But there's nothing I can say to justify this. This is the moment when my mom realizes how serious my problem is, and it's the same moment I confront just how deeply Oxy has taken over my life.

Even going through the horror of withdrawals hasn't kept me from stealing more pills. Oxy has wrapped its cunning arms around me and is squeezing with all its might. It's like I'm under a spell. I'm trapped, and I can't get out. When I'm not high, I'm scheming on how I'm gonna get high. And when I am high, I can't even enjoy it, because I'm only thinking about how to keep getting high. I'm consumed by it.

It takes my mom days to even speak to me again, which is unheard of in our relationship. She's my best friend, but she is rapidly losing her trust in me, no longer looking at me with pride in her eyes. I've always been her "Sweet Pea." A star athlete, a good person, and an even better son. But I can see all that fading away. Now she can hardly look at me, and honestly, I can't blame her.

Her silence isn't just about disappointment; it's about protecting herself. She starts taking the pill bag with her everywhere she goes, no longer trusting that it's safe in the house. And she's right. I'd have flipped the entire house upside down to find that bag if I thought she'd left it behind. Because, let's face it, I'm better at finding her bag than she is at hiding it.

21

Divine Intervention

A few weeks have passed since my mom caught me for the second time. Things are tense, and the distance between us feels heavier every day. But none of that stops the craving.

One Saturday night, I'm pacing around my bedroom, wracking my brain yet again to find a local connect for pills. I call and text everyone I can think of, hoping someone might point me in the right direction. Each call ends the same way, with no leads, no answers, nothing.

Frustration builds with each dead end, my desperation growing louder in my head. Then, out of nowhere, it hits me: what feels like the most brilliant plan of my life.

I know my parents will leave for church early in the morning, and my mom will take her pill bag with her. I figure there's at least a 50/50 chance she'll leave the bag in the car. She's not gonna take it into church, right? If I can get to her car while she's in church, I just might be able to get access to the bag.

My heart says, *Don't do it, Filly. This is crazy!* But my brain isn't listening.

After partying on ecstasy with friends most of the night, my 7 a.m. alarm jerks me awake. My body screams for more sleep, my mind still clouded, but I can't let that stop me. If I'm going to pull this off, I need to move now.

I peek out my window to confirm the coast is clear. My parents' car is gone.

Yep. So far, so good.

First, I need their spare car key. I know exactly where they keep it, tucked in a dresser drawer, and I'm relying on it still being there. My heart pounds as I race into their room. I yank open the drawer, and there it is, exactly where it's supposed to be. For a moment, I just stare at it, and then relief floods through me.

Next, I need transportation. The church is only five minutes away, but I don't have a car. It'll take 45 minutes to walk each way, and I can't risk being seen. I remember D-Weez has a 20-year-old bike out back. It's a wreck, barely functional, with flat tires and a rusted chain that squeaks like a dying mouse. But it's all I have.

It's not ideal, but I don't hesitate. I grab the bike, convincing myself it'll get me there and back.

I grip the handlebars, ignoring the creaks and groans as I take off. With every push on the pedal, the wheel rim grinds into the pavement, making loud crunching, screeching sounds. As cars speed past me, I must look like a madman.

When I finally reach the church, I spot my parents' car parked right out front. I leap off the bike before it even stops, letting it crash hard onto the sidewalk behind me. I click the unlock button on the fob, practically diving into the passenger seat. My eyes scan the interior like a cyborg, programmed to locate Oxy and every other opioid in existence. Almost immediately, I lock onto a bag on the back seat floor.

No way, could it really be?

The quiet of the church feels strange, almost like it's mocking me. Outside, cars rush by, oblivious to the chaos unfolding inside the car.

With one eye on the church door, I crouch down and rummage through the bag. The rustle of plastic and pills shatters the silence.

The moment I see the Oxy bottle my eyes widen, and I nearly shit myself.

I'm seconds away from pulling this off.

Something tells me this may be my last hurrah, so like a complete jackass, I take at least 25 Oxys and a fistful of Xanax. Then I carefully place the bag back exactly where I found it, lock the door, and race home on the bike, feeling like I've hit the lottery.

I have a pocket full of pills, and my parents have no idea how flawlessly I've executed this insane plan.

*   *   *

When I get home, I crush two pills, mix in some Xanax, and snort a fat line to celebrate my impossible heist. The ecstasy from last night still lingers in my system, but I don't care. I deserve this.

Four days later, I'm outside smoking a cigarette when I hear D-Weez yell my name from inside. His voice has an edge that puts me on alert. I stub out the cigarette and head inside. The sight stops me cold. My mom is on the floor, sobbing next to the open pill bag. Her face is pale, her hands trembling as she grips the bottles. When she looks up at me, her eyes are full of hurt and confusion.

"How did you do it?" she asks, her voice breaking. "How did you get to them?"

Her words hang in the air, cutting through my excuses as I scramble for a way out.

"Do what, Ma? What are you talking about?" I reply, trying to play dumb. Stalling before all hell breaks loose.

"Jason, how could you? You've run through all my fucking scripts! The doctor can't legally write me another one for weeks. I went from having reserve bottles to not having enough to get through this month. You think your withdrawals are bad? I've been on opioids for pain since you were a baby. I can't believe you. How dare you. How the fuck could you do this to me?!"

Seeing her on the floor, crying like this, kills me. The way she's looking at me, her eyes full of disbelief, like she doesn't even recognize the person standing in front of her. Then, without a word, she slowly lowers her gaze to the floor, refusing to look at me again. Her tears begin to flow even harder, the kind of sobbing that shakes your whole body, a pain so deep it's like I've ripped something out of her.

D-Weez stands silently, shaking his head. He's pissed off, and he's never pissed off. The look on his face tells me everything. His usual composure is gone, replaced by anger and disappointment.

"You're out of control, Jason," he says, his voice low but steady. "We've tried being patient with you, but this—this is too far. You gotta go!"

I don't argue. I can see it in their eyes: they've had enough. They don't care where I go; they just know I can't stay here anymore.

*   *   *

I call my brother Ryan to explain the situation. I don't sugarcoat a thing; I need a place to stay. The silence on the other end of the line says it all. He's shocked. He had no idea how bad it had gotten, how deep I was in. I can almost see his facial expression through the tone of his voice on the other end of the phone. I'm embarrassed but grateful that he doesn't blow up on me, even though he probably should. Instead, there's this pause, like he's trying to process the fact that his little brother, the one he loves so much and has always looked out for, has turned into a junkie.

It's not easy for me to admit everything I've done, to lay it all out for him like that. And I can tell it's tough for him to hear. He lives with his girlfriend and his best friend, Zach. His place is already full. But even with all that, he doesn't hesitate to let me sleep on his couch.

I show up at Ryan's looking ragged and feeling defeated. My life is in a suitcase, and with three pills left in my pocket, all I do is worry about running out.

Ryan's apartment is the spot in L.A. where all our friends meet up. He's got a full studio for creating and recording music, so the place is always jumpin'. It's filled with energy: friends popping in and out, drinking, smoking, and partying until the wee hours of the morning. We're all in our early 20s, living for the music and the party.

That first night, I let myself get lost in the partying. I drink too much, snort my remaining Oxys, and for a while, it feels like I'm back in control, masking my growing depression under the haze of a high. But the illusion doesn't last. When I wake up the next day, the weight of reality crushes me. My pills are gone, and so is my access to my mom's stash. I've known this day was coming, but there was no way to actually prepare for it.

Ryan and Zach are at work, leaving me alone in the apartment. My head throbs, reeling from the heavy combination of alcohol and pills the night before. And no matter how hard I think about it, I can't figure out what to do next.

Withdrawals are on the horizon, and I have no connect. The game is officially over.

By midafternoon, the sweats kick in, followed by the nausea, the body aches, and everything else. I'm in bad shape and getting worse.

As I lay there, I realize how far I've fallen. Barely surviving in my brother's living room, crashing on his couch, my relationship with my parents in ruins, and no way to get more pills.

Disappointment and embarrassment twist together into a slipknot, tightening with every thought, choking out any shred of pride or dignity I have left. I start questioning everything, wondering how I let it spiral this far.

How could I have made so many wrong moves?

It's like I'm standing on the outside, watching myself play Jenga with my life. Every bad decision is another block removed, each one weakening my foundation a little more, then a little more, until it all comes crashing down.

When Ryan and Zach get home, I do my best to act normal. I'd give anything for a bedroom where I could close the door and try to sleep, but I'm stuck on their couch.

Pretty soon, the two of them are back to making music. This may be the most uncomfortable I've ever been in my life. I'm sprawled out on their couch, in the middle of their living room, going through full-fledged opioid withdrawals while the two of them are busy making beats with the volume at full blast.

It's torture.

When I wake up the next day, my withdrawals are even worse, but at least the house is quiet and empty.

What can I do?

I toy with the idea of going to Skid Row to buy some heroin. Oxy is basically a pill form of heroin, so a lot of addicts end up switching from pills to heroin, because it's much cheaper and way easier to find. But heroin scares the shit out of me. I have no idea how much to do. I don't want to mess it up. I'm not ready to die.

Then I remember this little pharmacy about 20 minutes away. It's a small mom-and-pop kind of place, the kind where you'd expect fewer cameras and easier access. My brain starts racing. I could rob them for everything they have: Oxy, Percocet, every other opioid they've got stocked. I don't care about their money, just the pills.

The plan takes shape quickly. I drag myself off the couch, mustering up the strength and courage I'm gonna need to go through with this. I start pacing around the room, jumping up and down like I'm psyching myself up for a game.

I know exactly where my brother keeps his gun: a big silver .357 Magnum. I grab it from the drawer and set it on the coffee table. It's heavy and unfamiliar, and I realize I have no clue how it works. I'm too scared to even check for bullets because I don't want it to accidentally go off. Not that it matters; I don't plan on using it anyway.

I sit on the couch, drenched in sweat, my head pounding. My eyes are bloodshot as I try to think clearly, to wrap my mind around what I'm about to do. The fear is there, but it's muted by desperation.

Fuck it. I'm doing it.

I put on some basketball shorts and a hoodie.

Okay. You got this, Filly.

Then, as I'm tying my shoes, my phone rings, rattling the coffee table. I pay it no mind, too focused on the plan.

Instead, I shove it in my pocket, grab the gun, tuck it in my waistband, and head for the door.

But then it rings again, vibrating insistently in my pocket. I stop, annoyed, and check to see who it is. Damn. It's Mom. My finger hovers over the screen as I debate whether or not to answer.

What does she want? Probably to lecture me, maybe even yell at me. I'm not in the mood. But something—call it instinct, call it fate—makes me pause. A voice in the back of my mind whispers: *Answer it.*

*   *   *

Answering that call winds up being one of the best decisions I've ever made in my life. I'd never considered armed robbery before. I can't believe my brain went there.

A part of me had been hoping my brother would come busting through the door to put an end to that dumbass plan of mine. But in the end, it's my mom who saves me, just by calling to check on me, to make sure I'm okay. To see if I might be willing to go to rehab.

She starts telling me about places she's been researching, and while she talks, I sit back down on the couch. I pull the gun from my waistband and place it back on the coffee table. I listen to her, but I'm not really hearing the words. My eyes are locked on that big-ass silver gun, and all I can think about is the magnitude of the situation.

I was just about to cross a line I couldn't come back from. I've seen the videos: someone walks into a store planning to grab some cash, but fear takes over, and they pull the trigger, killing someone in the heat of the moment. Or a security guard sneaks up, no clue the robber isn't planning to hurt anyone, and eliminates them in self-defense.

That could've been me. I was desperate. And there's nothing more dangerous than a desperate human being.

If I hadn't answered that call, I might have done something that would have changed my life, and possibly someone else's, forever. The timing still freaks me out.

Divine intervention? Maybe.

What I do know is that connections with the people we love are real. That phone call saved me. It might have saved someone else too.

I interrupt my mom mid-sentence, forcing her to pause. "Okay, Mom. I'll go."

Agreeing to rehab is one small step back from the edge, a chance to stop the spiral before it gets worse. I've lost all control, and it's time to take action. It's time to try to reclaim my life.

22

Victory House

My options for rehab are limited. We need somewhere that can take me immediately. I can't last another day on my brother's couch, and D-Weez makes it clear he doesn't want me back in the house. Unfortunately, every place we contact has a waitlist that's two to four weeks long.

I don't have that long. I need something right away. I don't even know if I'll be alive in two weeks, given how I feel and the wild ideas my brain's been conjuring up to find pills.

The other issue is that most rehab facilities don't take insurance. They can cost thousands, anywhere from $12K to $60K for a 30-day stay.

Am I really going to have to spend every dime I have just to go away for a month?

Finally, we land on a place called Victory House. They take insurance, which makes them way more affordable than the other options. That alone feels like a win, but there's something else that draws us to them. The man on the phone hears the pain in my mom's voice and responds with care and empathy. He doesn't rush or brush her off. Instead, he listens, he tries to work with us, and he genuinely seems to want to help.

He doesn't know when a bed will be available, but he promises to call back soon. Less than an hour later, the phone rings. They have a spot for me, and I can check in tomorrow.

He encourages me to stay clean for just one more day, to show up first thing in the morning, and to let them handle the rest. And just like that, it's happening. I'm going to rehab.

The thought of it hits me hard. My habit has snowballed to the point where I've completely lost control of my life. It's hard to accept.

And as I sit with the reality of it, dark, berating thoughts run on an endless loop in my mind:

Look at you, a fucking loser.

Pathetic. A washed-up has-been.

Ain't nothing but a junkie now.

These thoughts overshadow the kindness happening right in front of me. My mom has gone out of her way to save my life. The man on the phone has moved mountains to make sure I'll have a bed in 24 hours, yet I don't feel any relief. Just the pain of withdrawal coupled with the harsh reality of where my choices have led me.

You'd think that would be enough to fight off any urges, but it's the opposite. My cravings are stronger than ever. I'm desperate for one final pill to soften the blow of what I'm feeling, to carry me through the night, to comfort me before I step into this unfamiliar chapter. Rehab may be the first step to reclaiming my life, but the reality of how far I've fallen is a hard truth to come to grips with. I want one last pill to say goodbye, a proper send-off, on my terms.

And in that moment, it's the only thing I can think of.

*   *   *

Once my spot in rehab is confirmed and the plan is officially locked in, my mom and D-Weez make an exception and let me stay at their house for the night. Desperate to escape my own thoughts, I sit at the computer in D-Weez's office, trying to distract myself from the withdrawal gripping me. My eyes wander across the room, landing on the wooden cabinet where my parents store work documents and office supplies. Something inside me nudges me to go through it, like the black pill bag could be tucked away in there. I crack it open and immediately realize there's no way it's in here. The cabinet is packed, wall to wall, with binders and notebooks stacked in every corner. Loose papers fill every gap, with rubber bands and a stapler balanced precariously on the edge of a shelf.

At first glance, it's obvious the bag wouldn't fit in this clutter.

I'm about to close it up, disappointed, but something tells me to dig deeper. I move a few things around, inspecting between the books, hoping for a miracle. And I kid you not, sitting behind a book, next to the inner wall of the cabinet, is a single 40 mg Oxy.

You've got to be shittin' me!

It practically has my name written all over it.

Like I said, I've always been better at finding them than she was at hiding them. But, damn. This one feels like a gift from the gods of addiction.

With zero hesitation, I grab it and sprint to my bedroom bathroom.

My last pill.

The feeling is bittersweet, like breaking up with somebody I thought was the love of my life. Somebody I've shared so many moments with. Somebody who's made me feel invincible.

And while I know how toxic and evil these pills are, I mourn letting them go the same way you mourn an ex during a breakup.

*   *   *

I wake up the next morning in my childhood bed, in total disbelief that I'm heading to rehab. My brain starts listing reasons I should back out, justifying the cold feet I'm getting. The magnitude of the situation begins to set in. I'm humiliated. But I'm out of options.

Before I know it, we're in the car, with Joe Budden's "Just to Be Different" playing through the speakers. The haunting piano and heavy bass line pull me into a trance, amplifying the heaviness in my chest. His raw lyrics cut through the noise, perfectly capturing the weight of everything I'm feeling but can't put into words. It drowns out the possibility for conversation, which is exactly what I need. The song plays on repeat, and my poor mom has to endure it the whole ride. As the car slows, I finally glance up and see that we are pulling up to a place that looks more like an office building than a residential treatment center.

As my mom opens the door for me, I hesitate and think about running. I don't know where I'll go, but I'm one breath away from dropping my bag and sprinting down the block.

Now, let's be clear. Victory House is not some Malibu treatment center with luxury living, a chef, massages, and ocean views. Hell, no. Imagine the exact opposite of that. The treatment center is housed in a commercial property that takes up almost half the block. The building itself is two stories, with a faded, dark brown awning hanging off the side. Seven other businesses are crammed into the same building, and at first, we can't even figure out which door leads to Victory House. None of the doors have visible addresses, and all the windows are covered. It takes a minute to figure it out, but we finally decipher which door is ours and step inside, where the reality of the place hits me immediately.

I'm greeted by the stale stench of cigarette smoke. The smell clings to the air as we move deeper inside.

A narrow, dimly lit staircase forces us upstairs, and when we reach the top, it's clear someone has turned this second-floor office suite into a makeshift living space. The hallway is tight, with plain white walls that force us to march in a single file line. The hardwood floors are stained and scuffed, and the bending of the hallways gives it the disorienting feel of a labyrinth.

I hear the faint clinking of pots and pans from around the corner, clearly coming from a kitchen we can't see from here.

On the opposite end of the hallway, I spot what seems to be an office door, almost hidden in plain sight. I glance at my mom, who's taking it all in just like I am. The look on her face says it all. It's a mix of concern and exhaustion. Her eyes struggle to hide the disappointment in the stark reality of this place, but they also carry a determination that tells me, despite everything, that she needs me to go through with this. We both know I'm out of options. There's no turning back now.

The office door swings open, and out steps Johnny, the man we'd spoken to on the phone. He's a recovering crack addict who's been through treatment here and now practically runs the place as a counselor. From the moment he steps out, Johnny's energy is contagious, inviting, and full of life, just like on the phone. Next to him is Sam, another counselor and the program director. Both Johnny and Sam are in charge, and they'll be responsible for my intake into Victory House.

Johnny introduces himself to me and my mom, then gently but firmly says, "We've got it from here, Mom," a not-so-subtle cue that it's time for her to say goodbye. I'm caught off guard by how fast everything is moving, but it's clear they've got a process and it's starting now.

I wrap my arms around my mom like I'll never see her again. Squeezing her with everything I have left. Whispering, "I'm sorry," in her ear.

And I am. In this moment, I am truly so sorry. Sorry for embarrassing myself and my family by almost getting raided and fleeing Hawaii the way I did. Sorry for stealing from my mom. For lying to her. Sorry for morphing into this version of myself that she can no longer trust.

The thought of her driving home alone, broken by all of this, almost kills me. I can see it clear as day. Her hands gripping the wheel, her heart breaking with every mile she puts between us. My poor mom, bawling her eyes out, suffering from the realization that she just dropped her baby off at rehab.

*   *   *

The pill I'd done the day before suppressed my withdrawals throughout the night, but as I sit in the office with Johnny and Sam, the symptoms start hitting me hard. All I want is to retreat into a cold, dark room and sleep for days.

When Johnny asks how I'm feeling, I tell him the truth. I explain that I used the night before and now I'm starting to feel like shit. He nods and suggests we go find my bed.

He leads me down a long, narrow hallway with closed doors on both sides, finally opening one and walking me inside. The room is tiny but neat, with two dressers, a closet, a bathroom, and two bunk beds pressed against the wall. On top of the dresser is a boxy CRT TV from the '90s, with a bulky frame and an antenna dangling loosely from the side.

I'm definitely not in Malibu.

Johnny gestures to the top bunk closest to the door, tells me I can sleep, and that he'll wake me up for lunch and dinner. But he makes it clear that regardless of how I'm feeling, my work starts in the morning.

I toss my bag in the closet and then jump on the top bunk, taking a moment to thoroughly examine the room, still in disbelief that my life has come to this. Then I close my eyes and sleep for hours.

At some point, I'm awakened by a herd of footsteps coming from the back of the building and a surge of voices echoing down the hallway, piercing the thin walls. I throw my pillow over my head, roll over, and go back to sleep.

*   *   *

The next morning, I'm startled by the bedroom light being switched on at 6 a.m. I jolt up in my bed, realizing I've slept for almost an entire day. I hadn't even heard my roommates come in.

An older Black man stands in front of the closet, getting dressed. He nods at me and says, "What up, youngster?"

His tone is comforting and inviting, like he's trying to say, *I know how you're feeling right now. We've all been there. Great job taking that first step!*

His name is Donald Champion, but everyone calls him Champ. Champ is a recovering crack addict in his early 60s, in his second attempt at recovery.

After a lifetime of battling his addiction, he managed to pull together 15 years of sobriety. Then one day, out of the blue, in the middle of his workday at USC, he bailed. He headed down to Skid Row and lived on the streets for five years, consumed by his addiction. Now he's here, trying to get clean, just like me.

Champ is a good-looking man, clean-cut and well-dressed. He's clearly educated; the tone and cadence of his speech make him sound articulate, wise, and slick, like one of those old heads with a plethora of knowledge and a fountain of street smarts.

He always starts sentences off with "Say, man," followed by the point he's trying to make or the question he wants to ask. Like, "Say, man, what time does the meeting start today?" or "Say, man, we can't sit in this room and watch this shit all day."

Champ not only becomes my closest friend in rehab, but he's also the reason I stay as long as I do.

From day one, Champ and I connect. He looks out for me, and I don't know if it's because he sees something in me or if he just has that parental instinct. Whatever it is, he seems to know that I need this extra support during one of the darkest times of my life.

My first week here, I lie in bed at night in total agony from my withdrawal symptoms, doing my best to suffer in silence. Then I hear a voice from the bottom bunk call out, "Say, youngster. You good, youngster?" or "Say, youngster. You awfully quiet up there." Never calling me by name, not once. It's always "youngster," his voice appearing out of nowhere, always checking on me at the perfect time.

In class, Champ always saves a seat for me right next to him. If I start dozing off or look disinterested, he taps on my desk and says, "Come on, youngster, you need this shit now. Don't be like the rest of these fools."

Champ and I stay up late into the night talking sports and swapping war stories about our addiction, with his stories always trumping mine. His life feels like something out of a movie, and I admire his strength, still here at 60, fighting for the life he deserves.

His presence is constant, grounding me in a place where everything else feels uncertain.

*　　*　　*

When done right, rehab is an opportunity to learn about addiction as a disease and to develop tools to get clean and stay clean. But to me, rehab feels more like a vacation. A chance to rest and take a break from the chaos and downward spiral I've found myself in. All I have to worry about is getting off pills and proving I can resist the urge to use on my own.

I know I'll need a lot of help, but I'm confident Victory House will be enough to get some sobriety under my belt. While I try to go in with an open mind, deep down I'm already making reservations, fantasizing about the next time I'll drink and wondering if I can do it without drugs.

*　　*　　*

Sam and Johnny run a tight ship, with strict rules and a grueling daily schedule. There's no gaming the system here; everyone knows the consequences. We have weekly drug tests, and Sam and Johnny know all the tricks. Sneaking food into rooms or trying to slip out at night isn't tolerated. Break the rules, and you're gone.

Most of us have been running wild for years, doing whatever we wanted, whenever we wanted, so these rules can feel harsh at first. But they're about more than control; they're about learning discipline. In the real world, rules exist for a reason, and Victory House makes sure we understand that.

This place isn't just about getting clean; it's about rebuilding habits and finding pride in the small things again. Wake-up is at 6 a.m., beds are made military style, and rooms must be spotless. Sam inspects every corner and crevice weekly to make sure everything is in tip-top shape. And I'll be honest, it feels good to care about something again.

Most of us here are on court orders and need Victory House more than it needs us. With a waiting list for beds, Sam and Johnny don't waste time on anyone unwilling to fight for sobriety. They're not here to babysit. Either we do the work, or we leave.

For the first 30 days in rehab, you're on lockdown. No phone privileges, no day passes. Every day looks exactly the same:

6:15 a.m. to 7:15 a.m.: Breakfast

7:30 a.m.: Meet at the van

8:00 a.m. to 2:00 p.m.: Daily classes

5:00 p.m. to 8:00 p.m.: AA and NA meetings

The days drag on, draining me both mentally and physically.

We're taught everything about the disease of addiction. How it rewires the brain, the science behind cravings, and the long road to recovery. Counseling sessions happen several times a week, and speakers come in to share their stories, which are raw, unfiltered accounts that leave the room silent. Some days, I feel like I'm learning something valuable. Other days, it's like being back in school, waiting for the bell to ring.

Despite the tightly controlled environment, my mind often wanders, resisting the lessons they're trying to teach me. I keep my head down, trying not to be a pain in the ass, but deep down, I feel like I'm just biding my time.

They teach us that addiction is a chronic disease, something I'll have to manage for the rest of my life. They tell us I'll never be able to drink again, not even casually. When they mention that 40 to 60 percent of people relapse after treatment, I can't help but wonder if I'm already part of that statistic.

At 24, the idea of never drinking again feels impossible to accept.

As part of our routine, outside organizations often come in to speak with us, sometimes about recovery, other times about the risks tied to our lifestyle. One day, a mobile HIV testing company visits to talk about the dangers of sharing needles and having unprotected sex while high or under the influence of alcohol.

Our group jokes around during the presentation, cackling like immature boys every time we hear the word *sex* or *penis*.

After the class, they have all of us take an instant HIV test, and one of the tests comes back positive. One of the guys in rehab with me finds out right there that he has HIV. It's crazy.

The poor guy is devastated. He's been a raging alcoholic for years and has repeatedly cheated on his wife while blacked out. This is such a harsh reality check. We've all been so careless in our behavior, reckless as hell, completely disregarding real-world consequences for our actions. Consequences like HIV.

*   *   *

During the week, we eat dinner around 4 p.m., then spend our evenings driving to AA and NA meetings around the city as a group. The routine feels relentless, and it starts to feel like I'm being programmed, conditioned to believe and accept things I'm just not ready for.

It's like they're drilling it into me, over and over: my life is unmanageable, my addiction is permanent, and I'll never be able to use again. But part of me fights against it, resisting the idea that my situation is beyond my control. I know I'm in a bad spot, but I'm not ready to accept this as my forever.

On Tuesdays and Thursdays, we finish class at noon and walk to a nearby park to play softball as a group. It's a welcome distraction, especially because there's a basketball gym nearby. After softball, a handful of us always head over to the gym to ball with the local kids who are hooping.

I'm still young and can hold my own on the court, so when we're playing, I almost forget I'm part of the rehab group. But that feeling never lasts long. Mid-game, Johnny walks into the gym, his voice cutting through the noise. "All right, fellas. Time to go," he says, rounding us up.

And every time, it's the same story. The looks on those kids' faces say it all: shock and surprise as they realize I'm not just another baller, but part of the rehab group. The group of kids tends to change every time I'm there. There are always a few of the same hoopers, but each time, I'm forced to relive their shock, and it never gets easier. One second, I'm running the court, balling like nothing's changed. The next, I'm walking off the court, standing by the exit, next to the guy in my group who looks homeless, missing all of his teeth.

It's brutal. A cruel reminder of where I am now. No matter how much I want to separate myself from this, I'm part of it, standing side by side with people whose stories are just as messy as mine. It's humbling, but more than that, it's a hit to my ego every time I have to line up with the group, feeling like I'm caught between who I was and who I've become.

And the irony isn't lost on me. As a kid, I spent my weekends at Pan Pacific Park in L.A., playing sports. Every Saturday, there was an AA meeting in the back room of the gym. After their meetings, I'd see the group trickle out, peeking into the gym to see what was going on. Back then, I didn't know much about what they were doing. But as I got older, I began to understand that they were fighting their own battles.

Now here I am, standing in their shoes, part of a similar group to the one I used to notice from the sidelines. I catch myself standing at the door of the gym, peeking in like those old-timers used to, only now it's the kids watching me as I ready myself to leave.

*   *   *

Eventually, my 30-day probation period is up, and I'm given a day pass. After class, I now have the green light to leave the facility and do whatever I want. The only caveat is that I'm responsible for going to an AA or NA meeting every single day, with no exceptions. I can go to any meeting in the city, but I have to get a signature from the meeting host on my attendance slip. This serves as proof that I've been there. It's supposed to help me hold myself accountable while I'm out on a day pass. If I miss a single day without a meeting, my day pass will be revoked, and I'll be back on probation.

On the first day I can leave, my mom picks me up. As soon as she sees me, her face lights up. I can tell she's happy with how I look. The dark circles under my eyes are gone, my skin is healthier, and I've even gained a few pounds thanks to the three full meals a day. Seeing her look at me with pride instead of worry fills me with a sense of relief I didn't realize I needed. For the first time in a long time, it feels like the dark cloud that's been looming over our relationship is beginning to fade.

She picks me up every day that week. We hang out at the house and then go to a meeting together. She's incredibly supportive and willing to do whatever it takes to make sure I get everything out of this experience.

On the weekends, Dev picks me up and takes me on long, beautiful hikes, knowing how much nature will help free my mind of everything I'm going through. We spend the day talking, laughing our asses off, and enjoying each other's company. Mom and Dev really go out of their way to make sure I feel supported and surrounded by positive energy. And for that first month off probation, I do a great job at going to a meeting every single day. No exceptions.

But by the start of the next month, I'm feeling a little burnt out by the whole "meeting obligation" thing. I don't want to lose my day pass, but I'm tired of meetings cutting into my personal time after class. So I do what any person who thinks he's smarter than everyone else would do: I forge my attendance slip with random signatures in different colored pens. Each day, I come up with some unique scribble for a signature that's hardly legible but looks legit to me.

Instead of going to meetings, I spend most of my time at the YMCA gym around the corner, trying to work off my extra pounds. In my mind, the exercise is way more therapeutic than the meetings. Working out is a form of therapy for me, and it feels so good to be back in a gym. After I work out, I head back to Victory House to turn in my forged attendance slip with a big smile on my face. Nobody questions it. Or me. So, in true addict form, I just continue to do it and completely stop going to meetings altogether.

*   *   *

By day 80 of my 90-day program, I've convinced myself I've got the system beat. So when Johnny calls me out of class, I'm caught completely off guard. The entire group goes, "Ooooh, what you do, Ferg?" It feels just like getting called to the dean's office in high school.

Johnny opens his desk drawer as I walk in, pulling out two handfuls of meeting slips.

SHIT! I know what's coming.

"Jason, man. I've been doing this a long time. I'm an addict just like you. You can't just scribble some random bull jive on the slip and think I won't be able to tell."

Johnny says all of this with a huge grin on his face. He isn't angry. If anything, he's getting a kick out of this. I think he actually enjoys busting us for this type of stuff.

All I can do is laugh. He's seen this behavior again and again and just wants me to be honest. So I am.

Then we debate my reasons for skipping meetings to hit the gym. I argue that the gym is just as important as the meetings. Johnny doesn't hesitate to shut me down, saying it's that kind of thinking that got me into this mess in the first place. Then, without missing a beat, he takes away my day pass and phone privileges. Pissing. Me. Off.

The thing is, Johnny's not wrong. But it's more complicated than he realizes. The gym isn't just a distraction for me; it's my way of starting to rebuild the confidence I've lost. Every workout feels like laying another brick in the foundation of the person I used to be. It's helping me care about my health and physique again, something I haven't done in years.

I get it. We spend all day in class hearing about the disease of addiction, soaking in stats and stories that drive the point home. But to me, skipping another meeting in my free time doesn't feel like a setback. The gym is giving me discipline, structure, and purpose. Losing it feels like losing something I desperately need.

*   *   *

I only have ten days left in rehab, but I become fixated on not being able to use my phone or hit the gym. Suddenly, ten days feels like an eternity, and the voice in my head starts making suggestions:

Let's get the hell out of here.

Our time here is up.

You're not here on a court order, so technically, you can leave whenever you want.

I'd say 80 days is close enough to 90.

What's ten more days really gonna do?

I sell myself so hard on these thoughts that by the time I get back to my room, my mind's made up. I'm out of here. A completely justified decision, as far as I'm concerned. But the truth is, I'm leaving early because I got caught. I'm punking out. (Writing this down now is the first time I've truly acknowledged that.)

It's really that simple. I got caught, had my privileges snatched, and instead of sticking it out for ten more days, I throw a tantrum and quit.

I walk back into the office to find Johnny and Sam there together. I'd been hoping I'd only catch one of them, so it might be a little easier to explain away what I was about to do.

Oh well.

I get straight to the point.

"Guys, I appreciate all that you've done for me. You've both been great. But with that said, my time here is done, and I'm going home today."

Johnny looks disappointed. Sam shows no expression at all. Johnny calls me out on what I'm doing, blaming my need to leave on the fact that I got caught. But I do what addicts do best. Deny. Deny. Deny.

I explain that's not the case. Tell him some lie about an upcoming trip. That I was never going to stay the full 90 days anyway.

Johnny sees right through me and calls bullshit. "You're not fooling anyone," he says, his voice firm but almost tired, like he's been through this a hundred times before. "You got caught, your pride's hurt, and now you're running."

Sam just sits there, quiet, watching us go back and forth like he's seen this play out before. The silence from his end makes Johnny's words hit even harder. I can feel the slow build of frustration in Johnny's voice as he refuses to let me bullshit my way out of this. He challenges every excuse I throw at him, cutting them down one by one, until I've got nothing left to say.

This goes on for several minutes until eventually, Johnny sighs, leans back in his chair, and seems to accept the fact that I've made up my mind. "This some bull jive, and you know it. You're only cheating yourself, man," he says, shaking his head.

Sam just nods, as if to say he knows it too.

As I leave the office, Sam follows me back to my room and finally speaks.

I'd heard horror stories about rehab counselors telling people they'd never amount to anything, that if they left early, they might as well consider themselves dead. But Sam doesn't hit me with any of that. He just looks me in the eyes and says, "You're a special kid, Jason. This doesn't have to be your future. You don't have to spend your life in and out of rehab. Some of these guys in here won't make it. But you can. You've got 'it.' Use what you've learned here and go live a full life, man."

This man sees something in me. He believes in me. And in that moment, his words breathe life into me. A dose of real hope. They make me feel like I'm the chosen one, like I'm truly destined for something bigger.

When Sam leaves, I pack my stuff up as fast as I can. Now that my mind's made up, I can't get out of here fast enough.

I make sure to say goodbye to all of the fellas. These guys have been my roommates for almost three months. We've shared not only the same living space but also almost every detail of our life stories with one another. I know so much about these guys, and it's weird thinking I'll probably never see them again.

I look around for Champ, knowing I can't leave without saying goodbye to my guy. That man was more than just my roommate; he was my anchor during some of the hardest days of my life. I am positive that God put him in this rehab facility, in my room, to look out for me during this brutal time. And for that, I'll always be grateful.

Who would have thought my closest friend in rehab would be a 60-year-old man? But that's what Champ is to me—a friend, a guide, someone who made the unbearable just a little more bearable.

We hug it out, and as I step back, I take one last look at him. A wave of emotion hits me as I realize this will likely be the last time I ever see him.

(Champ would wind up passing away a few years later. We never did speak again, but I've thought about him often.)

*   *   *

Too nervous to ask my parents, I call Ques to come swoop me up. Then I suck it up and call my mom to tell her I'm coming home. She doesn't question me, and I don't tell her about the forged signatures. All she wants to know is, "Do you think you're really ready? Can you stay clean out here?"

Her voice is calm, but I can feel the hope behind it.

"Yes, Ma. I'm ready."

That's all she needs to hear.

That night, lying in my childhood bed, I can't shake the weight of her question.

Can I stay clean?

I don't even know. Rehab felt like a bubble. It was structured, safe, predictable. But out here, the world feels loud, unstructured, and full of temptation. I stare at the ceiling, trying to convince myself I can handle it, trying to ignore the itch that's already creeping in.

The next day, I'm out with Donnie and my little brother Donovan, heading to meet up with some girls. In the car, Donnie glances at me and asks, "Jason, are you gonna drink?"

For a second, I hesitate. I've been clean for three months. Surely, I've got enough control now.

What harm could one drink do?

"Hell yeah, bro. I'm a drug addict, not an alcoholic," I reply, almost daring myself to test those limits.

When we get to the spot, it doesn't take long for that dare to turn into action. Less than 24 hours out of rehab, and I've already taken my first shot. We spend the next couple of hours flirting, laughing, and doing more shots. I'm convinced this is exactly the kind of energy I need, this feeling of being back in the real world.

But as we make our way to the car, the feeling of wanting something "more" begins to crawl into my thoughts. The drinks aren't enough. I know I can't do pills; that's not an option.

But what else is there?

With the rush of life fueling my spirits and the haze of alcohol clouding my judgment, I turn to my friend and say, "Think you can find me some coke?"

23
Glacier Freeze

Within weeks of leaving rehab, I'm fully reintegrated back into society. And by fully, I mean working all day for D-Weez and partying all night. My days start early, and my nights seem to never end. By the time I get home, it's practically time to go to work and start the day all over again.

The evenings blur into a string of loud bars, Hollywood lounges, or a Gyu-Kaku happy hour, where we race to see who can drink the most $1 Kirin. Clinking glasses and roaring laughter fill the air, drowning out any nagging thoughts that may be lingering in the back of my mind. I've been drinking, but I haven't touched pills, not since rehab. And that line still feels solid, even as I inch closer to it.

Each drink, and every joke, cuts through any fear of a potential relapse. The thrill of it all silences the doubts, making it easy to believe that everything is still under control. At least for now. It's an epic time, for sure. But the truth is, I'm testing how close I can get to the edge without falling off.

Then one day, my little brother gets a call from an old friend who works at a nursing home. He's just swiped a bottle of Oxy from one of the tenants and is looking for someone to buy them.

Until this moment, pills hadn't even crossed my mind. But now, my brain starts to race:

I could buy them. Not all of them ... Maybe just a couple?

I start fantasizing about the ritual that comes with using. Removing the film from the pill, crushing it down to powder, snorting the line, waiting for the drip to make its way through my nose and down the back of my throat. And how great the cigarette will feel a minute later.

But then it hits me:

What the fuck am I thinking?

Rehab wasn't that long ago.

I fought through hell to get clean.

Am I really about to throw that all away?

I try to remind myself of the struggle, the excruciating pain of withdrawals, the endless hours spent trying to claw my way out of the hole Oxy had buried me in.

I wrestle with these thoughts for a second, but the pull is too strong, overpowering the lessons learned in rehab.

What are the odds this guy would call my brother to talk Oxy at the exact moment I'm sitting next to him? It feels like destiny. "Take me there," I say.

Instantly, I'm guilty and excited at the same time. I'm disappointed that I'm letting myself down, but I'm so looking forward to what's coming next. Having your drugs in hand, the moment right before you actually get high, can be almost as exhilarating as the high itself.

The second the pills are in my hand, my mind is made up. There's no hesitation, no second-guessing. I can't get those pills up my nose fast enough. And yet, the high falls flat.

Don't get me wrong, I'm high, but it's not what I expected. It's not the euphoric burst of energy I've missed so much. Instead,

I'm paranoid, ashamed, and full of regret. Even the cigarette tastes like shit.

You'd think all of that would be enough to keep me away from the pills, right? Nope.

I become obsessed with chasing the old high. Yearning for that feeling I'd grown to love and know all too well.

So I call my brother's friend, looking for more. This time, I don't even make it home. The thought of waiting feels unbearable, like every second is stretching into forever. I pull into the nearest gas station, park, and use the face of my iPhone to crush down a pill. I eagerly roll up a dollar bill and sniff the line right there in the front seat.

I sit motionless in my car, surrounded by silence. The windows are up, radio's off, and I'm listening to the screech of L.A. traffic while I wait for the high to hit. No guilt. No shame. No regret. Just pure, unfiltered bliss.

This is it. This is the one I've been chasing.

It's like I can feel the Oxy surging through my bloodstream, heading straight for my head, lighting up my brain like a switchboard sparking to life. Each receptor triggers a flood of dopamine. Pleasure and euphoria, all crashing together in this beautiful catastrophe that consumes me in an instant. This is exactly what I've been searching for, that feeling I lost in the chaos of dependency, withdrawal, and then rehab.

But now that I've found it, and I can't shake the question: *What now?*

I've caught what I've been hunting, but sometimes, the thing we think we want the most comes with a price we're not ready to pay.

*   *   *

When I leave rehab, Dev and I start planning a trip to Hawaii, giving ourselves a few months to save up. Dev has been my best friend for nearly 16 years, but we've never taken a trip like this, and we're both super excited.

Our plan is to fly to Hawaii and stay with Apryle. Although we don't speak every day, Apryle and I have managed to stay in touch while I'm in L.A. During that crazy spiral right before rehab, I'd found myself pulling away from her. I knew I wasn't in a position to settle down, and I didn't want to string her along. She was too pure. She didn't deserve the shittiest version of me, and the last thing I wanted was to hurt her.

But now, our connection feels like a lifeline, and my love for her is still deep. I'm really looking forward to staying with her and her dad for a week.

Despite my excitement, part of me feels like an idiot for returning to the island so soon after fleeing to avoid a raid. It's been over a year since I left, but the paranoia still lingers.

*　　*　　*

When Apryle picks us up from the airport, all that tension fades. Being near her again feels like a breath of fresh air, and her energy and aura radiate a positivity I crave.

But even with her warmth surrounding me, another truth pokes at me. My relapse hasn't spiraled out of control, but it's been steadily escalating. Coming back to the island feels like permission to indulge, and I want to make sure I have enough pills to get through the trip without any hiccups.

I spend the entire drive to her house with the window down, soaking in the fresh Hawaiian air while texting my friend Lance. Lance and I have been through a lot together, often leaning on each other back when I was living on the island. These days, his addiction has escalated, and I know he can hook me up. He lives about 15 minutes from Apryle, so Dev and I drop off our stuff and head straight to his place.

The moment Lance opens the door, the energy feels off. He's lost at least 20 pounds, and his face is sunken in, highlighting his sharp cheekbones. His voice is raspy, his eyes are bloodshot, and he's obviously extremely high. He struggles to speak, his delivery is slow and lazy, and he's barely keeping his eyelids up. It's clear he's on something strong because the nods are kicking his ass. It's a bad look all around.

We sit in his living room for a while, me doing my best not to raise any red flags with Dev. I'm hiding the fact that I'm back on pills because I know Dev won't be okay with it. He's always been the friend who calls me out and holds me accountable, which is exactly why he can't know what's happening.

Lance catches my eye and gives me a quick glance, and I know exactly what it means. Without saying a word, I casually get up, muttering something about heading to the bathroom, and make my way toward the back. Dev stays on the couch, completely unaware.

Once Lance and I are alone, I start pressing him about his condition. He brushes it off, blaming stress and not hitting the gym like he used to, but I can't shake the suspicion that he's graduated to heroin, like so many Oxy users do.

When he hands me a bag of pills, my suspicions are nearly confirmed by the track marks running up and down his bicep. The bruising and scabbing from the needles are highly visible on his light skin. I'm not sure if he's using heroin or pills, but whatever he's doing, he's injecting it.

Seeing track marks up close for the first time scares the hell out of me. My love for Lance runs deep; he's like my little brother. We were roommates back when he was new to the island, still trying to find his footing. He was younger than me, far from home, and chasing his dreams with the same uncertainty I'd felt when I first arrived. We clicked immediately, and I always looked out for him.

Now he's a rising star on the UH football team, but the demons he's battling are tearing him apart. I'm torn between saying something and pretending I haven't noticed. Who am I to judge? I just got out of rehab. The only real difference between us is that I snort my drugs, and he's clearly shooting his.

*   *   *

Despite the unspoken weight hanging between Dev and me, our Hawaii trip is nothing short of epic. We spend our days hitting the beach or hiking Hawaii's beautiful trails, and at night we hit Waikiki to dive into the island's nightlife. I keep my pill usage hidden, a secret I carefully guard from Dev and Apryle, slipping away when no one's watching to feed the habit that's growing by the day. My Oxy appetite is escalating, creeping up on me faster than I want to admit.

By day 3, I'm doing one in the morning to kick off the day, a half in the afternoon, another to pregame before we go out, and one more in the club or bar bathroom. It's my new daily routine.

One night in a club, after my fourth or fifth shot of Patron, I head to the bathroom to bust down a pill. It reeks of stale urine and mildew, like something's been wet for weeks.

I head straight for a stall and quickly realize the lock is broken, so every time I try to close the door, it swings back toward me, leaving a crack wide enough for anyone to peer in.

I survey the space and notice the walls are covered in stickers, with random names and curse words etched into the metal. The floor is drenched in piss, making my feet slide as I attempt to maneuver around this cramped space. This has got to be the worst stall ever.

I explore every inch for a hard surface to crush my pill on. Usually, the toilet paper dispenser works great, but this stall doesn't have one. I'm drunk off my ass desperately searching for something, anything, when finally, the back of the toilet seat catches my attention. Not the toilet seat itself, because, of course, there isn't one. I'm talking about the disgusting flat surface just behind the rim.

Even though I'm wasted, I notice everything. A brownish-yellow film stains the edge of the bowl. Inside, the murky liquid reeks of urine, bubbling with globs of soaked toilet paper, practically overflowing like a brewing cesspool.

The filth doesn't stop there. The back of the toilet is splattered with piss, shit, and pubic hair, every kind of nastiness imaginable. I grab a wad of toilet paper, ball it up, and try to clean off the grime as best I can. My feet are still slipping and sliding on the wet floor as I try to steady myself, my focus blurring in and out. Then, my drunk ass fumbles, and the pill slips through my fingers. Time slows as I watch it spin in midair before landing in the toilet with a soft "ca-plunk." That tiny sound crushes my soul.

Without a second thought, I plunge my arm in elbow-deep. The pee is still warm, and the smell hits me instantly, making me gag. Wet toilet paper swirls around my arm as I move it to the side, searching frantically for the pill I just dropped.

Finally, there it is. I snatch the pill from the bottom of the bowl, hold it up like a champion raising a trophy, and pat it dry with toilet paper. I squat down, crush it on the now "clean" surface, and snort the line with an old dollar bill. The burn hits instantly, but it's nothing compared to the thought of what I just did.

This is, without a doubt, the most disgusting thing I've ever done. But I don't care. I'm seconds away from blastoff.

A minute or two later, I black out. Oxys have this way of triggering episodes where you seem coherent, but you're far from sober. You can hold conversations, and often, no one can tell you're in a blackout. Right now, I'm completely gone.

I don't snap back to reality until I'm driving home, Dev sitting in the passenger seat, and we're in the middle of a heated argument. It's like I was in Narnia one second, and the next, I'm back, fully engaged in an argument that's already spiraling. I can't remember what led to this moment, but I feel the emotional weight of it immediately. Dev's voice is sharp, cutting through the fog as he lays into me, disappointment and frustration dripping from every word.

"So, D-Weez is wrong, your mom's wrong, everyone's wrong but you, huh?"

His words hit hard, and even though I'm not exactly sure what we're talking about, I can feel it. Physically, emotionally, he's calling me out. He's done this before, holding me accountable in ways only your best friend can. That's the thing about Dev; he loves me enough to call me on my bullshit. He never holds his tongue when he feels like I'm slipping, because he knows I need it. Right now, he's going in on me, and as much as it stings, it's part of what makes him such an incredible friend.

But today, in this moment, I'm irritated, agitated, and on edge. As much as I know he means well, hearing him bring up my mom and D-Weez feels like a cheap shot, and it triggers something in me. The frustration builds, and my instinct is to lash out. As we approach Apryle's house, I've had enough. I throw the car in park, turn to him aggressively, and say, "Get the fuck out the car."

Before he can even move, I burst from the car and march to the front, where Dev meets me, trying to calm things down. In a fit of rage, I shove him as hard as I can, causing him to trip and crash onto the concrete. He falls hard, and for a split second, I don't even know how to feel about it. I'm torn between "I told you to shut the fuck up" and instant remorse. I didn't mean to shove him that hard. I approach him slowly, fists unclenched, wanting to check if he's all right. But before I can fully assess the damage, he reacts. Without warning, his hand flies out, and he open-hand slaps the shit out of me across the face.

I drop to the ground, clutching my head, overwhelmed by a high-pitched ringing in my ear. Dev's face shifts from anger to concern as he realizes he might've seriously hurt me. He starts apologizing immediately, checking to see if I'm okay. But I can't even focus on his words. My ear feels like it's been split open, throbbing with pain, and I'm too riled up to hear anything over the ringing in my head.

Dev quickly realizes I'm not listening and decides to remove himself from the situation. He walks off down the street, leaving me alone to stew in my pain and anger. That night, he finds a long branch in a tree at a park to sleep on, while I crawl into bed with Apryle, half my face swollen and a wad of toilet paper stuffed into my right ear to stop the bleeding.

The next morning, I'm asleep when Dev jumps on top of me, grinning ear to ear, eager to see how I'm doing after last night's chaos. We instantly start laughing our asses off, hugging it out as we realize just how out of control we were. He feels terrible, I feel even worse, both physically and emotionally. But that's the beauty of our friendship: we move past things quickly.

This is how we've been for nearly two decades. We're more like brothers than friends. Even though this time was a little more outrageous, we still treat it the exact same way. We laugh about it and move on.

But as I sit up, the reality of last night hits me. I take a good look at my ear. It's clearly a mess. It's swollen, still bleeding, and ringing like crazy. There's no denying it now—I need to see a doctor.

Unfortunately, I can't see a doctor for a few days, and we're supposed to fly back to L.A. tomorrow. I don't think I can fly with my eardrum in this condition, so Dev heads back without me while I stay behind to get checked out.

At first, it feels like a minor inconvenience, but after a couple of days, the idea of staying starts to take hold. Living here with Apryle feels comfortable and easy. Why would I leave? The police aren't after me anymore. Staying in Hawaii means I can avoid facing my parents and their inevitable disappointment when they discover I've relapsed again. I wouldn't have to answer any hard questions or deal with anyone judging the choices I've made. Out of sight, out of mind.

And then there's Apryle. Being with her again feels like a lifeline, a small corner of the world where things still make sense.

This perforated eardrum becomes more than just a physical setback. It's the justification I was looking for to stay. Hawaii feels like a clean slate, a chance to hit pause on reality, and I convince myself it's exactly what I need.

*　　*　　*

Now that I'm staying in Hawaii, I need a job. I quickly find one at a school for autistic students, and to my surprise, it feels meaningful, so much more rewarding than working as a janitor for D-Weez. The work is challenging, but it gives me a sense of purpose, something I've been missing for a long time.

But as the days roll into weeks, my routine starts to settle into place. Early mornings, the demands of the job, and the quiet moments when my thoughts wander. It all becomes familiar, almost automatic. Slowly but surely, I fall back into old patterns. A pill here to take the edge off, another to help me wind down after a long day.

Before I know it, I'm back to using every day, leaning on Lance to keep my stash full. I see him multiple times a week, always making sure I have enough to get by.

One day, Lance picks me up from work, and we head to his dealer to grab pills for the week. On our way home, Lance pulls over on a side street to get high. He opens his middle console and takes out a syringe, a spoon, a Q-tip, and a bottle of water. His "kit" is kept in a small bag that discreetly ensures his essentials are by his side at all times. He preps to shoot up right there in front of me, but by this point, the shock of it has worn off.

Several months earlier, I'd watched him shoot up for the first time with a friend. They even shared the same needle, passing it back and forth like a joint. It was all so casual. I couldn't believe it. Watching someone cook up and inject themselves was terrifying. But what was even scarier was how quickly I became desensitized to it.

Lance had become my main source for pills ever since Old Man Bob disappeared. We spent hours together on these half-day missions to find them. Drug dealers are the most inconsiderate, untimely people on the planet. They know you need them more than they need you, and they treat you like shit. We'd be left waiting for hours on end, hopping from one shady spot to the next, scrambling to get in touch with one of Lance's connects. And only Lance could deal with them, which meant I was stuck riding shotgun in his world, on their time.

Usually, it wasn't just me and Lance. The car was packed with addicts who were antsy, anxious, and desperate for a fix. Our withdrawals intensifying, like a ticking time bomb ready to blow. Every second of waiting felt like pure torture. And when the pills finally came, everyone scrambled to do them as fast as they could. We tore into the bags like zombies ripping into flesh, our desperation on full display

My method was still up the nose. I'd crush it down on the face of my iPhone and sniff it with a rolled-up dollar bill. But the others? They'd graduated to something darker, more dangerous. In the beginning, I'd sit there in disbelief, watching them pass the same needle around like it was nothing.

I can't believe how fast I adjusted. How quickly it became normal.

Now, I watch Lance go through his routine without even flinching. If anything, curiosity is creeping in, slowly overtaking the fear.

Does it really feel that much different?
How fast does it hit—are we talkin' seconds?
How strong will it be?

The idea of something so powerful, so immediate, has me wondering if this is the ultimate high I've been chasing. I can feel myself preparing to take the leap, mustering up the courage to tell Lance.

But then fear grips me, and the risk becomes crystal clear.
What if this kills me?

There's a brief moment of pause, I hesitate, but it's quickly drowned out by that familiar pull.

"Fuck it, bro. Hit me," I say, sizing up my biceps, already evaluating which arm to stick the needle in.

"You sure, Ferg?" he asks.

This is a massive step into a world of darkness that Lance is all too familiar with. He's concerned about me; I can hear it in his tone.

"Yeah, bro. Let's do it!" I say, reaching out my right arm and waiting for further instruction.

Lance's face says it all. Shock and concern flicker across his expression as he stares at me, his eyes searching mine for any hesitation or doubt, something to give him a reason to stop. He doesn't say a word. He doesn't have to. I can tell he desperately wants to tell me no.

"Come on, bro. I'm ready," I say, cutting him off before he has a chance to object.

Lance sighs, his movements slow and deliberate, as if he's still processing my decision. He grabs a Q-tip and dabs his blood off the end of the needle. For a split second, I'm transported back to rehab. To the moment that guy found out he was HIV positive. I remember how his entire world changed in an instant, and it rocked me to my core.

I think about Lance sharing needles right in front of me, and every voice in my head screams, *Abort. Abort. Abort.*

But I can't. The magnetic pull is too strong, like I'm locked into a path I can't veer off of, even though I know better.

I watch with fascination as Lance drops the little blue pill into a spoonful of water, flames it with his lighter, and uses the butt of the syringe to mix in the dissolving pill. It's like watching a chemist at work, precise and methodical, while the rest of me prepares for what's coming next.

He dips the clean end of the Q-tip into the spoon, then slides the needle through it, using the cotton as a filter to catch every last bit of powder. I'm mesmerized as I watch the liquid vanish through the needle and up into the syringe. It's light blue, like Glacier Freeze Gatorade.

There's still time to back out, Filly.
You could stop this right now.
What the FUCK are you doing?

These thoughts rattle in my head, but I don't say a word. I'm locked in, unable to pull away.

Lance shows me how to use my seatbelt as a tourniquet, wrapping it tightly around my arm until my vein bulges beneath the skin, practically begging for the hit. It's strong, and I can feel the pressure building.

Then, with one swift move, Lance slides the needle into my arm, and I'm stunned by how smoothly it goes in, like a steak knife slicing through warm butter.

Lance pulls back on the syringe, and I watch in a trance as my blood mixes with the blue liquid, signaling we're in the vein. He presses down slowly, injecting the mixture straight into my bloodstream. I loosen the seatbelt around my arm, and as the blood rushes back in, I feel the intensity start to build instantly.

Then, it hits.

Every hair on my body stands at attention. A wave of warmth surges from my toes, up through my spine, and straight into my brain. It's like a switch has been flipped, and suddenly everything is bright, almost too vibrant, as if I've been thrown into a world that's more alive than anything I've ever known. It's all-consuming, every nerve firing in sync, sending pleasure to every corner of my body.

Damn. I think I fucked up.

I know I fucked up.

There's no going back now. How could I? I've crossed a line, taken a step into a new chapter that comes with the type of crazy I don't even know how to prepare for. But it's too late; I'm in it now.

                    *   *   *

Sticking that needle in my arm for the first time ends up being one of the biggest regrets of my life. What follows is a year and a half of pain and bad decisions. During this time, I don't revert to snorting pills; that feels like a waste.

I quickly learn how to cook a pill down and inject it on my own, keeping a spoon, Q-tip, and syringe with me at all times. Even at work, I keep my kit with me, tucked away in one of the many pockets of my backpack. Every day at recess or lunch, sometimes both, I shoot up in the faculty bathroom, then head right back out to work with the kids.

One day, I'm in the bathroom, getting high like usual, when I forget to lock the door. It's a single-person bathroom meant for faculty, and just as I'm finishing up, putting my kit back in my backpack, the door swings open. It's my boss. He apologizes right away, turns around, and leaves.

I was so close to being caught. If he'd walked in 30 seconds earlier, he would've seen me pulling the needle out of my arm. But even that doesn't stop me. The only thing that changes is I start compulsively checking the door, making sure it's locked before I even think about pulling out my kit.

Outside of work, things begin to spiral. I'm running with a crowd whose entire lives revolve around finding and using drugs. Every paycheck disappears the moment I get it, spent entirely on pills. When the money runs out, I start abusing my bank's overdraft policy, which allows me to overdraw up to $250 for a small penalty, as long as I pay it back quickly. It becomes a way to keep my habit alive, even when I'm completely out of cash.

But then, the safety net snaps.

One day, I walk into the bank, counting on being able to overdraw again, and I'm denied. The same teller I've been seeing since my college days, who's almost become a friend to me, has to break the news. She looks uncomfortable, but tells me straight up, "Jason, your account's been flagged. We can't let you overdraw anymore."

Her words crush me, but I'm not totally surprised. I knew I had relied on it way too much, and lately, every time I went in, I almost expected to get cut off. But it never came, until now. She breaks the news, and it's a blow.

Damn.

I have no access to money. My account is deep in the negative, and I'm completely broke.

After the denial, she walks out from behind the counter and follows me outside. "Are you okay?" she asks. "I'm not trying to get all up in your business, but you've been coming here for years, and I can tell something's off."

I brush off her question, forcing a smile and assuring her I'm fine, practically walking away mid-sentence. After that day, I stop going to that bank altogether, going out of my way to avoid her.

That moment at the bank feels like another nail in the coffin of what little stability I have left. With my finances in shambles and my body increasingly dependent on pills, the cracks in my life start showing everywhere.

I start calling in sick at least twice a month, sometimes more, crippled by the sweats, the nausea, and the brain fog brought on from being dope sick. The kid I work with has extreme behavioral issues, so I assume my boss thinks it's the job wearing me down. He cuts me some slack, especially since he's a big UH fan and knew all about me back in the day. He treats me well and lets a lot slide, but he has no idea what is really going on.

Most days, when I don't have pills, I'm at work battling withdrawals, doing my best to pass it off as fatigue. And no one has a clue. At least that's what I tell myself.

*   *   *

Apryle starts supporting both of us financially, and I take complete advantage of how naive she is. She knows something is up, but she can't quite put her finger on it. She works as a bartender and usually doesn't get home until 3 a.m., leaving me with hours to myself. It's almost too easy to hide my habits with her gone so late into the night. I'm always asleep by the time she gets home, and as long as I don't leave anything incriminating out, I'm fine. I've got needles stashed in several spots around the room. Little hiding places that give me access no matter where she is. As long as I'm careful, always putting things back exactly where they belong, it's like nothing ever happened.

With Apryle gone until late, the house is quiet, and the hours stretch endlessly. That's when I come alive. It feels like I'm in my element, sitting alone in our room with the lights off, lost in the familiar loop of the same Drake song. The track is called "The Resistance," and it starts with Drake singing in a soft, melodic tone that pulls me in immediately. Then, the dark synths kick in, and it's like the music is speaking directly to my soul.

As the song plays on repeat, I scan my arms for a vein that isn't completely blown out, desperately searching for a new entry point. My arms are a map of abuse, scarred and swollen from months of relentless punctures.

In that moment, the music drowns out everything. The sonics elevate my high, making me feel untouchable, even as the rest of me is falling apart.

This ritual pulls me into a deeper, darker headspace. I'm just as addicted to the process as I am to the drugs.

My money problems get so bad that I start stealing from Apryle. She keeps a lot of cash under the bed in a safe that's never locked, so I begin taking a few $100 bills at a time, hoping she won't notice. Eventually, she catches on and stops putting money there. But she never questions me, never brings it up. I'm not sure if she's giving me the benefit of the doubt or just avoiding conflict. Either way, the money disappears from its usual spot, and I know she's caught on.

With my usual source of cash gone, the desperation ramps up. I need money fast, and the withdrawals are brutal, pushing me further than I ever thought I'd go. That's when I start pawning Apryle's jewelry. One night, during a particularly brutal withdrawal episode, I take the most sentimental piece of all: a beautiful white-gold diamond ring her grandfather gave her for high school graduation. A man who had just recently passed away.

I walk into the pawn shop with tears in my eyes and hand over the ring, knowing exactly what it means to her.

And for what?

I only get $150. A ring easily worth thousands, reduced to barely enough for seven measly pills. I've become completely unhinged. My conscience doesn't even faze me anymore. Nothing seems to stop me.

The days blur together as I spiral deeper into my habit, crossing lines I never thought I would. Desperation consumes me, and nothing else seems to matter.

And then, one night, Apryle comes home to find the bedroom empty and the bathroom door shut. A strip of light slips through the crack beneath the door, a clue that I might be inside. She knocks softly at first, calling my name, but gets no response. Her quiet knock turns urgent as she rattles the doorknob, realizing it's locked. Concern sets in, and her gentle tapping turns into assertive pounding, fists slamming against the door as she yells my name.

Desperate and confused, she grabs a paper clip and slips it into the small hole on the knob, popping the lock. The door flies open, banging against the side of my leg. I jolt awake, blinking against the harsh bathroom light, and see her standing over me, frozen in the doorway. Her face is twisted in horror and disbelief.

I scramble to regain my senses.

Where the hell am I?

I glance around and notice the sink above me.

Am I on the bathroom floor?

Out of the corner of my eye, something catches my attention. I look down and nearly choke. My belt is loosely wrapped around my left arm, and a needle is dangling from my vein.

Damn.

The dose was too strong. It must have knocked me out cold the second it hit my bloodstream.

Now I understand the look of terror on her face. She thought I was dead.

This is big. How the hell do I come back from this?

My secret is out. She sees the truth. She knew I was using again; she's not dumb. But she had no idea I had graduated to using needles, no idea I was cooking four to five pills at a time and shooting up multiple times a day. Even though my track marks were getting worse, I managed to keep them hidden, most of the time right in plain sight. The thing is, most people don't actively inspect the bend of your arm for track marks. As long as I didn't draw attention to them, they flew under the radar. I used makeup to cover the bruising, wore long sleeves, or casually positioned my arm to keep the marks out of view. I navigated it all so naturally, hiding my addiction in broad daylight.

And now, it's all right here in front of her.

Apryle used to look at me like I was a god, like I could do anything. She'd stare at me like I was the coolest, smartest person in the room. Not anymore. Now, all I see in her eyes is disappointment mixed with sadness and fear. And after what just happened, I can't blame her.

I dodged a bullet, barely. I got lucky this time, but I could've just as easily died. I would've been gone forever. I never would have had the chance to see my mom, D-Weez, or my brothers again. I would've never known the trauma I caused Apryle, forcing her to find me dead, laid out on the bathroom floor.

The gravity of what happened hangs over us, unspoken but palpable. Apryle doesn't say much, but the weight in her eyes speaks volumes. I know I can't keep going like this.

*   *   *

Apryle and I spend the next day scouring the internet for rehab facilities. We're desperate to find something like Victory House, but the options on the island are slim. None of the facilities take insurance, and with me being completely broke, inpatient treatment isn't even on the table.

Eventually, we come across an outpatient program that prescribes Suboxone, a synthetic opioid designed to suppress withdrawal symptoms and curb cravings. It's not a perfect solution, but it feels like a lifeline.

I know Suboxone gets a bad rap. Some people say it's just trading one addiction for another. And yeah, if you're reckless, it's easy to abuse. But with proper guidance, it can be a game-changer. Something I desperately need.

That's where Dr. Turban comes in. From the moment I meet him, I feel like I'm in good hands. He's patient and sharp, and he knows addiction inside and out. He's also no-nonsense, running a tight ship that leaves zero room for excuses.

His program is strict, almost military-like. I have to see him three times a week, every week, and he only gives me just enough Suboxone to last until the next visit. He also runs urine tests at every session to keep me honest. There's no faking it with Dr. Turban. The only way to earn his trust is through consistency and showing up every single time.

At first, the structure feels overwhelming, like yet another thing I've boxed myself into. But as the days go by, I start to notice the difference. The Suboxone works wonders. No shakes, no cold sweats, no racing to the bathroom every ten minutes. For the first time in forever, I almost feel normal. Almost.

But the cravings strike when I least expect them.

I'll be driving home from work, passing my dealer's apartment or an old meetup spot. The second I see it, I begin to sweat. My jaws tighten, and I'm forced to clench everything. That devilish voice in my head creeps in, whispering from the shadows. It's like an invisible hand grips my throat, pulling me in, daring me to turn back with the promise of euphoria.

Then there's the park. The one I used to shoot up at and sit until two in the morning, headphones on, gazing aimlessly while bobbing my head to the rhythm of my music.

Driving through Honolulu now feels like I'm navigating a minefield, with triggers placed strategically across the city, ready to detonate if I take one wrong turn.

As time passes, Dr. Turban gradually loosens my leash, cutting my sessions from three times a week to two, then one.

He fuels me with good energy, reminding me of the savage I once was when it came to hard work and big dreams.

At first, it feels like waking up from a long, hazy sleep. I didn't realize how far gone I was until the fog began to lift. Little by little, I start reclaiming who I was before addiction took over. For the first time in years, I'm not thinking about partying or chasing the next high. Instead, moments of clarity creep in, nudging me to think about my future, what I want to do, and where I want to go.

The changes aren't just internal. Apryle and I dive into a workout routine, and the extra weight I've packed on starts to melt away. I'm beginning to recognize the person staring back at me in the mirror, stronger and leaner than I've been in years, even better than when I played football. The transformation feels like reclaiming pieces of myself I thought were gone for good.

Apryle sees it too, and she's proud, really proud. She doesn't just tell me; she shows me. I notice the way she looks at me, those familiar glowing eyes filled with admiration. She's been my rock through every session with Dr. Turban, every meeting, every step of this fight. Seeing her pride reminds me how far I've come and why I keep pushing forward.

By the end of six months, I'm off Suboxone completely. For the first time in five years, I'm entirely sober. And for the first time in what feels like forever, I feel ready to conquer the world.

24
We All Take the Stairs

The first thing I've got to do is figure out a long-term career plan.

What do I want to do with my life?

I'm still working with autistic kids, which is rewarding in so many ways, but I realize I'm a lot more financially motivated now that I'm sober and thinking clearly. I need a change. Something inside of me is kicking and screaming to be let loose. My spirit is talking to me, and I'm finally ready to listen.

One afternoon, just after Apryle and I finish a workout, my phone vibrates, rattling the wood on my desk and catching my attention. It's a 510 area code that I don't recognize, though I know that's from Northern California, where several of my friends now live.

Now, let me be clear—I never, ever, answer unknown numbers. In fact, I hardly ever answer my phone, period. I blame this on being an "ambivert." In social settings, I'm the life of the party, clearly an extrovert. But when I'm within the four walls of my home, I'm extremely introverted. I don't want to talk to anyone most of the time, so it's easier to just not answer my phone.

But something feels different today. So I pick it up.

"Ferg!" the voice on the other end screams, full of energy and enthusiasm.

"Dez?" I reply happily, instantly recognizing it's my close friend from college.

Dez and I had fallen out of touch as my drug habit escalated. It's so good to hear his voice again. We spend an hour catching up on each other's lives. Reminiscing, laughing, and crying.

He had no clue about the extent of my struggles. He feels guilty for not being there to support me, but I tell him he's lucky he wasn't around. That I'd been a nightmare and could have easily dragged him down with me.

When I ask him what he's doing for work, he says he's a medical device sales rep.

What the hell is that?

He explains that he spends his days selling medical equipment to hospitals and doctors. When he's not out canvassing his territory in Northern California, he's in an operating room with surgeons, serving as the equipment expert.

My mind is blown. While I've spent the last five years of my life getting high, messing around, and drowning in my sorrows, Dez has been getting after it. I still don't fully understand his job, but I can't stop the competitor in me from thinking, *If he can do it, I could do it.*

Curious, I ask him what he's making. When he says $90K a year, my jaw hits the ground. It's 2011. I'm 26 years old. I'm making $24K a year. That $90K sounds like a million bucks to me.

I put him on speaker, open up the calculator on my phone, and work the math backward. He's bringing in $3,750 per paycheck, while my checks are just under $1,000. He's making nearly 4 times what I'm making.

Dez is still chatting away on the other end of the phone, but I've totally tuned him out. My eyes are fixated on these numbers.

Damn, he hasn't been playing around.

Dez has been out here grinding, building something real for himself. Meanwhile, I've been stuck in the same cycle, spinning my wheels.

What the hell am I doing?

That question hits hard, and the answer feels obvious, almost immediate: *I need to break into sales!*

I've been asking the universe for a sign, some kind of push toward a new career path. I've never really given sales much thought, but somehow, it immediately feels like something I could be passionate about.

People often tell you to follow your passion, but that's not always the best advice. If what you're after is financial freedom and new career opportunities, I think it's more important to find something you could become passionate about, and then go all in.

This call from Dez wakes me up and has me fantasizing about my future again. Over the next few days, I dive headfirst into learning about sales. The process, strategies, career paths, and industries to explore. The more I dig, the clearer it becomes: there's a natural connection between sports and sales. At first, I didn't see it, but as I research, it's like a light bulb goes off.

In sports, every day is a competition. Whether it's a game or a practice, you're constantly battling, trying to outwork and outperform your comp. Sales is the same. Every call, every pitch, every deal, it's all a competition. The best athletes live to be number one, driven by the desire to win, to prove themselves on the field or court. Salespeople chase that same thrill, pushing themselves to dominate the leaderboard and earn recognition.

In sports, you track stats and follow a ranking system. There are trophies and accolades for those at the top, a tangible way to measure success. Sales operates in the same way. The numbers don't lie, and every deal closed is another step toward being the best. Athletes are coached relentlessly on fundamentals, drilled until the basics are second nature. From what I'm learning, sales managers take the same approach, coaching their reps, honing their skills, and demanding coachability.

It's wild to realize that all those years of discipline, training, and competition on the field weren't just about football. They were preparing me for this. The drive, the relentless focus on improvement, and the hunger for results have always been a part of me. I just needed to recognize the connection and channel that energy into a new arena.

*　　*　　*

A couple of days later, Dez and I hop back on the phone to strategize my entry into sales. I'm sober, my mind is clear, and I'm hungrier than I've been in years. Lucky for me, Dez is all in, willing to go out of his way to help. It's like he's fully adopted this mentor role, and I'm his protégé. Every night for a week straight, we're on the phone, breaking down everything meticulously, from building a standout résumé to nailing the interview process. He's thorough in how he coaches me, making sure I understand every detail.

His only ask in return is that I show up and fully commit with the same level of tenacity I brought to football. No half-assing it. He's pushing me like we're back on the field, the same way we pushed each other during those grueling summer workouts in college.

But bringing that same drive to sales presents an unexpected hurdle: my lack of experience. It's hard to create an impressive résumé when I've never had a formal sales job. I pitch an idea to Dez, half joking but also half serious. We could spice it up a bit, maybe invent a job or two. At first, Dez hesitates. He's not thrilled about it and suggests we play it safe. But I push harder, determined to make it work. Eventually, he gives in, and together, we doctor my résumé until it's flawless. By the time we're done, I don't just look employable. I look like the *man*.

On paper, I look like a guy with years of experience: A top performer. Coupled with my time playing Division I football, I'm convinced that any sales manager would be completely nuts to pass on me.

Now Dez and I turn our focus to interview preparation, and we role-play interview scenarios daily. I'm in awe of his professionalism. This is the same guy I partied with all night in college, cruising around in his Mazda 929 with just $5 between us. Now he's light-years ahead of me professionally. He pushes me to step out of my comfort zone, challenges me to become obsessed with the process, and teaches me a valuable lesson: *Finding a job should be treated as a job itself.*

*   *   *

When Dez gives me the green light, I start firing off my résumé to every sales job I can find, most of which are in L.A. Each submission feels like a step closer to something bigger. Then, one afternoon, my phone buzzes with a notification. It's an email from ADP. They want to interview me. I quickly pull up the job listing: $48K base salary, plus another $21K in commissions if I hit my goal.

This is three times what I'm making now.

The stakes feel massive, and I know I can't afford to blow it. I dive into preparing for the phone interview, going over everything Dez drilled into me: speak with an enthusiastic and confident tone, lean into my story as an athlete and how that translates beautifully into the role, and be clear about the value I can bring to the team. I even memorize Dez's sales process, planning to recite his steps word for word.

On the morning of the interview, I do one more thing to set the tone. I put on a suit, even though it's just a phone call. There's something about wearing it that shifts my mindset. It makes me feel sharp, professional, and ready to step into this next chapter. It's a mental edge, and I'll take any advantage I can get.

By the time the call comes, I'm ready.

The phone interview begins, and it's game time. I pace the room, fully locked in. Sharp, confident answers fall from my lips effortlessly the moment they part. Each word seems to flow from my brain to my mouth, with no buffer in between to scramble my train of thought or hinder my delivery.

By the end of the call, I know I've nailed it. I haven't felt this alive in years. My brain, which had felt like mush for so long, is fully activated, firing on all cylinders. I delivered everything we worked on, and I did it with a swagger I forgot I possessed.

Maybe I am cut out for this sales stuff after all.

A few days later, the call comes in. They want to fly me out to California for an in-person interview.

Before I go, there's one more thing I know I need to do. There's an ace I haven't played yet. Someone I trust to help take my skills to the next level and make sure I'm ready to nail this interview. I hit up my friend Colin Coggins, who's like a big brother to me and, at the time, a rising sales director making waves in the tech world.

I first met Cog back at John Burroughs Middle School. I was in sixth grade, and he was in eighth. He quickly became best friends with my brothers Ryan and Dominic, since they were all in the same grade. Naturally, I got pulled into their circle, and almost all of their friends became my friends too.

Cog was one of the coolest kids on campus. There was something about his aura and confidence that drew people in, me included. And on top of that, the dude could rap his ass off. We spent countless hours freestyling at lunch in high school, with a crowd circled around us, feeding off the energy.

At first, I looked up to Cog as a friend of my brothers, but over time, we built our own relationship, independent of them. He's more than just a friend; he's a brother and mentor I'm grateful to have in my corner when I need him.

(Today, Cog is a sales monster. He's been part of multiple acquisitions and successful exits as a VP of Sales and CRO. He's also the author of the *Wall Street Journal* best-selling book *The Unsold Mindset*, which he cowrote with his good friend Garrett Brown.)

Cog spends nearly two hours on the phone with me breaking down every aspect of the sales process: from qualifying the partnership fit on the front end of a conversation, to discovery questions to help identify a customer's pains and needs, to active listening, tonality, and closing, which he refers to as "asking for the money." Cog has a unique way of making complex things sound simple, emphasizing that while the process is critical, the delivery is where the magic happens.

Just before we get off the phone, he shifts gears, saying, "Filly, all of this sales process stuff is great and necessary, but your superpower lies in all the personality traits that make you *you*. That's the secret to winning at this. When all else fails, remember to be authentic."

This last bit of advice is a gem I'll come back to for years. By the time our call ends, I'm replaying his words in my head, hyping myself up.

This is your moment, Filly. Don't fuck it up.

When I touch down in L.A., I'm locked in. I'm wearing the same suit I put on for the phone interview, channeling that same energy.

The moment the interview starts, it's like flipping a switch. I crush the in-person interview, including the impromptu role-play they spring on me last minute. My years of freestyle rapping with friends and being forced to think on the fly really pay off. Role-playing is just like freestyling, only easier because I don't need to rhyme. I leave that office knowing I am, without a doubt, a natural born salesman.

Next thing I know, they've offered me the job. But there's one massive problem. ADP's business model is built on HR expertise, which means background checks. And I've lied on 75 percent of my résumé. There's no way I can provide references for the jobs I claimed to have held.

I'm mortified, knowing I can't back up a single position listed on that résumé. The shame eats at me, and instead of facing the fallout, I ghost them. After all that prep, all that excitement, having to walk away is brutal.

I was so close. I was right there on the one-yard line. I had it. *Damn.*

That was my first major lesson in winning in business or in life: *There's no elevator to success. We all take the stairs.*

Recovery, growth, and building something that lasts require patience, effort, and the willingness to embrace every step of the journey, especially the hard ones. Shortcuts are tempting, but they lead to bad habits. Habits like cutting corners, stretching the truth, and skipping the hard work that is necessary for real growth.

I tried to skip levels and interviewed for a job that required three to five years of outside business-to-business sales experience. Experience I didn't have. Even though I nailed the interview and proved I could do the job, I hadn't earned the opportunity. Shortcuts don't just cheat the process; they cheat you. They rob you of the lessons you gain by showing up day after day, doing the work, and embracing the grind.

That being said, the experience wasn't all bad. Without hesitation, I prepared and did the work. I tapped into the mindset I had when I was striving to be the best on the football field, a mindset I hadn't revisited in years. I nailed the interview, and more importantly, I crushed the role-play. I walked away feeling confident that sales might truly be the right career path.

If I wanted true success, I had to build my sales muscles the right way, through real wins and tough losses. I needed to know what it felt like to push through failure and keep going. I needed to feel the pressure of hitting sales targets over and over and the weight of accountability that comes with making 150 calls just to book one product demo. That kind of grind can't be faked. The experience, the grit, and the polish that come from showing up for those battles are things you have to earn.

What I needed now was an entry-level sales position to build my skills, foster authentic confidence, and set myself up for long-term success. Dez had been right, of course, and I should have listened to him about not lying on my résumé. But in true J-Ferg fashion, I had to learn the hard way.

I knew in my heart that I could do it. Now it was time to grind it out and embrace the stairs.

* * *

On Oahu, sales opportunities are limited, making it tough to get a foot in the door. My big brother Ryan works for T-Mobile, earning solid pay and enjoying great benefits. He suggests it might be a good way for me to jump-start a sales career. At first, I resist, convincing myself that working for a cell phone company is beneath me. An ironic thought, considering where I'm at in life.

Who am I to judge?

Eventually, I stop fighting it and submit résumés to Sprint, T-Mobile, and Verizon.

And you want to know what's funny? Sprint and T-Mobile won't even consider hiring me. I get an automated "thanks, but no thanks" email, letting me know they appreciate my time but are moving in a different direction. I thought I was a shoo-in. Turns out, I'm not even on their radar. Here I am thinking I'm too good for them, and they don't even want me. Despite everything I've been through, my ego is still the size of the Pacific. I think it's finally time to humble myself.

Verizon is my last hope, and I put everything I have into killing the application process. I'm extremely thoughtful in my answers, carefully proofreading every line to make sure I come off as excited, hungry, and as articulate as possible. After two screening interviews over the phone, I'm told the only place hiring is the kiosk in Kahala Mall.

A kiosk? Really?

Here I'd been hoping to skip a few levels, thinking Verizon was beneath me, and now my only sales job option is at a kiosk in the middle of a damn mall. The universe knows exactly how to serve me a double dose of humble pie.

Going after this job means humbling myself, being fully grateful, and embracing the opportunity if I'm lucky enough to get it. I have to want this, own it, and see it as a stepping stone to becoming a true sales savage.

Sure, it's a kiosk, but it's not just any kiosk. It's massive, well-managed, and operates more like a store. There are seven sales reps, which means I'll have competition, stack rankings, coaching, commission bonuses, and stats to track, just like in a traditional retail setting.

With my mindset flipped, I go all in and fight for this job. During the interview, I shift into full-blown terminator mode. I leave everything on the field, because I know I need this.

The next day, I get the call: I'm in.

*   *   *

The job at Verizon changes my life. From the start, I'm given an incredible lesson in humility, one that forces me to reflect on how often people miss opportunities because of their egos. I almost did the same. Here I was, thinking I was too good for a kiosk job, feeling like Verizon should hand me something bigger, something better. But the reality is that my ego almost blinded me to the opportunity right in front of me. I'd been so caught up in where I thought I should be that I nearly missed where I needed to start.

I think about how often people pass up jobs, positions, or chances to learn because they think they're above it. They're too focused on skipping steps or obsessing over what others might be thinking. And the reality is that most of the time, nobody's thinking about us in the first place. It's all in our heads.

Verizon ends up giving me the best foundation in sales training I could've asked for. Fundamentals that stick with me throughout my career, and skills I'll go on to teach as a coach and leader later in life.

Verizon quickly becomes home, and the team feels like family. We compete against one another, work our asses off, and push one another, just like the teams I grew up on. After a month or two of ramping into the role, I start crushing it. I'm putting up store-level sales numbers from a kiosk. Our performance is measured by how many phones, tablets, and accessories we sell each month, all going toward our quota. I'm pitching to nearly everyone who walks by. I'm that guy at the kiosk in the middle of the mall you try to avoid making eye contact with because you know he's going to try and sell you something.

Out of nearly 4,000 sales reps nationwide, I finish in the top 10 on several occasions and consistently land in the top 10 percent of all Verizon sales reps.

I'm a man possessed. I'm learning, winning, competing, failing from time to time, and getting stronger. I'm also getting close with some of my coworkers, so it's not long before I'm going out for drinks with them after work. But I don't allow the drinking to derail me. I don't relapse. I manage to keep the urge to use at bay.

*   *   *

In just two years, I've worked my way up to assistant manager, and I'm gunning for the general manager position. I've just interviewed for it, and they're about to make me an offer for the role. And throughout all of this, my relationship with Dez has never been stronger. We talk almost weekly, and he's been keeping close tabs on my success. He knows exactly how hungry I am for this next step.

One day, he calls to check in, and we start talking about the general manager position. The conversation naturally shifts into weighing the pros and cons of the role. Eventually, we get to the numbers, salary plus commission. I tell him it's just shy of six figures.

Over the last two years, I've made huge financial strides, and cracking six figures has become my ultimate goal. If my team exceeds our yearly target, I'll finally hit that mark for the first time ever. He sounds impressed, but there's a pause. A subtle hesitation that tells me he's not completely sold.

"You're killing it, bro," he says. "But think about it. You've caught on so fast, got promoted in no time—I'm not convinced Verizon is really it for you."

There's a silence. I wait, curious to see where he's going with this.

"You should move out here and live with me. I know your experience is still a little light, but somebody out here will take a chance on you. I know it."

I'm thrown off for a second.

This was the last thing I expected him to say. I repeat it back, almost as if I'm trying to process it out loud. "Move out there with you? Like, actually move?"

He doesn't miss a beat. "Yeah, man. I'm serious. Move out here. I've thought it through. You and Apes can stay with me, Tash, and the boys until you figure it out. Somebody will take a chance on you, bro. I know it."

There's no hesitation in his voice. It's clear he's already carefully considered this.

And just like that, it's on the table. He's offering a lifeline. It's not every day somebody invites you to stay in their home with their wife and kids in an attempt to help change the trajectory of your career. Even bigger, the trajectory of your life.

Can I really just pack up and move to Northern California at the drop of a dime?

What do I do?

It's a massive decision, and I'm torn. Do I stay in Hawaii to become a GM for Verizon? Or do I move to California in an attempt to go big, with Dez at my side?

Apryle is in nursing school, so a move doesn't just affect me; it changes her trajectory too. But she's willing to put her own goals on hold, knowing how rare opportunities like this are on the island. Her belief in me is unlike anything I've ever known, a strength I can always count on. It's why she stuck by me through everything, always certain this version of me was waiting to emerge.

Now she sees it. The sparkle in my eye she's been waiting for. Proof that I'm locked in and laser focused.

When I bring up the possibility of moving, she doesn't hesitate. It's not an easy decision, but she's ready to drop out of nursing school and follow me while I fight for the career I want. She makes it clear: "I love you, and as long as you're sober and focused, I'll follow you to the end of the earth."

Her words mean everything. With her support, I feel unstoppable. I remind myself why I had taken the Verizon role in the first place, as a stepping stone toward breaking into medical device sales. That had been the plan from the start, and now Dez was offering me an opportunity to live in an area where that industry was booming.

Should I stay, or should I go?

*   *   *

I decide to go, but the idea of making such a big move and failing is overwhelming. Doubt creeps in, and I start having second thoughts. I'm passing up a sure thing by bailing on the GM job and taking a huge risk by betting on myself. It's terrifying.

I can't seem to get out of my own head. My thoughts begin to ping-pong back and forth, bouncing from fear to hope and back again.

What if it doesn't work?

What if nobody pulls the trigger on me?

What if we have to move back?

The fear is real. I almost back out on several occasions.

What stops me, though, is thinking back to that day in high school when I'd been up all night, paralyzed by the fear of getting hit on the field. I didn't back out then; I didn't quit on myself. Instead, I got hit, and I learned about fear and the cunning tricks our brains play on us when we're on the verge of doing something new or embarking on the unknown. Embarking on something big.

With all that in mind, I know it's time to "get hit" again. So that's exactly what I do.

Before I know it, Apryle and I are on a plane heading to Northern California. I've just placed the biggest wager of my life, betting everything on myself.

25

Disneyland for Executives

Brentwood, California, is nothing like Hawaii or L.A. It's a newly developed city that's pretty isolated, about two hours outside of San Francisco. There's nothing out there but houses and land. From the moment we arrive, I'm focused on one thing: not failing.

To break into medical device sales with so little experience, I know I'll have to work twice as hard to stand out. Every morning, I'm up at 5 a.m., combing through job postings, tailoring my résumé, and sending out applications. The afternoons are filled with phone interviews, and every evening is spent deep-diving into research about the companies I've managed to secure interviews with.

Dez becomes my secret weapon. Before every interview, we huddle up, going over my pitch, anticipating questions, and mapping out strategies to leave a lasting impression. During the calls, he's right outside the door, listening intently to every word. Afterward, we break it all down. He doesn't sugarcoat it; he tells me exactly where I messed up and how to do better next time.

After a month of grinding like this, I feel stuck. The recruiters love my energy and always pass me straight through to the hiring manager. Those interviews feel solid too. I walk out confident they'll take a chance on me. But every time, my lack of "outside sales" experience comes up. No matter how well the conversation goes, I never hear back. It happens so often I lose count.

I interview for almost every medical device company out there: Johnson & Johnson, Stryker, Medtronic, Smith & Nephew. I even drive three hours in traffic to San Jose to interview with Boston Scientific in person. But each one ends in rejection. It's brutal.

The constant rejection is taking a toll on my optimistic spirit, but I refuse to give in. I make a conscious choice to push back against the doubt, to keep believing that this will work out. When I was younger, with fewer scars, optimism came naturally. Now it's something I have to fight for. Every time doubt tries to creep in, I catch it and flip the script, fighting hard to focus solely on the possibility of success.

When I catch myself thinking things like:

What if nobody takes a chance on me?

What if I'm not the type of person any of these companies want?

I recognize it and quickly pivot to something more like:

What if the right person loves me?

What if I break through and hit six figures in my first year?

It's easy to be positive and optimistic when things are great. Not so easy when everything is going to shit. These are the moments when being mindful of your thinking matters the most.

This process is testing my mental endurance, but I refuse to quit. I know I can do the work. There are hundreds of companies out there; I just need one leader to take a chance. One opportunity, and I'll prove I'm the best investment they've ever made.

*　　*　　*

One night at the dinner table, Dez suggests we might be looking at this all wrong. "We live in the tech capital of the world," he says, gesturing broadly. "Silicon Valley is right in our backyard, with start-ups and well-known companies everywhere. Why not try tech sales? It's the number one market here."

He's absolutely right. It's time to pivot. The idea sparks something in me. Tech is innovative, fast-paced, and filled with opportunities to grow. I throw myself into this new direction, sending out résumés to Uber, Google, Salesforce, Oracle, and just about every other company I can think of.

At first, I feel reenergized. But then, weeks go by without a single callback. Not a peep. Months of rejection like this bring on a tremendous amount of self-doubt.

I think I fucked up!

Why didn't I just take the GM role at Verizon?

These thoughts get louder and louder with each failed attempt. All I can do is continue to get up at the crack of dawn and keep trying to push through the doubt.

*　　*　　*

At a BBQ one afternoon, I'm introduced to Kendall, a friend of a friend who happens to ask me about my career. I share with her, in great detail, my efforts to apply and interview for every possible sales position known to man. Then she casually mentions that she works for one of the largest tech giants in the world, a company renowned for its cutting-edge technology and its high-performing sales teams. She tells me they recently acquired a groundbreaking cloud networking company and are actively looking for sales reps. Kendall says she'll put in a good word for me.

Drinks are flowing, so I don't put a lot of stock in her promise. I don't really expect her to follow through. I know how these things tend to go.

But when Monday comes around, Kendall is true to her word. She connects me with a recruiter at the newly acquired company, and before I know it, we're on the phone for an interview. I'm locked in, delivering every answer with confidence and enthusiasm, completely in the zone. By the time we hang up, I'm certain I've crushed it.

I'm quickly moved along to speak with the hiring manager, Henry, another conversation I crush. The rapport between Henry and me is instant, and this time, I'm sure that I'm a shoo-in.

But at the end of the call, he derails our conversation by addressing the elephant in the room: my experience.

Not again.

I can't catch a break.

Right before we jump off the phone, Henry pauses for a moment, and I can feel there's more he wants to say. He takes a breath and then says, "You know, there's actually another opportunity I think you'd be a perfect fit for. Our web conferencing division is building out a large sales team. The best part is that it's based right here at the same office." His voice shifts, and I can hear the enthusiasm as he goes on. "They're putting together something big, and I'd love to put in a word for you."

Although getting rejected for the first position stings, there is still a flicker of hope. I'm not entirely convinced Henry will follow through, but later in the evening, an email comes through. It's an introduction to a recruiter for the new sales team, with Henry giving me a glowing reference.

I'm still in the game, baby, let's go.

I can't let myself get too excited just yet. I need to focus and make the most of this opportunity. This could be the one, and I've got to give it everything I've got.

*   *   *

Rather than schedule another phone screening, the recruiter sends me straight through to their in-person mixer. This is an event held at a bar for all the candidates who've made it to the final round. I haven't even spoken to a manager yet, but the recruiter pushes me through anyway, trying her best to give me a real chance. This is my shot, an opportunity to get face time with senior leaders and win the job.

I've never been to anything like this before. The objective seems to be to stand out from the pack while mingling over cocktails and leaving a lasting impression on all the bigwigs in attendance.

Are you shitting me?

I thrive in environments like this. It's what I do. I just need to be myself, because, honestly, if this doesn't work, I don't deserve the damn job.

I give myself a strict two-drink max rule going into the evening, to make sure I'm clear and focused. And immediately, it's a race for face time. A battle between recruits to get in front of every leader there.

Picture two candidates standing at a bar. They both spot a VP across the room. They both take final sips of their respective beers. Then they glance at each other for a split second before racing across the room toward their target.

Now multiply that by ten. This is what my evening is like. I make my rounds unapologetically, grabbing whatever time I can with every manager, director, and VP in the room. Very intentional about leaving a lasting impression. And by the end of the mixer, I genuinely feel like I've left it all on the field.

I'm proud of myself. Not just for how I've shown up at this event, but for how far I've come from the guy sitting in a park at 2 a.m., searching for a healthy vein to stick a needle in. Every step forward feels like reclaiming another piece of the life Apryle and I have been dreaming of.

Through it all, Apryle has been my rock. She's proud of the effort I'm putting in, and her constant love and support fuel me to keep going. It's like having my own personal cheerleader in my corner, always rooting for me, always believing in what I can become.

Apryle's also been on the job hunt, and she's got something promising lined up at KB Home. It's a bit of a relief for us financially. We need the money. But as for me, it feels like the pressure is mounting. I've got to come through. This is my shot, and I've got to nail it.

*　　*　　*

A few days later, I'm asked to come interview in person. I've experienced so many *L*s up to this point, so many setbacks. Some were just the luck of the draw, and others were totally self-inflicted. Right now, I am desperately in need of a win. I've interviewed with almost 40 companies and submitted hundreds of résumés. I don't think I can take another *L*.

I show up early to the interview in downtown San Francisco. As I wait in my car, I remind myself that authenticity is my superpower, and I just need to be myself.

Before getting out of the car, I glance in the rearview mirror, checking my face and hair one last time. As I stare into my own eyes, something clicks. Without hesitation, words spill out, almost as if they've been waiting for this exact moment:

I am strong.

I am a natural-born salesman.

I am built for this.

I am a bad mothafucka.

I've never done an "I am" statement before. Hell, I don't even know where it came from, but in the moment, it feels real. It feels right. I take a deep breath, hop out of the car, and head into the building.

The elevator spits me out into a large lobby, where a friendly receptionist instructs me to sign in. The lobby itself feels like a window into another world, sleek and modern, yet warm in a way that draws you in.

Glass walls stretch from ceiling to floor, spotless, giving me a clear view into the office and beyond. To my left, a handcrafted wooden staircase catches my eye, winding its way up to the second floor. It's polished, clean, and sharp. Simple, but somehow still fancy.

I take it all in, feeling both impressed and a little out of place. The hum of voices surrounds me, blending with the soft rhythm of footsteps and the occasional hiss of an espresso machine. There's a pulse here, an energy that moves through the space and brings it to life.

I glance at the furniture just beyond the glass walls, and at first, it doesn't even register as furniture. It's bold, artistic, like someone dropped sculptures in the middle of the room and told people to sit on them. And they do. Shoes off, sprawled out, laughing like they're in their living rooms. It's clear this place isn't just meant to impress; it's meant to be lived in.

The hiring manager meets me in the lobby and takes me further in. For a second, it feels like I'm at Disneyland for executives, a place where work and play blend seamlessly. I've never experienced startup culture before, so I'm completely unprepared for how immersive and intentional these office spaces are.

The deeper we go, the more impressive it becomes. Huge concrete beams frame the open floor plan, giving it a raw, industrial vibe. People sit cross-legged on built-in sofas that are carved into the walls, with their laptops balanced on their knees, looking focused but chill.

In the center of it all is a life-size chessboard, with pieces so big they look like they belong in a museum. They're bigger than me.

Behind it, I hear the sharp crack of a ping-pong ball and bursts of laughter that make me want to laugh too. There's a lightness here, a playful energy that feels infectious.

And then, something surreal catches my eye. A strange machine glides past me, like a Segway with an iPad mounted on top, displaying someone's face. It maneuvers around us with precision, as if it's alive. For a moment, I just stand there, trying to make sense of it. Someone is navigating the office remotely, physically absent but digitally present, like something straight out of a sci-fi movie.

The hiring manager keeps walking, unfazed, while I'm still frozen, watching this futuristic scene unfold. The space is dope, buzzing with innovation, and I'm standing at the edge of it all, reminding myself I belong here.

The hiring manager explains that lunch is catered every day, and they bring in the good stuff: sushi, steak, burgers, pasta, you name it. They even have a fully stocked kitchen, like a mini 7-Eleven, but it's all completely free: unlimited chips, candy, protein bars, bagels, cereal, and soda. The level of thought behind every detail here is next level.

When we finally get to the cloud networking division's sales floor, it's jumpin'. At least a hundred desks are packed tightly together, practically elbow to elbow, and nearly every rep is at their desk, fully locked in. They're working hard, feeding off one another's energy, the conversations blending into a symphony of hustle. It feels like big things are happening right before my eyes.

In the middle of it all, one sales rep, deep in conversation with a customer, effortlessly tosses a football across the room to another rep on the far side, blending focus and play like it's all part of the job. It's casual, loose, and competitive all at once. It looks like a scene out of a millennial tech sales movie that hasn't been made yet.

I don't know a thing about their products, but I'm ready to grab a headset and close a deal right now.

Whatever career I thought I wanted before this completely vanishes from my mind. I can't believe I was in the tech capital of the world thinking about medical device sales. Not anymore. This is it. I don't just want this; I need this.

The hiring manager gestures around, explaining his vision to grow the web conferencing team to mirror the energy of the cloud networking team's sales floor. His goal is to scale to 100 reps, and if I get hired, I'd be number four. He wants his team to embody the same energy, collaboration, and drive that makes the cloud networking team so successful.

After the tour, he walks me into a small meeting room where the VP of Sales is already waiting. I can feel the potential in the air, fully aware of what's at stake here. Every question they ask feels like a chance to prove myself, so I focus on giving everything I have, making sure my drive and experience are undeniable. Thirty minutes after I leave the office, my phone rings.

I got the job.

When I hang up, pride and relief wash over me. I did it. I give myself a moment to take it in, but it's quick. I know what's ahead won't be easy, but this is my launch into the next chapter of my life and career. The excitement is undeniable, but it's quickly tempered by the realization that this opportunity comes with its own unique challenges.

New Jersey is part of my territory, which means I have to work East Coast hours from the West Coast. I need to be in the office by 6 a.m., Monday through Friday, which makes for a grueling commute. I live over two hours away, so my mornings start early. I'm up at 3:00 a.m., out the door by 3:30, and dropped off at the BART station by 4 a.m. for the two-hour train ride into downtown San Francisco. Apryle is a trouper; she wakes up with me every day to drop me off at the station by 4 a.m., ensuring I get there on time.

I spend my time on the train immersing myself in everything sales. I dive into sales books, devour podcasts, and scour YouTube for anything that will help me enhance my scripts and email cadences. I use every second of my commute as a means to improve my sales skill set.

It's one thing to talk about what you'll do for an opportunity, the sacrifices you'll make, and the lengths you'll go to, but I'm living it. And I don't complain. Not once. I never ask for my territory to be changed, never look for an easier way. I focus on making the most of the opportunity, grateful for every grind-filled minute of it.

Still, no amount of preparation can ready me for what I face in my first week on the job. On my third day, just as I'm about to attack my cold call list, a senior leader from the office walks by. He slows his pace, hesitates, then looks my way with an expression I can't quite read. Finally, he pulls me aside, shifting uncomfortably.

"Jason, please don't take this the wrong way, but ... you sound too ... urban."

I freeze, blindsided. Unsure how to respond, I manage a hesitant "okay," hoping that might be the end of the conversation. But he goes on.

"You need to be mindful of how you communicate," he says. "Your tone, your style; it might not sit well with the CTOs, IT directors, and VPs you're talking to."

I'm left stunned, struggling to find the right words to respond with. This leader isn't even my supervisor, just a higher-up who felt the need to offer his unsolicited advice. I head back to my desk, replaying the exchange in my mind.

Did he really just tell me I sound too Black?

The thought hits hard, forcing me to second-guess every word that leaves my mouth. Growing up in West L.A., I know I have a subtle accent, one I'm already self-conscious about in spaces like this. And in an area of the office with just four people, where I'm the only Black person, there's nowhere to hide. Between calls, the silence feels heavy with an awkward stillness that makes every sound sharper. Here, when you speak, every word seems amplified, echoing back louder, carrying an unnecessary weight. His comment lingers, casting a shadow over every conversation that follows.

For the next month and a half, I completely change the way I speak, mimicking the rep next to me. I copy everything, from his tone and his cadence to his phrasing. The problem is, he's a middle-aged White dude from Northern California. He has a completely different personality and set of characteristics than me. We're nothing alike.

I'm brand-new to sales, totally green in this role, and on top of that, I'm trying to pretend to be someone I'm not. Every day, I show up doing my best "Mike" impersonation, trying to mimic his style, and I'm failing miserably. I can't book a demo to save my life, and I'm stumbling through all of my calls. It's brutal.

As the days drag on, the pressure builds. New reps get a three-month ramp-up window, a grace period to learn the ropes without the full weight of a quota. But I'm nearly at the end of that window, and I haven't booked enough demos or closed a single deal on my own. The clock is ticking, and I'm running out of time to prove I belong here.

One night, while lying in bed, my thoughts won't let me rest. I've always been the best, or at least among the best, at everything I do. And now my inconsistency is eating me alive.

Ain't no way I'm losing this job. No way.

As I lie there, my mind keeps circling back to everything I've been doing wrong. I think about how hard I've been trying to be someone else, this "Mike" version of me that doesn't feel real. That's when I remember my coaching call with Cog, how he said my personality is my superpower.

I grab my phone and call him. Thank God he answers, because I'm spiraling. I tell him everything: the early morning grind, the comment that messed with my head, and my growing fear about still not closing a single deal. He listens without judgment, letting me vent until he finally cuts in with his raspy, high-energy voice that always seems to light a fire under me.

"Filly, you're the coolest dude in the room. People want to be you, bro. They always have. But the real you, not this version of you you're trying to force. Just be that person. Keep failing, keep learning. You'll be fine. Relax. You're built for this."

His words hit hard. They're simple, but they're exactly what I need. The next day, I walk back into the office with a clear commitment. I'm going to be Jason Ferguson. If I fail, if I lose this job, I'm going out being unapologetically me.

At first, nothing happens. The change isn't instant, but I stay the course. Then, little by little, I start to notice a difference. I stop obsessing over how "urban" I sound and lean into the qualities that make me who I am: my raspy, charismatic voice and my natural enthusiasm. I know I'm articulate, that I can connect with people, so I focus on letting that shine. Instead of trying to be perfect or sound a certain way, I speak with honesty and a genuine care for the customer.

The shift is undeniable. The more I embrace who I am, the more confident I feel, and that confidence radiates through every conversation. My calls flow naturally, and I can sense a genuine change in how customers respond. Those same IT directors and CTOs, the ones I was told wouldn't respond well to how "urban" I sounded, end up loving me. Being raw, imperfect, and a little eccentric wasn't a flaw; it was my edge. The connections I was forming proved that authenticity is not just acceptable, it's magnetic.

It's remarkable how the simple act of being authentic can change the game. Research from *Psychological Science* shows that people who act authentically are perceived as more trustworthy and likable, traits essential for success in any area of life. Being authentic isn't about being perfect; it's about being real. It creates trust, fosters connection, and lays the foundation for meaningful relationships and opportunities.

This connection isn't just emotional, it's practical. Authenticity breaks down barriers and creates an environment in which collaboration and understanding can thrive. By being real, you invite others to do the same, creating a ripple effect that can transform ordinary moments into opportunities for impact.

For sales, authenticity isn't just a feel-good concept. It's a measurable advantage. Top-performing salespeople are known for consistently building relationships rooted in honesty and empathy. Customers don't just buy products; they buy trust, connection, and a sense of alignment with the person on the other end of the conversation. These qualities come directly from being real. It's not about being polished or fitting into a mold. It's about being relatable.

My raspy voice, my enthusiasm, even the eccentric parts of my personality, all the things I thought I had to suppress, turned out to be my biggest assets.

This journey taught me that embracing authenticity doesn't mean avoiding growth. It means growing as yourself. When you lean into your unique strengths, even the ones you once saw as flaws, they become your superpowers. Authenticity connects you to people on a human level, and in sales or in life, that's what wins.

Eventually, I close my first deal, and then another. Before long, I've exceeded my quota for the quarter, triggering the biggest commission check I've ever seen: a little over $10,000. That's just one month's commission check, not even including my salary pay.

What?!

I call Apryle, fighting back tears as I tell her about the check. It's surreal. For the first time in years, it feels like everything is coming together, just like we'd always hoped.

* *Discover the values, beliefs, and traits that make you one of a kind. Go to JFinspires.com/TheBlueprint to download the free Authentic Self Blueprint and start living as your most authentic self.*

26

Sabotage

With things finally on track at work, life outside the office starts to feel just as fulfilling. Being able to live with Dez and his wife, Tash, is incredible. Not only do they provide me with an opportunity to advance my career, but we have a ton of fun living together. BBQs on the weekends, and every now and then, Dez and I get a boys' night out in Walnut Creek. Our friendship picks up right where it left off. We're back to being joined at the hip, and I'm grateful to have him back in my life.

But even as things seem to fall into place, there's a subtle undercurrent I can't quite shake. A lingering itch, faint but persistent, that reminds me how fragile progress can be. Sometimes it's just a passing thought, but other times, it feels like something heavier. A crack in the foundation I've worked so hard to build.

That itch, that subtle pull, finds its shape one afternoon when Dez mentions he's switching medications after surgery. The Percocet he's taking makes him itch uncontrollably, so he has to stop taking it. He tosses the bottle onto the counter like it's nothing, but to me, it's something impossible to ignore. A completely full bottle of pills, just sitting there. My brain locks onto it, filing it away in that dark corner where temptation lives.

At first, it's just a passing thought, drifting into my mind at random moments. Late at night, I find myself staring at the ceiling, thinking about that bottle, how no one would even miss it. I fight the temptation, reminding myself what's at stake, and I acknowledge this new sense of control I've managed to build. But control can be deceptive. It feels solid until it doesn't, fragile in moments you least expect.

One day, I get home from work to find the house eerily quiet. I call out for Dez, Tash, and their boys, but there's no response. The place is empty, and something shifts inside me. A thought breaks through, with unexpected intensity.

Now's your chance. Go find them.

That thought, prompted by space and opportunity, becomes unbearably loud. I know they're just sitting there, untouched, and the idea of a fresh, unopened bottle under the same roof becomes impossible to ignore. Suddenly, I'm in it. I'm spiraling, fixating on that bottle.

I pace around the living room, fighting hard to resist the temptation. But the pull is fierce, an invisible force drowning out all rational thought. I have no foundation, no system to fight off this voice that manages to twist and bend all reason. Before I even realize it, the decision is made.

I peek out the living room window, scanning the street to make sure the coast is clear. My heart pounds as I sprint up the stairs to Dez's bedroom. The thrill is undeniable, an intoxicating reminder of the rush that comes with the hunt.

I barely even have to look. It's right there in plain sight, sitting on top of Dez's nightstand. And just as I thought, the bottle is completely full.

So now what?

I stare at it, torn. I can't just take these pills without covering my tracks; it would be too obvious. I pour them out into my hand, staring at the chalky capsules.

They look just like Tylenol.

Then a bright idea pops into my head. I sprint to my bathroom and grab my Tylenol bottle.

Leaning over the bathroom sink, I grip a pill between my fingers and use my thumbnail with a little water to scratch the word "Tylenol" off the surface.

Adrenaline rips through my veins as the voice in my head screams at me.

Hurry the hell up; they could be home any minute.

My hand trembles while my thumbnail scrapes frantically, back and forth against each pill like the needle on a polygraph test.

Then another thought breaks through the madness.

I should stop.

There's still time.

What the fuck are you doing? This is crazy.

The contrast is jarring. One moment, I'm racing against the clock, and the next, a sliver of reason tries to pull me back. But I'm not in control anymore. My body has gone rogue, driven only by instinct, like a zombie chasing after the scent of flesh.

I take a second to meticulously inspect each Tylenol pill, making sure there's no trace of the letters. Then I fill my Tylenol bottle with his Percocet, and his Percocet bottle with my modified Tylenol pills.

Self-sabotage at its finest.

It's not like I'm going through withdrawals or feeling depressed. Life is great. But suddenly, I've lost all control. At the snap of a finger, I'm on a mission of self-destruction. Maybe part of me just wants to see if I can get away with it. *They say insanity is doing the same thing over and over again and expecting different results.* Well, this is obviously pure insanity.

Still, I make promises to myself. I tell myself I won't go crazy. I'll just do a little each week. Only when I'm drinking. I won't let it get out of hand.

But who am I kidding? That plan doesn't even last a day.

*　　*　　*

The next morning, I chew up a pill with my coffee as soon as I get to work.

Big mistake.

This changes everything.

I have one of the best working days of my career. I feel like a different person on the phone, like I somehow tapped into my alter ego, unleashing a side of me that's been hibernating, waiting to be set free.

What I don't realize in the moment is that I've accidentally set a new standard for what a workday should feel like: a dangerous thrill, exhilarating yet risky.

Who I am as a seller morphs into an even bigger personality, effortlessly delivering sharp, impromptu lines that seem to come out of nowhere. The pills pull that quick-witted, on-the-fly talent I spent years cultivating through rapping and freestyling right out of me. All those years of searching for clever words to rhyme in real time are finally paying off, only now it's even easier. I don't even have to rhyme. I just open my mouth, and it feels like the Percs unlock those perfect words, making them magically appear. I'm unrestrained and unfiltered.

I was already doing well, but something shifts, and the results are undeniable. My productivity skyrockets as I crush demo after demo, booking them faster than ever. It doesn't take long before I start to believe the Percs are the secret behind it all.

One morning, I chew up a pill, chase it with my coffee, and feel an unstoppable charge as I grab the phone.

"Hey, Allen, it's Jason again. How's it going today?" I ask, my voice vibrant and enthusiastic.

"Jason, not today. I'm really busy," Allen replies.

"I hear you, but I've been reaching out for months because I truly believe my software can make a difference for you and your team. Just give me a quick minute to explain?" I persist, refusing to let his brush-off deter me.

"All right, but make it fast," he concedes.

"Straight to the point, I like it. Look, I know you're comfortable with GoTo Meeting, but you've got to at least see what we can do for your teams. Not only can we save you money, but we also offer much better functionality and top-notch security, and we even come with a messenger app similar to Slack, but better. Imagine having all your communication needs integrated smoothly," I explain.

Allen's voice grows firmer. "Jason, we've had this conversation before. I don't see a need to change right now."

I lean back in my chair, refusing to give in. "I get it. Change can be a pain in the ass, but imagine having a tool that not only keeps up with your team's needs but actually propels your sales forward. That's what we're doing for sales teams just like yours, across the board. But you haven't given me a chance to show you yet."

There's a brief pause. I hear him take a breath. "Look, I appreciate your persistence and enthusiasm, but I'm really swamped right now. Maybe another time."

I glance around, noticing a handful of colleagues starting to gaze in my direction, eyes peering at me over the top of their monitors. I shoot my manager a confident smirk as we lock eyes, then throw a quick "watch this" gesture before making my move.

"Allen, before you hang up, let's make this interesting. I saw on Facebook you're a big-time Golden State Warriors fan. Man, they're running the league right now. Steph and Klay are going crazy. I actually work in downtown San Francisco, and they're building the new stadium right next door to my office. It's gonna be sick. Anyway, I'm from L.A., and the Lakers are playing the Warriors next weekend. How about a friendly bet?"

The line goes silent, and I can almost hear Allen raising an eyebrow. My colleagues perk up; some are even standing now to get a better listen.

"A bet? What kind of bet?" he asked.

In a friendly yet competitive tone I say, "Look, if the Warriors win, I'll buy pizza for your entire office, and you'll never hear from me again. But if the Lakers win, you gotta carve out 45 minutes for me to show you what we can do for your team. Deal?"

Silence again.

As the silence stretches, my heart begins to pound.

Damn, did I push too far? Is he about to hang up on me?

I hold my breath and wait patiently.

Come on, Allen. Take the bait.

I can hear the faintest rustling on the other end, almost like he's thinking it over.

More silence.

Then, finally, a chuckle breaks the tension. "All right, fine, you've got yourself a deal. The Lakers are a mess this season, but if this bet keeps you from bugging me and gets my team some pizza, then consider it done. I'm in."

I grin and give a nod to my manager, who is smiling ear to ear. "You've got it, Allen. Enjoy the game, and I'll be in touch. Have an amazing rest of the week."

Cog had given me the idea for the "pizza bet" over six months ago, but until now, I had never had the guts to try it. The rush from that call is unparalleled. The risk I take pays off, and my confidence soars. The truth is, I could execute the pizza bet and variations of it without being high, but I start to believe otherwise. The high amplifies everything: the thrill, the focus, and the edge that makes taking calculated risks feel effortless. It fuels a momentum that seems almost unstoppable, building a confidence in me that makes me forget how easy it is to lose control.

*   *   *

I wind up running through the bottle of Percs in just under a month, and as I chew up the last pill, reality starts to set in.

What do I do now?

How will I succeed without my Perc superpower? My secret weapon that allows me be whoever I want to be, or need to be, on the phone?

I need a solution, and my mind starts searching for answers. Then it hits me—a friend of a friend had once mentioned a doctor in San Jose, one who'd write an Oxy prescription for anyone with a history of surgery. He'd brought it up casually, not knowing I was an addict, but that was all it took. The detail slid effortlessly into that part of my brain where every addict's secrets live, stored alongside years of dangerous information I'd held onto without a second thought.

I've been sitting on this information for weeks, agonizing over what to do. I go back and forth, thinking about all the times I've lost control.

But I'm different now, right?

I'm certain I can handle it this time. My focus is sharper than it's ever been. I'm not that same guy anymore. I'm winning now, thriving. Too focused, too driven to let it slip again.

I repeat this to myself, almost like a mantra, willing it to be true. The fear of losing everything I've worked so hard for lingers, but I shove it down. This isn't about escaping; it's about winning. And the more I think about it, the more I start to believe it.

Every time I take a pill, I feel like the Terminator. I can almost hear that iconic beat pound in my head the second the high kicks in. The need to tap into that confidence, the need to win, outweighs everything else.

Before I know it, I'm sitting in the doctor's office, walking him through my medical history. I talk about the two ACL tears, the four surgeries in total. I show him my knee, how disfigured it is, pointing out the permanent swelling and how it barely bends. The scar alone should seal the deal. It's raw and runs jagged from the bottom of my kneecap to just above the top. A cruel reminder of everything it's been through. I play it up too, not willing to risk getting denied. I overemphasize every symptom, wincing at the right moments, grimacing when asked to bend or straighten it. I paint a picture of constant, unbearable pain, something that can only be eased with what I'm here to get. I make it impossible for him to say no.

This is going to be even easier than I thought.

After a 15-minute examination, he's convinced. I'm prescribed 60 pills a month, two 30 mg Oxys a day. These pills would go for over $25 each on the street. And here, with this doctor's blessing, I'm getting the whole bottle for six bucks.

Now, once a month, I leave my office and drive down to San Jose for a quick visit to the doctor to refill my script, and I'm back in the office before lunch. It's a perfect system. It keeps me in my zone and keeps Apryle in the dark.

At first, everything goes as planned. I keep it under control: two pills a day—one in the morning, a half around lunchtime, and a half before the long commute home. But as the months roll by, the intensity of the high starts to dwindle. The buzz that used to carry me begins to fade quicker and quicker. I start wanting more. I crave a high that's stronger, one that lasts longer. So I up the dosage. A little more here, a little more there.

While Apryle has no idea about my monthly trips to San Jose, she knows something's up. The way she looks at me when I get home says it all. The once naive, innocent island girl has evolved into a junkie detector. She's gotten so good at sniffing it out that she can even hear it in my voice over the phone. I can literally say one word, not even a full sentence, and she's on me. Instantly suspicious.

Lately, her frustration has been mounting. I can feel it in the way she watches me when I walk through the door after work, her eyes scanning me like she's piecing together a puzzle. Tonight is no different. My shoulders sag under the weight of exhaustion, my eyes are red and heavy, and my face is worn and disheveled, like I've been through something only I can explain. I know I look exactly like someone with something to hide.

"Fergie, what's going on?" she asks one night as I step through the door. Her voice is steady, but there's an edge to it. It's a mix of irritation and suspicion. I can feel her gaze, scrutinizing my every move.

I force a smile, shaking my head. "Nothing, Babe. Long-ass day, that's all."

She crosses her arms and her eyes narrow in. "Don't lie to me. You look different, disheveled. I know when something's off."

My stomach twists, but I shrug it off, keeping my voice as calm as possible. "I'm serious, babe. It was just a long-ass day. That commute sucks, I'm tired, and I'm starving."

She takes a step closer, refusing to let it go. "Come on, Fergie. This isn't just work. Do you think I'm stupid?" Her voice cracks, as a hint of vulnerability slips through.

I sigh, tossing my bag onto the couch. "Why you always trippin'? I told you, it's nothing. Fuck, am I not allowed to be tired after a long day?" My tone turns aggressive, annoyed, trying to deflect and make it about her, hoping it's enough to end the conversation.

She stares at me for a moment longer, her face a mix of frustration and fear. I can see the questions piling up behind her eyes, the doubt clouding her trust. But she's got no solid evidence. Just instincts and worry.

She finally shakes her head, her voice barely a whisper. "I just hope you're not lying to me."

I look her in the eyes, then nod in silence.

Deep down, I know she doesn't fully buy it. She wants to, desperately. All she can do is hold on to hope, and I keep giving her just enough to hold on. It's a delicate balance, and I can feel the cracks starting to form.

It eats at me. The truth is, I feel like absolute shit, standing there, looking Apes in the eye, lying straight to her face. The embarrassment cuts deep; my secret isn't much of a secret anymore. Even worse is how I flipped it on her, making it seem like she's overreacting. That only adds to the guilt. But it's the only way I know to avoid facing the truth, to keep from owning up to my relapse. I do what I have to do to keep it hidden, even if it means slowly unraveling the things that matter most.

*   *   *

Back at the office, the cracks are invisible. I'm getting away with it, thriving even. Our culture is built on hard work, high performance standards, and a whole lot of partying. We grow fast, scaling to nearly 75 sales reps, and the sales floor is dynamic. We're an electric group of salespeople from every background you can imagine, each one of us competing to close bigger deals and hit bigger targets.

The competition is fierce. This isn't just a job; it's more like a battleground. Every morning, we hit the sales floor like warriors, each one of us laser-focused, hungry, and ready to grind until the day is done. But once the day is done and the targets are hit, the office transforms. We go from being professional killers to partying like rock stars in a heartbeat. We have regular team happy hours, both in and out of the office. No one can outwork us, and no one can out-party us either.

Startup tech culture is unlike anything I could've imagined. We're all in our twenties, making a ton of money. It's a rush, a high that makes us feel untouchable. As the team scales, I get close with a group of guys from the office. We're all top performers, the hitters on the team. We find one another almost by fate, drawn together by our hunger for success and our love for the chaos that comes with it. It's wild to think that some of the best-selling degenerates in all of San Francisco ended up on the same team, but here we are. And we own it.

We find a way to take that degenerate spirit to another level, putting a small refrigerator on the sales floor and stocking it exclusively with beer. If someone's dumb enough to put anything else in there, it gets tossed immediately, no questions asked. It's our space, our rules.

It doesn't take long for our partying to escalate. We're animals, and we know it; we bask in it. Before long, we're sneaking off to do cocaine in the office, even giving it a nickname: "prospecting." A twisted inside joke that makes us feel clever. In sales, prospecting is all about finding new opportunities, cold-calling, and hustling to secure leads. So, giving our chaos, that nickname makes it feel like it's almost part of the job.

By now, I'm willing to put almost anything up my nose to keep the party going. To keep that electric edge that makes the sales floor feel more like summer camp instead of work. We try to be responsible by setting a "No prospecting before 9:00 a.m." rule, but it quickly turns into a loose guideline, something we hardly ever stick to.

Most days start slow, but by midmorning, someone will give the signal. A nod, a glance, a grin that says, "It's time, bro; you coming?" Four of us slip away, moving in silence like conspirators, each of us taking different routes to the same empty demo room that's become our go-to for prospecting. Drinking beers openly on the sales floor is one thing, something we can pass off as a harmless part of the culture. But doing coke out in the open? That's a different level. None of us are willing to be that reckless. A fireable offense like that calls for secrecy, calculation. So, we make sure to stay discreet. I cut through a row of desks, practically ducking as I pass my manager. Another one heads around the back, slipping behind a cluster of meeting rooms. We meet up in the hallway, exchanging sly smiles as we quietly open the door.

The demo room is small and dimly lit, with a flickering blue light from a panel on the wall casting shadows across the cramped space. It's tucked away on the far side of the office, offering a sense of isolation that keeps us hidden from the rest of the team. We huddle together, passing around a tiny vial. We're talking about nothing and everything all at once, laughing hard, savoring the moment as everything feels lighter. It's a twisted kind of camaraderie, a bond built in secret, but right now, it's everything.

The rush hits, and suddenly, we're invincible. The coke sends my heart racing, and the Oxy smooths out the edges. It's a dangerous mix, a speedball that I know can end badly, but in the moment, the risk doesn't matter. The feeling is everything: my body's wired but weightless, charged and calm all at once. I keep the Oxy use to myself; none of the others know that it's my secret weapon. A hidden layer that keeps me balanced while we ride the madness.

As the high settles in, we swagger back out to our desks, still riding the rush, still laughing. We're a mess, but we're crushing it. The numbers don't lie. We're obliterating our targets. I'm making four times what I made at Verizon, bringing in well over a quarter million dollars a year, a number I never even considered.

I feel like the fucking man.

We're reckless for sure, but it's some of the most fun I've ever had, personally or professionally.

Being a top performer also has its perks. One day, my manager asks if I know anyone who would be a good fit for the team. He's looking to hire another rep and doubles down, saying, "I need another you, Ferg," half joking, half serious. I laugh and tell him there is another me out there: my brother, Ryan. He's literally just like me.

A couple of weeks later, Ryan comes in for an interview, crushes it, and earns a spot on the squad. And I was right; he's a beast. I show him the ropes and teach him everything I've learned. Now I've got my favorite person in the world working right beside me, and he's killing it in no time.

We commute to and from the office together every day, catching up, laughing our asses off at whatever sick, twisted jokes my brother comes up with. Between *The Joe Budden Podcast*, Howard Stern, and me belting out the same Tory Lanez songs at the top of my lungs, every ride feels like it could be a reality show. What used to be a torturous commute has become something I genuinely look forward to. Those hours spent in traffic suddenly aren't so bad; they're time I get to spend with my brother, just the two of us, like it used to be. I cherish every bit of it.

At this point, I feel unstoppable, like I'm on top of the world.

But life has a way of bringing you back to reality, and it hits me with something that shakes my entire foundation.

Apryle is pregnant. We're having a baby girl.

H-o-l-y shit!

Finding out Apryle is pregnant is both thrilling and terrifying. Nothing feels better than being able to confidently tell her she doesn't have to work anymore. I'm making enough now for her to be a stay-at-home mom as long as she wants. We had already moved out of Dez's place and into our own apartment, a space that's finally ours, and it's perfect for starting a family.

I feel this deep sense of pride knowing I can provide for my family, but I also feel this sinking dread. I've been slipping big time, and the reality of becoming a father comes with a sobering burn. I know I need to slow down. I need to get a grip, not just for myself but for the baby on the way. Each month, I promise myself that next month I'll stop. But when the next month rolls around, I crumble under the weight of the cravings and wanting to perform, and I tell myself I still have time.

The truth is, quitting feels harder than ever, almost impossible. I've convinced myself that my success, my ability to keep up, to excel, is tied to these pills. They're what get me through long days, what keep me on point in the office, fueling a lie I've come to believe. It feels like I'm in a race against time, torn between the father and husband I want to be and the ruthless grip of these pills that promise to keep me performing. But with a baby on the way, the truth presses harder: my life isn't just mine anymore. A quiet urgency gnaws at me, forcing me to confront how quickly time is slipping through my fingers. Now I'm not just fighting for myself but for a family that deserves me whole and present. I keep promising myself that I'll slow down, I'll stop, but if there's one thing I've learned through years of addiction, it's that escape is never that simple. And as the clock ticks louder, the weight of this dilemma settles on my shoulders. I know I'm running out of excuses, and I'm definitely running out of time.

27
My Origin Story

By now, I've been the top performer for nearly two years, consistently holding down the number one spot on the team. I've refined my process to a science, knowing exactly what it takes to close deals and keep my pipeline packed. A lot of my success stems from mastering a system our company refers to as "channel sales."

The channel is all about working with resellers, partners who act as middlemen, selling our products directly to customers in addition to us doing it ourselves. I've learned how to leverage these resellers effectively. When done right, it means having four or five different reps out there selling for you, each bringing deals directly to your desk to assist in the close. It's a complicated system to navigate, but if you crack it, it's an absolute game changer. And I've cracked it.

As I continue to succeed from working the channel, I take it upon myself to share what I've learned. I start running training sessions for the new hires, showing them how to work the channel. I coach them on how to build strong relationship with the right partners and find their own rhythm in the sales process. I don't believe in winning at the expense of others failing. I learned that from battling with Davone on the football field. We can all win together. So I've been going out of my way to run these training sessions after hours, staying late to help the newer reps get up to speed.

And beyond that, I've got my sights set on the next level. I want to be a manager. I know that to get there, I need to prove I can lead, to do the job before I officially have it. This is my way of doing just that.

One day, I invite a few new hires to stick around for one of my after-hours training sessions. On this particular day, I'd started drinking much earlier than usual, and just before we sit down, I head to the bathroom to bust down an Oxy. I snort the line, feeling the familiar burn as it sears through my nostrils, and then I march into the conference room, ready to attack the training.

By the time we all settle in, I'm already wrecked, a sloppy mix of drunk and high, teetering on the edge of control and total collapse. My enthusiasm and my knack for staying articulate usually mask just how far gone I am. I've learned to be completely wrecked and still demolish a sales call or a training session. The more I do this under the influence, the more comfortable I become. It's almost like I've built a tolerance, not just to the substances but to the improv of keeping up appearances. This has started to feel like my new normal, and I care less and less about how coherent I actually am.

We jump into the session, and everything starts to feel like it's moving in slow motion. My slightly slurred, raspy voice echoes in my head, stretched and warped. The new hires' faces blur together as they nod along, their expressions melting together, becoming difficult to decipher. My hands move automatically as I jot down notes on the whiteboard. I hear myself talking, but it's like I'm listening from underwater, distorted, and distant.

Then, suddenly, everything goes black.

This wasn't the first time I blacked out at the office. By this point, my Oxy blackouts had become almost routine. From the outside, I seemed completely coherent, delivering my lines and staying in character, but inside, I was gone, a blank slate running on autopilot. The next day, I would struggle to piece together what happened, my memory wiped clean like someone had hit the factory reset button.

At first, I was alarmed by how frequently it would happen. Each blackout was unpredictable, you never really knew you were in one until the next day, piecing together the gaps. I became terrified by how easy it was to function without actually being present, like I was nothing more than a puppet going through the motions. But as it happened more and more, it started to bother me less.

I was out of my mind, yet somehow keeping it together well enough to slide under the radar, raising very few red flags. A part of me even began to secretly welcome the oblivion, finding comfort in the mayhem. I learned to function at a high level there, and the risk of it all kept things interesting. It was like a twisted game I'd play with myself. A game to see just how far I could push it without losing everything.

A couple of days after that particular training, I arrive at the office, and my manager calls me over. His face is stiff, and his eyes are cold. The expression parked on his face makes it clear that he's pissed off. My stomach sinks as I make my way over.

What the hell have I done that would make him pull me aside like this, into an isolated room?

I walk in and sink into the seat next to two other reps, both staring at the floor, looking like kids waiting to see the principal. These were my guys, my prospecting buddies. But today, no one's joking around. As I settle in, my mind races. Possibilities flash through my head as a knot forms in the pit of my stomach.

Our manager's fury simmers in the silence. He finally leans in, fixing each of us with a look that leaves no room for excuses. "We've got serious complaints," he says, voice low but sharp, "about inappropriate comments to colleagues in the office."

I hear his words, but they don't seem to register. It's like he's speaking another language.

What did I say?

When did I say it?

Whom did I say it to?

I can't quite believe I'm even part of this conversation. This is serious.

The room shrinks around me. I feel the blood rush to my face as I try to process my manager's words. I glance at the other two reps, but they avoid making eye contact, like I might drag them down with me. After a few tense moments, he waves them out of the room, demanding that I stay for further discussion. My heart pounds in my ears as he shuts the door behind them.

"Jason. You asked Michelle if she likes anal?!"

The words hit me like a brick to the face. My initial reaction is to laugh, a nervous, instinctive chuckle. It's what I always do when I'm uncomfortable, like I can defuse the tension with humor. For a split second, I think he's got to be fucking with me.

This has to be a joke, right?

"Hell, no," I say, smiling nervously, trying to alleviate the tension.

"Dude, this shit isn't funny." His voice cuts through the room like a blade. "Michelle told us you asked her if she likes anal during the training the other day."

Impossible.

I scramble through every crevice of my brain, trying to remember anything that could explain this. I close my eyes, like I'm trying to teleport myself back to the training, retracing my steps, every word that left my mouth. But I come up with nothing—just blackness.

I remember snorting the Oxy, walking into the training, and making my way over to the whiteboard. But then … nothing. I can't remember a single thing after that.

He keeps talking, highlighting the details of what was shared, his every word adding to my growing horror.

I'd apparently walked in and, almost out of nowhere, kicked off the training by blurting out, "We're going to *anal*-ize this data," oh-so-cleverly turning "analyze" into an anal joke.

Michelle had been the only woman in the room, and she didn't find it funny. And instead of backing down, instead of reading the room and realizing I messed up big time, I doubled down. I looked her in the eye and said, "What, you don't like anal?"

As my manager lays all of this out, I sit there, feeling my world tilt off its axis, trying desperately to remember, but there's nothing. A dark void where my memory typically lives.

And the worst part is, even though I can't remember saying it, deep down in my soul, I know I did. It sounds exactly like something I'd say to my brother, or to one of my friends, thinking I'm being hilarious. Oh-so-clever, witty, and inappropriate.

But there's nothing hilarious about this. It's sexual harassment. Pure and simple.

My manager and I stand there, both trying to make sense of it. I'm frozen stiff, my back turned to him as I process. He pauses, allowing me to catch my bearings. The silence between us is almost unbearable. There's no excuse I can make, no joke to pull me out of this one. The realization sinks in like an anchor dropped into deep, dark water. Heavy and unyielding.

*   *   *

To say I'm disgusted with myself is an understatement. I'm mortified. The moment I truly wrap my mind around what I've done, I feel sick to my stomach. And it's not just because my job is in jeopardy. It's because I know better. I was raised by a single mother, one of the strongest people I know. I've always prided myself on respecting women, on recognizing their struggle and supporting them. And yet here I am, someone who disrespected not just a woman, but a Black woman.

Michelle was working twice as hard to make her way in tech, an industry that hasn't always been the most inviting for women of color. There were only five Black people in the entire office, including Ryan and me. The fact that I made her feel uncomfortable, that I undermined her in that room, knowing how hard she had to work just to be there, crushes me. She was already navigating her way through a room full of people who don't look like her, and I made it worse. I made it harder. I turned her environment from tough to hostile.

The idea that I have it in me to make someone feel that uncomfortable, that weirded out, is devastating. And the worst part is, I can't remember it. I can't even defend myself or provide any kind of explanation. I'm forced to face the harsh truth: I'm completely out of control again. The drinking, the coke, the Oxy. It's all caught up to me, and now there are consequences.

Several months later, Michelle files an official sexual harassment claim against me. When I hear the news, I'm not surprised. It had been a long time coming. I deserved it, without question. A part of me had hoped, deep down, that maybe she'd let it go. But my luck has never been that good.

All of this is unfolding at the worst possible time. My daughter is a month old. My wife is a full-time stay-at-home mom. And here I am, watching everything I've built crumble.

I can't lose this job, my dream job, the job I fought tooth and nail for.

I can't let it slip from my grasp, not now.

But there's nothing I can do. I have to face the consequences, knowing full well that I did this to myself.

*   *   *

The decision was made. They had to let me go. I would've never known if it wasn't for my manager, who by this point had become more than just my boss; he was a real friend. I was his guy, and the whole situation sucked for everyone involved.

The day before I'm set to be fired, he pulls me aside, giving me the heads up. "It's coming," he says, and I know what he means. The writing's on the wall.

I walk into work that Friday, fully aware it's my last day. Knowing that I'm about to get the axe.

Fifteen minutes in, my manager tells me the VP of Sales is on his way to get me. The wait feels endless, every second dragging on. I do my best to maintain my composure on the outside, but inside I'm unraveling. Any movement from the kitchen causes a knee-jerk reaction, forcing me to glance in that direction, knowing that's where he'll be coming from.

When he finally arrives, we walk to the opposite side of the office, into a tiny, windowless meeting room. It's cramped, and the tension is suffocating. It takes a second for it to dawn on me that this is the room. Our go-to room, where we sneak off in packs to go "prospecting."

Damn, of course it is.

The fluorescent lights beaming from the ceiling make it almost unrecognizable. Everything feels too bright. I didn't even realize this was the same room at first. It feels like a cruel joke. I feel exposed.

The head of HR is already seated as we enter, her eyes glued to her laptop, refusing to look my way at first. Once we're settled, she finally looks up, her eyes stern and unflinching. She wastes no time.

"Jason, we have to let you go. We conducted two full investigations, and after careful consideration, this is the decision we've reached. You need to pack up your things immediately and then please exit the premises."

I try to play dumb, probing for details on what they were told or what they found out during the investigation.

Maybe I can wiggle my way out of this if I know exactly what they were told.

But she won't budge. The decision is final.

I steal a glance at my VP. I can see the hurt in his eyes. I was his hitter, and we'd gotten along great. He loved me from the moment we met at that mixer. He took a chance on me when nobody else did. I let him down. He knows I've got a good heart, but I deserve this. He has to do what he has to do.

I walk back to my desk and notice the entire sales floor is painfully still. A space that is usually loud, full of life and energy, now feels like it's frozen. The silence amplifies every sound. I can hear the gossiping whispers from faceless voices hidden behind their monitors, everyone trying to piece together what the hell just happened. Nearly 75 sales reps watch as I silently pack my things into a cardboard box. I can feel the weight of every stare. Most eyes are filled with sympathy, while others are harsh and judgmental. I try to bury my humiliation as I shove my notebook, my Nerf gun, and all of the other objects that occupy my desk into the box as fast as I can.

Then I walk out. Just like that.

My manager lets Ryan leave with me for the day. Instead of heading straight home, we make our way to the bar around the corner. The place is empty except for a couple of regulars hunched over their drinks. I've got my Oxy bottle in my pocket, and by the time we order our drinks, an IPA for me, a whiskey for Ryan, I'm already three pills deep.

We sit there in silence. My brother knows when words aren't needed. He lets me be. I stare at the condensation on my beer glass, and the tears come, quietly at first, but then I'm crying, shoulders shaking, tears dripping into my drink. Ryan places his hand firm on my shoulder, consoling me.

"Let it all out, Filly, let it out," he says.

When I finally stop, Ryan leans back, takes a sip of his whiskey, and looks me in the eyes. "All right, bro," he says, his voice calm but serious. "This is it. This is your moment."

I don't say anything in response. I'm almost at a loss for words. I just listen.

"The way I see it, you've got two options," he says. "You can say 'Fuck everything.' You can give up. Give up on yourself, give up on the fam, give up on your dreams, your career, and go all in on the drugs. They're kicking your ass, and you can keep letting them kick your ass. You can keep doing what you're doing, unapologetically. At this rate, you're going to end up dead, homeless, or in jail. It's inevitable."

He pauses, letting the weight of his words sink in.

"Or ... this can be your origin story," he says, his eyes never leaving mine.

I nearly laugh at that. My brother's not even into superhero stuff. How does he even know what an origin story is? I'm impressed.

He continues, "You can use this experience as fuel, bro. You can learn from it. You can choose to fight for your future, for your career. You can take this fucked-up moment and turn it into something big. Something huge. Somehow, some way, this can be the best thing that's ever happened to you, to us, if you let it. I'm dead serious, Filly. This could be the moment that changes everything."

Ryan's voice is steady, full of conviction. He believes in me. He believes that I can turn this around, that I'm far from done. And the craziest part is that in this moment filled with shame and embarrassment, I believe him.

*   *   *

Heading home to Apryle after getting fired is one of the hardest things I ever have to do.

How do I explain to my wife that I've just lost my dream job, the job I worked so hard for, the job we moved across an ocean for?

How am I supposed to explain that I've messed it all up by being an inappropriate junkie at the office?

That I sexually harassed someone at work?

Before going into the house, I walk around our block for hours, pondering my decisions, my life, all of the circumstances that have led to this exact moment, this horrible situation I've put myself and my family in.

When I was in rehab, I was going through the motions. I didn't put everything I had into the work. Deep down, I knew that when I got out, I was going to use again. I'd been making reservations to use, which meant I was planning my relapse. I hadn't truly hit rock bottom.

But today, in this moment, I have. This is it. This is what rock bottom feels like. Rock bottom isn't just one moment; it's an accumulation of mistakes and failures that crush you over time, one after another. It's almost getting raided, barely escaping Hawaii. It's the stealing fiasco that got me kicked out of my mom's place, then almost robbing the pharmacy. It's Apes finding me on the bathroom floor with a needle in my arm, then a second stint at recovery. And now, it's this. All those moments have compounded, stacking up one after another, and I'm officially exhausted.

I have a one-month-old baby, a wife depending on me, and now, I'm jobless. This has to be what rock bottom feels like. I need to change my life and commit to a new version of myself, or I'm not going to survive, and I'm not just talking about surviving in the workforce. I mean truly survive. At this point, this is life or death.

I need to take an honest look at who I am and who I want to become. The current version of me is no longer working and hasn't been for some time. I've allowed my environment to dictate my thoughts, my actions, and my emotions. What I need is the exact opposite: I need my thoughts, actions, and emotions to dictate my environment.

I'm going to have to shift my entire way of thinking. I need to change the operating system I've been running on for the past nine years. I have to find it in me to see this moment in time not as the end but as the beginning. An opportunity. That all of this is happening *for me,* not *to me*, and that this can be the catalyst for a much-needed transformation, the very thing that could save my life and possibly salvage my career.

28
The Life Contract

If I was going to survive, I had to stop playing defense, scrambling to pick myself up every time I hit the ground. I needed to go on offense, to set the terms of my life and seize control, moving beyond just reacting to setbacks. Reacting wasn't enough; I needed a system to anchor me, something proactive, designed to keep me from slipping while pushing me to grow stronger every day.

Instinctively, I knew I needed something real, something tangible to hold myself accountable and keep me steady. This wasn't just about setting goals; it was about reprogramming, a complete shift toward lasting transformation.

To break free from destructive habits, I had to get crystal clear on the man I wanted to be in all areas of my life and believe I could become him. That clarity would serve as my compass, guiding my choices and actions. But clarity alone wasn't enough; I needed a visible tool to keep me grounded when that devilish voice tried to sabotage my progress.

And that's how the idea for the Life Contract was born.

At first, there was no grand title or elaborate plan, just a simple intention to design my future self. I began by defining exactly who I needed to be, how he would think, feel, and act.

It wasn't just about imagining an ideal version of myself; I also had to confront the habits and beliefs that had sabotaged me for years. This process felt like staring into a mirror and facing the unfiltered truth.

But once I identified the man I wanted to become, I was left wondering, *What now?* My next thought was a hesitant, *Where do I go from here?*

I needed a game plan, something actionable and achievable. It didn't have to be perfect; it just had to be real, something I could build on day by day to lay a foundation for growth. I didn't overthink it. Instead, I turned to what I call "my spirit."

My spirit is the positive, intuitive part of my mind that always seems to know exactly what to do. Experiencing my spirit isn't about hearing voices or any black magic nonsense. It's that gut feeling, that subtle whisper urging you to go right when everything else is pulling you left. This voice isn't just abstract intuition; it's also backed by neuroscience. What neuroscientists call the "quiet coach" is your subconscious mind, the part running in the background, shaped by your experiences, values, repetition, and beliefs. It operates almost automatically, steering you toward the best version of yourself.

My spirit became my internal guide, nudging me toward better choices and serving as the author of the step-by-step playbook I desperately needed to turn my life around. Too often, we silence this voice, tuning out its guidance in favor of comfort. But this time, I chose to stop second-guessing and finally listen.

When I didn't know where to start or what to do next, my spirit gave me the clarity and courage to take the first step. It aligned my actions with the vision I was determined to create for my future, laying the groundwork for what would become the Life Contract.

THE LIFE CONTRACT: A PACT WITH MYSELF

The Life Contract serves as my guide, my daily compass, pushing me toward action and reminding me of the direction I need to go, especially when the path feels impossible. I call it the Life Contract because it has to feel like a non-negotiable agreement with myself. Writing it out in complete detail and signing my name at the bottom, just like a real contract, transforms it into more than just a plan. It becomes a pact with God, with the universe, and with me. A declaration that I will stick to this path no matter what. Once it's signed, I'm locked in.

Creating the Life Contract didn't happen all at once. It took trial and error, figuring out what worked and what didn't. Over time, I developed a three-step system that turned my intentions into consistent action. These steps became the foundation of my Life Contract, and I hope they can serve as inspiration for anyone looking to spark meaningful, lasting change.

Step 1: Designing My Future Self

I knew that if I wanted to change, I had to take a brutally honest look at myself. I couldn't just wing it or hope for things to fall into place. *I needed a clear blueprint for the man I wanted to become.* This wasn't about setting vague goals or chasing quick fixes anymore. It was about reimagining every part of my life, stripping it down to its core, and rebuilding it with intention. Each area of my life needed to be defined in detail, with the future version of myself fully visualized. So I broke it down into five components:

a. What kind of man am I?

The first line on my Life Contract is a declaration of the man I need to become, a direct contrast to the self-centered, dishonest, and addicted version I've been. At the top of the contract, I list qualities that define this future self, ensuring they're the first thing I see and reaffirm every single day:

I am a man of character.
I am a man of integrity with strong moral fiber.
I am disciplined.
I am sober.
I am someone my family—and most importantly, I—can be proud of.

These are *I am* statements, powerful tools for reshaping identity and mindset. Written in the present tense, they help you visualize and embody the person you're striving to become, as if you already possess these traits. This practice is widely supported in psychology, where seeing yourself as this person naturally guides your actions to align with that vision.

To craft these statements, reflect on the qualities you admire most and those directly tied to the future self you're working toward. Ask yourself, "What kind of person do I need to be to show up as the best version of myself?" Be specific. Think about values like integrity, resilience, or kindness, and write your statements as though they're already true. These declarations should push you to grow while staying authentic to who you are becoming.

b. What kind of relationships do I want to have with others?

I reflect on my relationships and visualize myself as an incredible husband, the best father on the planet, a loyal son, an amazing brother, and a damn good friend. For too long, I've fallen short of the standards I hold for myself. I think about how I've treated Michelle, remembering how carelessly I spoke, showing little regard for her as a person, let alone as a woman deserving of respect. That behavior mirrored who I had become, and it's far from the man I want to be.

I take the time to journal about the man I aspire to be in each relationship. I want to be someone who lifts others up, who listens deeply, who is dependable and present, and who shows respect to everyone around him, especially women. I vow to be better, not only to meet the standards I once set for myself but also to raise them.

c. What do I want to see when I look in the mirror?

Now I shift my focus to my appearance. I've spent the last ten years hating the man in the mirror, partly out of shame for not reaching my potential. The rest is rooted in my physical appearance. My lifestyle is etched onto my face and body: my skin, my eyes, my fitness. Right now, I look like shit. It's so bad that I've started going to the bathroom in the dark just to avoid catching a glimpse of myself in the mirror. There's pee all over the floor and the side of the toilet bowl because I can't bear to see my own reflection, and I'm left constantly cleaning it up.

Who goes out of their way to avoid their own reflection?

I need to design a version of myself that I'm proud of, someone so undeniably on his game that when I look in the mirror, I see a man who's fully alive and think, *You're that motherfucker!*

I map out every detail of my ideal appearance, starting with being fit and in shape, down to the tattoo sleeves I want running along my right arm and leg. I'm determined to get rid of the bags and dark circles for good, to see my eyes healthy and clear. I meticulously outline every aspect of the man I want staring back at me in the mirror.

d. What do I want from my career?

Next, I get ultra-clear about my career goals: what I want and why I want it. I visualize where I see myself in five to ten years, no matter how ambitious or far-fetched it seems. I think about the financial freedom I crave, not just for myself but for my family, and the deeper why that keeps pushing me forward. I write it all down, one aspiration at a time, refusing to hold back or worry about the how.

e. What happens if I don't become this person?

Lastly, to fully understand what's at stake, I take the time to journal what my personal hell would look like if I didn't change. I don't sugarcoat it; I force myself to paint a painfully honest picture of my worst-case scenario. I see myself on Skid Row, the infamous stretch in downtown L.A. where thousands live in desperation, homeless and forgotten, swallowed by despair. Or in a cold, concrete cell, cut off from everything and everyone I love, bitter and filled with regret. Or, even worse, dead.

Fucking *dead*.

The high finally taking everything from me, leaving my family shattered. I'm brutally honest with myself about these potential outcomes to make it painfully clear what I'm up against. This is my reality if I don't fight to become the man I need to be. I have to confront what's waiting for me if I fail: a bleak, wasted existence. And that clarity, as terrifying as it is, is essential. It's a stark reminder that this transformation isn't optional; it's a matter of life or death.

Step 2: Addition by Subtraction

The first step of my Life Contract is about defining who I want to become. The second step is just as essential: identifying everything that's holding me back and making the deliberate choice to let it go.

Real transformation requires clearing out the destructive forces that keep us locked in patterns of self-sabotage.

I call this process *addition by subtraction.*

To evolve, I had to be brutally honest with myself. I wrote down every destructive vice holding me back from growth, including the drugs and the people tied to the lifestyle I was desperate to leave behind.

But removing those external factors wasn't enough. It wasn't just the substances or the people that kept me shackled in chaos; it was my mindset that allowed those behaviors to flourish in the first place. It was the self-deception, the endless justifications, the negative self-talk, and the destructive habits that reinforced my worst impulses. Facing these truths, I realized that these patterns weren't unique to me. Everyone has forces working against their growth.

If you're looking to subtract areas of your life that hold you back, start by reflecting on the patterns and behaviors that keep you stuck. Consider the habits that drain your focus and energy, like having one too many drinks after work, losing hours to endless scrolling, or turning to junk food for comfort. Maybe it's the toxic relationships that weigh you down, the people who fuel your insecurities or drain your strength. Or perhaps it's the internal battles: the excuses that stop you from taking risks, the fear of failure that keeps you paralyzed, or the self-criticism that eats away at your confidence.

Whatever it is, write it all down. Acknowledge it fully, without judgment, and face the ways it's keeping you from becoming the person you want to be.

For me, the process was deeply personal. My inner voice, my spirit, had been urging me to make these changes for months, maybe even years. It was a quiet but persistent voice, pushing me to slow down, to get honest, to seek the professional help I had been resisting. The more I ignored it, the louder it got, refusing to let me stay comfortable in my denial. Deep down, I knew exactly what and who needed to be subtracted from my life. I just hadn't been ready to face it.

But now, I am. My life depends on it. I write down every single thing that needs to go, acknowledging them fully for what they are. The substances, the people, the lies, the anger, the constant need for external validation. None of it has a place in the future I'm building.

In the process of subtraction, I'm not losing anything essential. Instead, I'm practicing addition by subtraction, letting go of what weighs me down in order to create space for the habits, values, and relationships that will push me forward. The more I remove what no longer serves me, the closer I get to becoming the man I'm meant to be.

Step 3: Building the System

The third and final step of my Life Contract focuses on execution: the specific plays I'll run to turn my vision into reality.

I know who I want to be and what I need to remove from my life. But the real question is this: What specific steps do I need to take to ensure I become this new version of myself?

For me, it all comes down to taking massive action. I need to be *radically accountable* for every step of my journey. This kind of accountability means fully owning every outcome: success, failure, and everything in between. Nobody's coming to save me; it's up to me. If something's not working, I have to figure it out. If I fail, I have to learn, adjust, and keep going. This level of ownership leaves no room for excuses, forcing me to confront my shortcomings and fully commit to my transformation.

Radical accountability is about choosing to be the author of my own story, no matter the obstacles in my path. It requires looking inward rather than outward, staying hyperfocused on what I can control. I recognize that *the system I need to develop to pull me out of this hell will have to be just as crazy and unrelenting as my behavior has been.*

The first tangible step I take is seeking professional help. Historically, therapy has been stigmatized within the African American community. Growing up, my identity was shaped by my father's Black heritage and my mother's Jewish faith, but it was the cultural norms of the Black community that strongly influenced my thinking. According to the National Alliance on Mental Illness (NAMI), only 25 percent of African Americans seek mental health treatment, compared to 40 percent of White people. For African American men, the rate is even lower, with studies showing that young Black men are almost 70 percent less likely to seek therapy than their White counterparts. A lot of this comes down to how we're taught to think about masculinity, like asking for help is a weakness. The stigma is real, and for many of us, it creates this unspoken rule to just deal with it on our own, no matter how much we're struggling.

I believed I could handle it on my own, that I was strong enough to push through. But I couldn't have been more wrong. Recognizing that I needed help became the first step in a tangible plan to create lasting change. Therapy is more than just talking; it's a path to self-discovery, healing, and growth, and despite the stigma, its impact is undeniable. My first experience with therapy came as a kid, trying to process the trauma of watching my mother nearly beaten to death by my biological father. But back then, I couldn't connect with the process; I was numb, too young to understand, let alone heal. Since then, I've kept moving, refusing to slow down or face what's buried beneath: the pain of burying Domo, the agony of tearing my ACL not once but twice, and the devastation of losing the game I had built my identity around. This time, though, I'm finally ready to confront it all.

Let me tell you, my therapist is nothing short of incredible. She's sharp, patient, and unafraid to call me out. In those first two months, I struggle to stay sober and even show up high to one of our sessions, but she doesn't let me off easy. She holds me accountable, challenges me to dig deeper, and helps me set boundaries I've never had before. She gives me a space to finally unload the emotions I've buried for years, pushing me to confront them head-on.

Alongside therapy, I start seeing a new outpatient Suboxone doctor. Twice a month, I show up, determined to get off opioids and stay off for good. Each session with my doctor becomes a lifeline, a key part of my system to stabilize both my mind and body as I confront the physical and psychological grip of addiction.

But as essential as therapy and medical support are, they can't be the entire solution. Lasting change requires daily commitment, and that means bringing radical accountability to my daily habits. While therapy and medical support set me in the right direction, turning that ownership into real progress demands something more. It demands a system that keeps me grounded, focused, and fully accountable.

As James Clear explains in *Atomic Habits*, "You don't rise to the level of your goals; you fall to the level of your systems." I know I can't rely on motivation alone. I need a framework I can count on, built around nonnegotiable mission-driven habits to anchor me and drive my progress.

Mission-driven habits are daily actions that are aligned with a greater vision. They're executed on purpose and with purpose, and they reflect the person you aspire to be.

These nonnegotiable mission-driven habits form the backbone of my system, the daily practices that fuel my focus and keep me moving forward.

THE SYSTEM: MY MISSION-DRIVEN HABITS

1. Get Your Ass Up: The Power of "Win Stacking"

My system begins with an early morning wake-up. It started at 5:30 a.m., eventually evolving to 4:00 a.m. From the moment I'm out of bed, I'm "win stacking." Every small task I complete from my morning routine counts as a "win," creating momentum that drives me forward all day. Psychologists refer to this concept as the "success spiral," where early accomplishments make you more likely to succeed in later tasks. Each small victory, no matter how basic, boosts your motivation and sense of accomplishment.

But that first win doesn't come easy. Each morning, the moment my alarm clock goes off, there's a voice urging me to stay under the covers, whispering, "Just five more minutes," or "Hit snooze and start fresh tomorrow." It's the same voice that convinced me to take "just one more pill" for years, and every time, I gave in. Getting up early forces me to confront that voice immediately, retraining myself to choose discipline over comfort. If I can win that battle with the alarm at 4:00 a.m., I've already conquered a significant part of the day.

Studies confirm that early-morning wins do more than build momentum; they literally rewire your brain. Neuroscientist Dr. Andrew Huberman explains that completing tasks first thing in the morning, even something as simple as getting up on time, triggers the releases of dopamine, the body's reward chemical. This release creates a positive feedback loop, reinforcing productivity and focus for the rest of the day. Win stacking isn't just a strategy; it's a biological hack that primes your brain for success.

While early rising might not be for everyone, the principle of starting your day with a meaningful win can set the tone for success. It's about taking ownership of your morning, silencing the self-sabotaging voice, and building discipline on your terms.

2. The Mental Gym: Reprogramming Your Subconscious

While we consciously set goals, much of our behavior is actually driven by our subconscious mind, which operates largely on autopilot. Neuroscience reveals that the subconscious governs up to 95 percent of our daily behaviors, often driving us to repeat familiar patterns unless we consciously intervene. This subconscious programming functions like mental software, running in the background and influencing our actions without us even realizing it. It's the reason we often slip back into familiar habits, even when we're consciously striving for improvement.

To reprogram my mental software, I made reading a daily habit. I started a book club with close friends, which we call the Winner's Circle, where we explore self-help books, memoirs, and stories of resilience. Studies show that consistent reading can rewire neural pathways, fostering new ways of thinking and acting.

Memoirs offer powerful stories of triumph that build empathy and inspire resilience, while self-help books provide actionable frameworks to tackle challenges and create habits that align with the person I want to become. Immersing myself in these genres has helped me fill my mind with lessons of growth and tools for success, replacing old limitations with a new belief in what's possible.

Reading isn't just about collecting ideas; it's about shifting perspectives and challenging old beliefs. Memoirs remind me of the power of perseverance, while self-help books arm me with the strategies to put that perseverance into action. This practice, my "mental gym," keeps my mind sharp and focused, strengthening my commitment to personal growth. Just like lifting weights in a physical gym builds muscle, this daily mental workout strengthens my mindset, beliefs, and values. By reading two to three books each month, I'm actively reprogramming my subconscious, reshaping my behaviors, and cultivating the resilience needed to thrive.

* *For a list of 20 must-read books that changed my life and could transform yours too, download The Legends Library for free at JFinspires.com/TheBlueprint.*

3. Your Future Self: Visualization as a Daily Practice

In addition to reading, I dedicate five to seven minutes each morning to visualizing my future self. This practice has completely reshaped how I approach my day. Rather than simply meditating, I use Dr. Jose Silva's three-scenes technique. I visualize my current reality, my ideal future self, and the steps I need to take to bridge the gap. It's not just daydreaming; it's a guided exercise that creates a mental road map toward the person I am determined to become.

Visualization doesn't just spark motivation; it sharpens focus. The American Psychological Association emphasizes that visualizing not only the outcome but also the steps required to achieve it can significantly boost goal attainment.

When I see myself as the man I want to become, I don't just imagine the surface-level achievements. I also see his habits, his strength, and his resilience in vivid detail. These sessions often leave me deeply emotional because each day, the vision feels more attainable, and I feel more connected to the future I'm building.

For years, I wrote off meditation as something only Instagram-influencers-turned-motivational-experts would preach about. Just another cliché that made me gag. Still, I couldn't shake the fact that some of the people I admire most swore by it.

It wasn't until I hit rock bottom that I became willing to try anything, even the things I'd once dismissed. What started as a reluctant experiment is now a non-negotiable part of my day. Visualization isn't just about picturing success; it's about grounding myself with purpose and ensuring that my actions align with the long-term vision of who I'm becoming.

4. Get Your Ass in the Gym: Building Physical and Mental Resilience

Finally, getting back in the gym is about more than just physical exercise: it's where I release frustration, push my limits, and train my mind as much as my body. Studies have shown that regular physical activity not only improves brain health but also reduces anxiety, sharpens focus, and builds resilience, making it one of the most powerful tools for mental and physical strength.

Every workout presents two key moments where that same familiar voice creeps in: first, just before I start the workout, it whispers that I should skip it, that it can wait until tomorrow. Then it reappears halfway through the workout, urging me to quit early, insisting I've done enough. Each time, the gym becomes my battlefield, the place where I face that devilish voice head-on and choose discipline over comfort. Each rep isn't just physical; it's also a small but deliberate act of defiance, silencing that voice one choice at a time.

For me, exercise is about more than health; it's where I prove to myself, day after day, who I am and who I'm becoming. In the sweat and struggle, I'm not just building a stronger body; I'm also forging the resilience and focus that define the person I'm determined to be.

At the same time, let's be real. I enjoy being in shape and looking good. There's something undeniably satisfying about seeing the man in the mirror and feeling confident and alive again. Honestly, I'm far too vain to walk around looking like shit these days, so staying in shape isn't just a bonus; it's a must.

*   *   *

Each step in the Life Contract—designing my future self, practicing addition by subtraction, and committing to a system of mission-driven habits—has become more than a blueprint for transformation. It is a declaration of who I am determined to be. This is not about chasing perfection; it is about showing up every day with intention, grit, and relentless focus.

The truth is, change rarely feels linear. Some days feel like climbing out of quicksand: messy, uncomfortable, and painfully slow. I have learned to lean into the discomfort, to embrace the grind, not for instant results, but because it is in the work itself that I find my strength. Progress is not measured by how fast I get there; it is in the discipline to show up and the courage to keep going, even when it feels like I am barely moving.

That discipline is what gives the Life Contract its power. It is not just a document. It is my promise to myself, a daily reminder that every choice I make matters. Every habit I build, every step I take, brings me closer to the man I know I can become.

The best part is that I am still becoming, constantly learning, evolving, and finding clarity. Every day I recommit, not to the finish line but to the process. Because the process is where the growth happens. One choice, one step, one habit at a time.

* *Gain total clarity and create a practical game plan to become the person you've always aspired to be. Go to JFinspires.com/TheBlueprint and download the free Life Contract Worksheet to start your transformation today.*

29
Today

Looking back, my journey to becoming the person I am today has been anything but straightforward. It has been a path marked by adversity, with some challenges self-inflicted and others beyond my control. Along the way, there have been mistakes, setbacks, and moments of triumph. Each obstacle became a stepping stone, guiding me closer to my true self. I've learned to embrace this evolution, recognizing that growth is a constant process and that my journey is still unfolding.

Today, I am a different person.

Since October 28, 2017, I've been sober from pills and drugs, with no relapses and no lingering doubts about slipping back. Each morning, I stick to my system: I'm up at 4 a.m., centering my mind with meditation, filling my mental gym with some of the dopest books out there, and pushing myself through a workout. Addiction is a cunning disease; just when you think you've beaten it, it reappears. Consistency is my shield, and so far, I am winning.

Today, I'm a different husband and father.

I see it in Apryle's eyes. The trust that was once shattered is being rebuilt, piece by piece. I'm no longer the unreliable, unpredictable man I used to be. I'm the man who gets up with our daughter in the mornings, who makes time even when the day feels stretched thin. I'm there for school events and present in the moments that count. I'm the provider, not just financially but in every sense, offering stability, love, and a vision for our future.

The life Apryle and I are building is more than a home; it's a testament to everything we've endured, every sacrifice we've made, and every victory we've earned. Our daughter is growing up with a dad who is present, engaged, and unwavering in his love. We're not just surviving; we're thriving.

Today, I'm a senior sales leader in tech.

After getting fired, Apryle and I packed up everything we owned, and with our one-month-old daughter Zsa Zsa, left the Bay Area for Los Angeles. There was nothing glamorous about it. My confidence was shattered; I had risked everything, moving across the ocean for this job, only to lose it all. Everything had unraveled so quickly that I barely had time to process it. But one silver lining was that we would be close to family again, especially my mom, which felt like the reset I desperately needed.

That's when my boy Cog stepped up and saved my ass. As VP of Sales at a startup in Santa Monica called Bitium, he knew I needed a real opportunity to rebuild. He also knew I was a beast in sales, and he was eager to bring me on board. He set up a meeting with the CEO, and after a solid conversation, Cog hired me on the spot as a sales manager. Just like that, I was back in tech, and this time I was leading my own team.

Working under Cog wasn't just a job. It was more like a sales bootcamp, a chance not only to sharpen my skills but also to deeply understand the art and science of all things sales. Every day, I showed up ready to absorb everything he taught, from mastering the art of selling to honing my leadership skills. Cog pushed me hard, challenging me to refine my approach, knowing it would make me stronger. It felt like a second chance to prove what I was capable of. I was fully committed to the role and determined to honor the opportunity he had entrusted to me.

Then, just as I was hitting my stride at Bitium, building momentum and feeling like I was finally in my element, everything changed. Bitium was acquired by Google. The news came with a flood of emotions: excitement at being part of something so successful as well as bittersweet, knowing my time there was nearing its end. I still remember the exact moment it hit me, the realization that I would have to start all over again. Suddenly, I was back on the market, searching for my next leadership role.

Even though it ended abruptly, my time with Cog was invaluable. Working alongside my big bro every day wasn't just meaningful; it was also transformative. I gained insights I hadn't had before, seeing how leadership and vision could drive a company's success. Additionally, it was a crash course in the bigger picture of the tech industry. Scaling companies, acquisitions, IPOs, and owning equity opened my eyes to what was possible. I began to see how being part of a company's journey, from the ground floor to transformative milestones like an acquisition or maybe even an IPO, could reshape not just my financial future but my family's financial legacy.

After Bitium, I knew what I wanted next: to get in on the ground floor of a company and be part of building something that could really take off. I had a few solid leadership opportunities lined up, each with impressive perks and benefits. But then a recruiter called about a position with a small software company in Glendale called ServiceTitan. They were looking for a sales rep, and honestly, going back to a rep role wasn't exactly in my plan. Still, something told me to check it out anyway.

The moment I walked into ServiceTitan, I knew. It wasn't your typical startup office. There wasn't a life-size chess board, no cushioned seats carved into the walls, and definitely no robots rolling around. The space was simple, but their mission stood out bold and clear. The leadership was strong, and the product was groundbreaking. They were transforming the home services industry, an industry often underserved when it comes to tech, and that hit close to home with D-Weez running his maintenance company. As I left that interview, I caught myself thinking:

I can sell the shit out of this.

The software was sexy, and every part of the company's vision resonated with me.

I decided to take a step back and bet on myself. I joined ServiceTitan as a sales rep, putting my ego aside. From the start, they were clear: if I made an impact, there would be room to grow. So I got laser-focused, working my daily system and immersing myself in all things ServiceTitan. I was employee number 186 and one of the first six sales reps, joining a team that would scale rapidly and redefine how we approached sales success. In no time, I became the top seller, winning President's Club and several other performance awards. As the team grew, they kept their promise, promoting me to one of the first sales manager roles.

As ServiceTitan scaled, so did my role. I wasn't just watching a multibillion-dollar company take shape; I was helping to build it. With each win and every milestone, my responsibilities expanded, and I saw firsthand what it takes to scale a unicorn startup from the inside. Today, I'm a director of sales, focused on driving strategy, optimizing performance, and fostering a customer-first culture that defines who we are.

Just as I had done in San Francisco, I found a way to bring my brother Ryan onto the team. He was thriving at Adobe and hesitant to leave, but after a lot of convincing, he took the leap. Ryan crushed it right out of the gates, and he quickly grew into a leadership role as well. Now we work side by side every day, building something we both believe in and creating a legacy we're proud of.

Then, on December 12, 2024, the craziest thing happened. ServiceTitan IPO'd. It wasn't just another moment in my career; it was *the* moment. I was personally invited by our chief revenue officer to join the executive team and a group of "Titans" in New York to witness it all live. What I experienced that day will stay with me forever.

The IPO was a massive success, breaking a long drought in tech IPOs and soaring 42 percent above the offering price. The company was valued at nearly $9 billion, a staggering validation of everything we had worked for. But beyond the headlines, what I'll always remember is the feeling. The pride of knowing we built something extraordinary, the energy in the room, and the awe of watching a dream become reality.

I stood on the floor of the Nasdaq, surrounded by our founders and fellow Titans, as the opening bell rang. My wife was by my side to share the moment. For a brief second, time seemed to pause. I thought about those childhood dreams of financial security, the ones I feared I had blown right along with my ACL. Yet here I was, witnessing a moment that would forever reshape my future. The IPO didn't just symbolize success; it delivered a level of financial security and freedom I had once only dared to imagine. Now, it was real. Tangible. Earned.

Thinking back to that day at the bar after I got fired, I remember Ryan's words as if he said them yesterday. "Filly, this could be the best thing that ever happens to you, to us, if you let it." He couldn't have been more right. Losing my job wasn't the end; it was a reset. Though painful and humiliating, it forced me to reevaluate my life and become crystal clear on the man I needed to be. That clarity reshaped everything personally, professionally, and financially.

Big Fucking Danza.

From Needles to Nasdaq
ServiceTitan IPO – Nasdaq MarketSite, Times Square,
New York City, NY | December 12, 2024
"Every passing minute is a chance to turn it all around."

Today, I'm a motivational speaker.

After a year of sobriety and clarity, I felt a pull to share my journey with others. I wanted to reach high school athletes, to pass along the mental conditioning gems I had picked up in sports and the powerful lessons that translated directly to the corporate world. My goal was to show them the dangers of putting all of one's identity in one basket, as I had with football, and to open their eyes to possibilities beyond the game. I wasn't there to crush their dreams of going pro; I was there to plant seeds that life after the game could be even bigger than they imagined.

As I wrestled with the idea of becoming a speaker, my friend Miles Norvell, also known as Millz, attended his company's annual sales kickoff. There, he heard the motivational power-house Inky Johnson, whose story and delivery left Millz in awe. Immediately after, he called me and said, "Bro, I just heard this cat speak, and he was unreal. Filly, he's you, man. His energy, his story. Have you ever thought about being a speaker?" I couldn't believe the timing. Just the day before, I had told a coworker that I wanted to reach out to Coach Cox, my old high school coach, and see if I could talk to the football team. That call from Millz felt like a whisper from the universe, giving me the green light to go for it.

Millz and I teamed up right away. We spent weeks in my living room, building a presentation that captured my story while emphasizing the mental conditioning gems I wanted student athletes to walk away with. Soon, we realized these lessons could reach beyond just athletes. We expanded our focus to students of all backgrounds, convinced that the tools I had developed could apply to anyone willing to grow.

For three years, we knocked on doors at nearly every high school in L.A., pitching my story to principals, teachers, and coaches, offering to speak for free. Those early days were rough, with rejections piling up faster than we could count. But then, finally, someone said yes. And soon after, another yes came, and another. It didn't matter if I was speaking to five kids in a classroom or five hundred in an auditorium; if they would listen, I was there, pouring my heart into every word.

In addition to working my system, the "service" of speaking and committing to changing lives has been instrumental in helping me stay clean. There's something about helping others that grounds you in your own journey. Sharing my story helps me as much as it helps the kids I speak to, maybe even more. It reminds me of where I've been, what I've overcome, and what I'm still fighting for. Helping others is one of the most humbling and rewarding things you can do, and every time I speak, it strengthens my resolve to stay on the path.

And through all of it, Millz was my anchor. A coach, a brother, and a friend who had my back at every turn. Together, we reached countless lives, creating an impact that felt as real and meaningful as the journey I had been on to get there.

Today, I speak on much larger stages: corporate events, yearly sales kickoffs for companies across the country, universities, national summits at both the corporate and university level, and retreats. I've even had the opportunity to bless a TEDx stage, which was awesome.

Beyond the stage, my purpose is rooted in coaching and consulting, where I empower executives to overcome challenges, reignite their passion, and build habits that align with their goals. I also partner with early-stage founders to cultivate high-performing cultures and craft strategies that drive success in the fast-paced world of technology.

The journey that began on a high school football field has expanded to rooms filled with industry leaders, and each step forward strengthens my commitment to this work. I still remember standing in a tiny classroom, in front of the chalkboard, sharing my story with a handful of kids, determined to make every word count. Now, I stand on these stages with the same determination, grateful for the path that's brought me here.

* To inquire about working with Jason or hiring him to speak at your event, go to JFinspires.com/speaking. Jason delivers powerful, results-driven talks on mindset, sales mindset, leadership, personal growth, and career readiness that inspire audiences to take action.

*   *   *

For the past seven years, I've been on a journey of reflection, digging deep into my experiences and redefining the beliefs that have shaped my transformation. The mental conditioning gems I share aren't just lessons; they are the foundation of the man I've worked hard to become. These principles were forged through my own battles, in both my triumphs and my failures, and they represent the tools that have helped me break through barriers, build resilience, and elevate my performance in every area of life.

Let's take another look at the gems outlined in this book. They are designed to help you build a toolbelt of principles you can draw from to unlock your full potential, both personally and professionally.

FERG'S TEN MENTAL CONDITIONING GEMS

1. Thoughts Become Things

You're not just a product of your environment; you're a product of your imagination. Good or bad, the thoughts you nurture shape your reality. If you can think it, you can create it. So use your thinking to craft opportunities aligned with the life you want. Think it, then go do it.

2. Get Hit

Life is a contact sport, and your dreams are on the other side of fear and adversity. You have two choices: watch others play or get in the game and face the challenges head-on. True growth lies in choosing to run through the contact, absorbing every hit life throws at you. The impact is an opportunity to prove to yourself that you're capable of more, that your dreams are worth the bruises that come with contact.

3. Be Obsessed

Fully commit. Go all in. Obsession, when channeled with purpose, makes you unstoppable. It's about putting everything on the line and refusing half measures. The line between obsession and chaos is thin, but when you walk it with intention, you harness a level of drive that separates the extraordinary from the average. Be obsessed with growth, with your goals, with your craft. Be obsessed or be average.

4. Pathological Optimism

Relentlessly focus on the upside. See possibility in every challenge and potential in every moment. Most people default to pessimism, but optimism sets you apart. Choose gratitude, find the good, and hunt down opportunity, even in adversity. Optimism isn't just a mindset; it's a power move, fueling you to keep pushing forward when others fall back.

5. Radical Accountability

Take full ownership of every aspect of your life. Don't fall into the "victim" trap. Eighty percent of people don't care about your excuses, and 20 percent are relieved it's you facing the struggle and not them. Focus on what you can control. Look inward, not outward. Own your actions, decisions, and outcomes. Growth only comes from facing where you've fallen short and then rising above it.

6. Gratitude

Gratitude isn't passive; it's active. Make a deliberate choice to recognize value in every experience, especially the tough ones. Cultivate a mindset that appreciates the journey, the lessons, and the growth along the way.

7. Focus on the Controllables

Pour energy into what you can control. Life is going to throw a million things your way, but only some of it is yours to shape. Master the difference. Control your attitude, actions, and effort. Let go of the rest. Focusing on the uncontrollable is wasted energy; instead, double down on what you can influence. That's where real power lies.

8. Authenticity

You're one of a kind; there will never be another you. Lean into that. Embrace the traits and experiences that make you unique. Authenticity isn't just about being yourself; it's also about using who you are as your advantage. Show up as your true self—imperfect, unfiltered, and unapologetic—and in doing so you unlock your superpower. That's your edge.

9. Know What Quitting Looks Like

Quitting doesn't happen all at once. It's a slow erosion that starts with minor mindset shifts, like missing a workout, letting a task slide, or not honoring your word. Each small choice weakens the habits that define you. When your standards slip, the mindset follows, and then the habits cement. Consistently follow through on your commitments, big or small, because you are the sum of your habits.

10. Danza

This isn't just a mindset; it's a lifestyle. Live with abundance, knowing someone else's success doesn't limit your own. Celebrate your wins, your tribe, and every milestone. Embrace the journey. Stop obsessing over the gap between where you are and where you want to be. Live in the now, recognize how far you've come, and enjoy every moment of the ride. Like my boy Cog always says, "You don't go to the movies for the ending. The middle is the best part. Danza!"

*   *   *

When I was young, in my football prime, people would often call me "J-Ferg, the Legend." I was an elite athlete, a good-looking kid surrounded by admirers, and that "legend" label, though flattering, ended up warping my identity. The attention made me feel like I was invincible, like the world revolved around my accomplishments on the field. But when football was taken away, that so-called legend seemed to disappear right along with it. I remember thinking and feeling like, "Man, I ain't nobody's legend." Without football, I was lost. How could I possibly live up to that standard without the very thing I built my notoriety on?

Through the ups and downs, my journey as an athlete, my battles with addiction, my rise and fall and rise again, I learned a harsh truth: worrying about how others perceive you, or focusing on maintaining an image based on other people's opinions, is a dead-end road. You can't control what people think, and building your identity around their expectations is like building a house on a foundation made of sand. It's unstable and unsustainable. Real growth only began when I stopped caring about that image and started discovering who I was beneath it all. My obsession with what I could have been or should have been slowly destroyed me from the inside out. I was stuck in the past, clinging to a ghost of who I used to be instead of embracing the new chapters waiting to be written. I was so blinded by my former glory that I failed to see the opportunities right in front of me. I had to let go of the "legend" I thought I needed to be and start living for the man I could still become, someone beyond the football field and beyond the addiction.

And through it all, I've become someone I can be proud of. Today, I see myself as a legend, but for reasons that go far beyond the football field. I've become a legend in resilience, in overcoming addiction, in inspiring others, in showing up for my wife and kid, and in my dedication to coaching and guiding others toward unlocking their true potential. These are the qualities I value today, the legacy I want to leave behind. The truth is, being a legend isn't about the applause, the highlight reels, or the trophies. It's about the impact you make, the people you help, the lives you touch, and the character you build along the way.

*　　*　　*

Writing these words and sharing my story hasn't been easy. It took me nearly four years to write this book. Four years of reliving, remembering, and immersing myself in my journey. I've shared everything with y'all: the good, the bad, the beautiful, and the ugly. I look back on some of my accomplishments with pride, admiring that young kid like he was someone else entirely, like a father admiring his son. There are other moments where I'm mortified and filled with shame, and times when my behavior was psychotic and chaotic. However, I know that in order to heal, you must reveal. For this book to hold any real value, I needed to be completely honest. And I was. I told it all. I held no punches. For that, I'm proud.

Early in my life, I developed a powerful set of tools that helped shape me into a disciplined, driven young man. But when things got derailed, I lost sight of those tools. They slipped from my grasp, and without them, I found myself in places I'm ashamed of over and over again. It took me years to realize how far I had strayed and even longer to create a new system, a way of living that allowed me to reclaim those tools and use them to build something worthwhile. Today, I'm proud of who I've become, even if it's different from what I once imagined. I'm a dad, a husband, a sales leader, a coach, a speaker, a writer, a fantasy football enthusiast, and a contributor to my community. I am many things, and I embrace every aspect of who I am. I refuse to minimize myself to a single label ever again. My journey took unexpected turns, but it led me to a place where I can finally look in the mirror and be proud of the man staring back.

So why did I write this book?

I wrote it to share what I've learned, how I learned it, and what worked for me, hoping that maybe, just maybe, it could help you unlock your own path. I wanted to offer insights and experiences that might guide you through your own challenges and help you achieve your own version of "legend."

I wrote it so you could see that no matter how far you've fallen, you can use the adversities and challenges life throws your way as fuel to discover your greatness.

And honestly, I wrote this book for my daughter, Zsa Zsa. I want her to know that while her dad is far from perfect, he's a fighter. I want her to read these words one day and know that the version of me described here isn't who I am anymore. She didn't get to choose her dad, and yeah, I'm crazy as hell, but maybe by reading this, she'll understand that she gave me the strength to change. She saved my life.

If you're reading this, know that my journey is ongoing. Addiction is a cunning disease, and maintaining a mental edge requires a grueling commitment. But as the late, great mental conditioning coach and author Trevor Moawad said, "It takes what it takes." My system, along with my mental conditioning gems, isn't "the" way; it's "a" way, one that you can build on and adapt as you navigate the unpredictable twists and turns of life. Remember, every passing second is a chance to turn it all around. Everything can change in an instant. You just have to decide.

Acknowledgments

Acknowledging the people who have shaped my life is incredibly important to me. Every one of you has played a role in helping me become the man I am today, and I wouldn't be here without you. The list is long, but that's the beauty of this being my book—I get to do it my way, haha. Writing this book made me reflect on every chapter of my life, and at each turn, there were people who stood beside me, lifted me up, and pushed me forward when I needed it most. This is my chance to thank you all, and trust me, I'm going to take it.

First and foremost, I have to thank my beautiful, amazing wife, who is the backbone of my family and the foundation of my household. I don't know how you did it, sticking around through all the craziness, but I thank God every day that you did. I'm not the man I am today without you, and I'm so grateful to call you my wife and best friend. You didn't just stand by me through all my crazy shit. You stayed long enough to experience the good. You watched me pull my fucking hair out over this book, waking up at 4 a.m. every day to write, pouring my heart into every word. And you poured right back into me, encouraging me to keep going and helping me believe that someone out there needed to hear this. In the words of Kevin Durant, "You're the real MVP."

My baby girl, Zsa Zsa, you are the best thing that has ever happened to me. My pride and my joy. I thank God every day that He chose me to be your daddy. I love you beyond words. You saved my life and forced me to become the man I was destined to be. Throughout this entire writing process, you encouraged me, always checking in, asking how it was going, and showing so much interest. You're a truly special human being, and I am so proud to call you my daughter.

To my parents, boy did I get lucky. I genuinely feel like I have the best parents on the planet. You have supported me through every chapter, the good and the bad, and none of it is lost on me. You are my motivation, the reason I am the way I am. Our household was unique in so many ways, but what stands out most is the love and fun we built together. I thank God every day for blessing me with Allison and Danny White as my parents.

Ryan, there's nothing I can say here that hasn't already been said a million times. We're 22 months apart but function more like twins. You raised me, bro. You were my dad, my brother, and my best friend. You were everything to me and still are. I literally want to be you when I grow up, haha. I can't imagine life without you as my brother, and my journey wouldn't be the same without you. Everything is better when a Ferguson bro is involved, and I'm the luckiest man on the planet to be the other half of that duo.

My brothers, Dominic and Donovan, I love you guys to death. Our journey wasn't always easy, but the bond we share is unbreakable. Blood couldn't make us any closer. Ryan and I were lucky as hell to get you two as brothers. Nic, thank you for always being real, for being authentic, and for supporting me and the girls the way you do. You're an incredible big bro, a phenomenal example, and I wouldn't be the man I am today without you. Love you, bro.

Grandma, Grandpa, and Uncle Jonathan, words will never fully capture how much you mean to me. You weren't just family in name; you showed up for me and Ryan every step of the way. You were intentional about being a real part of our lives, about helping my mom raise us, and about making sure we always felt loved, seen, and supported. I don't know who the hell I'd be without the three of you, and I'm so fucking grateful.

To the Walkers: Stacey, Dave (8ball), Dev, Donnie, and D'Andre. You basically got your own chapter in this book, so I don't have much left to say except that you changed my life the day we met. Dev and Donnie, you have been with me every step of my journey. Your relationship with Zsa is a direct reflection of the way you approach everything in life, with love, intention, and authenticity. The same care and intentionality you show her is what makes our friendship so strong and so special. I can even pinpoint mannerisms and personality traits in myself that are a direct reflection of the both of you, and that is something I carry with pride. You're not just my best friends. You're my brothers, and you push me to be the best man I can be. I love y'all to death and am so grateful to do life with you.

Karen White, I don't tell you enough, but I hope you know how grateful I am for the love you've shown Ryan and me. You treated us like we were your own, always going out of your way to love us and include us. I love and appreciate you more than you know, and I hope you realize the impact you've had on my life.

To my Mid-City brothers, the entire squad: Miles Norvell, Kevin Williams, Bomani Bragg, Mark Gardner, Zach Jordan, Ryan Yamasaki, Randolph Villamil, Colin Coggins, and Anthony Vincent. It's rare for a friendship to span two and a half decades, but nothing about our squad has ever been normal. We push one another to be better, we hold one another accountable, and we have created incredible lives for ourselves and our families. I wanted to call each of you by name because I truly believe that friends are the ultimate secret weapon to success. You become the aggregate of the people you spend the most time with, and my success is a reflection of y'all.

Steven Canales (Popz), Nancy Rauliuk (Momz), and Bobby Rauliuk (G-Rob), thank you for always loving me, never judging me, and treating me like one of your own. Your unwavering love and support over the past 16 years have meant more to me than I can ever express. I know reading this must have been hard, but please know that I wouldn't be the man I am today without Apryle or the three of you.

Marques Floyd, Kareem Dennis, Dana Garrison, my guys. Most of our high school shenanigans didn't make the book, but if they ever make a movie out of this, you guys would steal the show without a doubt. You've always been more than just friends; you're family. From the wild memories to the quiet moments of support, you've been there through it all. Love you boys and am grateful for the bond we share.

Desmond and Tash Thomas, you changed my life. Dez, we hit it off the moment we met in college, but you letting me move in and chase my dreams changed the trajectory of my life. I'm forever grateful, and I try to pay it forward as much as I can. Words can't express how much I appreciate you both. I wouldn't be here, doing what I'm doing today, without you. No fucking way.

To the Hobermans: Tom, Ellen, Eric, and Sarah. You took me in as family at such a young and impressionable age, pouring into me and exposing me to a family dynamic that was completely unfamiliar. You never made me feel less than or out of place, and the love and acceptance I found with you shaped so much of who I am today. Eric, our bond has lasted over 30 years, and I deeply appreciate the connection we share and the role you've played in my life. The influence of your family changed the way I view life, leaving a mark on both my mind and my heart in ways that are hard to put into words. I'm not the father, husband, son, or brother I am today without each of you.

Domo, not a day goes by that I don't think about you. I know you're in heaven, smiling down on us, pulling strings for me, and negotiating with God and the universe in ways only you can. It's comforting knowing you're up there watching over all of us, but fuck, I miss you, bro. I love you dearly, and I'm so grateful for the time we shared. Until we meet again ...

To my Mag 7 brothers: Davone Bess, Ryan Grice-Mullen, Jason Rivers, Jazen Anderson, Myron Newberry, and Gerard Lewis. There's no way I got through college without you. When I lost football, you guys were all I had. Each of you made me feel loved, included, and part of something bigger. From the unforgettable memories to the unbreakable bond we built, you turned some of the hardest times of my life into some of the best. Our brotherhood is something I'll carry with me for life.

I also want to acknowledge a few more brothers who were true pillars for me during my time in Hawaii: Ryan Mouton, Malcolm Lane, Tyler Graunke, Michael Brewster, and Brandon Eaton. While your stories didn't make the final edits, please know the profound impact you've had on my journey and my life. I'm forever grateful for each of you.

Colt Brennan, you were my brother, my friend, and an incredible human being. One of the most selfless people I've ever known. I catch myself smiling out of the blue, thinking about random memories we shared, both on the field and off. Fuck, bro, I wish we could hit Sandy's Beach just one more time together. You had a way of making everyone around you better, both as players and as people, and your impact will always be felt. I love you, I miss you, and I'm forever grateful for the time we had.

Manny Freitas, Steve Mills, Jay Jones, Jo Phillips, and Rikus Pretorious, you are incredible leaders who have shaped my journey in tech. Each of you took a chance on me at different stages of my career, and the trust and opportunities you provided continue to influence the leader and man I am today. I'm grateful for the chance to have worked with you and to still learn and grow alongside you.

Ross motherfuckin' Biestman, my mentor, my friend, and my brother. I had to throw the "motherfuckin'" in there because it's the extra sauce you deserve. It's the ultimate compliment, and you've earned it—you're that mothafucka. Calling you my CRO feels off because you're so much more than that. To Ryan and me, you're Ross the Boss, or RB. Your presence has impacted my life in so many ways beyond just being a sales leader. The access you've given us is special and never taken for granted. From asking me to give impromptu speeches seconds before introducing me to motivating us to hit sales goals that feel impossible, you've stretched the limits of what I typically think is possible. You're stuck with us, bro. ST500 for life.

Shane Cox, I am so grateful to have had you as a coach. You were an incredible mentor, a father figure, and a guiding force in my life. I can say without a doubt that I didn't earn a scholarship without you. I hope you know how much I love you and the profound impact you've had on my life, both as an athlete and as a man.

June Jones, you took a shot on me when nobody else would. I was a 5'5" wide receiver coming off an ACL tear, having missed my entire senior year. Only you would be crazy enough to do some shit like that. That decision changed my life. Grateful is an understatement. I still hold on to your teachings to this day, and while my playing days under you were cut short, the impact you had on me remains lasting and profound.

Barry Sanders, Maurice Jones-Drew, Tim Hardaway, Allen Iverson, and Baron Davis, thank you for fueling my imagination as a kid. Barry, you had me weaving through my house, juking every piece of furniture like it was a defender, and dreaming of making those cuts on the field. Allen, I spent countless hours in my backyard determined to perfect your signature crossover, the move that became my trademark all over L.A. Each of you gave me someone to look up to, someone to chase, and someone to push myself against in my own mind.

Joe Budden, Drake, and Tory Lanez, your music got me through my darkest times and was with me every step of the way. Every artist had their own chapter in my life, and when I hear certain songs, I'm immediately teleported back to that time. It's a reminder of how far I've come and how long your music has been a part of my journey. While I don't know any of you personally, it feels like I do, and I'm grateful for the connection your art gave me when I needed it most.

Jen Tate, you are a rock star. Thank you for being the best book coach ever and supporting me through this crazy writing journey. You were everything I needed and more.

Zach Richter, thank you for being a huge part of this process as my writing coach. You challenged me, brought out my best, and put so much care into this project.

To the city I love, my home, L.A., you raised me, molded me, and shaped me into the person I am today. Your streets taught me resilience, your people taught me grit, and your culture fueled my dreams. My love and gratitude for this city run deep, and no matter where life takes me, L.A. will always be home.

Hawaii, you embraced me as one of your own, offering love, belonging, and a sense of home. My time here has been filled with unforgettable experiences—some wild and chaotic—but I've come to realize those moments were never a reflection of you. They were a reflection of me and the mindset I brought with me. Despite it all, you remain a place of comfort, healing, and peace, and I'll always carry the aloha you've shown me in my heart.

Finally, to you, the reader. Thank you for choosing to spend your time with my story. Knowing these words might connect with you, inspire you, or remind you that we're all on this journey together means everything to me. You are the reason this book exists.

About the Author

Jason Ferguson is living proof that resilience can rewrite any narrative. From earning a Division I football scholarship to overcoming a decade-long battle with opioid addiction, Jason transformed his life through grit, determination, and an unwavering commitment to growth.

His professional journey has been just as dynamic, turning resilience into a competitive edge. As a senior sales leader in the tech industry, Jason was a leader on a high-performing sales team at Bitium that contributed to a successful Google acquisition. He later brought his expertise to ServiceTitan, helping scale it into an industry-leading software platform and paving the way for one of the most successful IPOs in recent years.

But Jason's story isn't defined by accolades alone—it's about clawing his way back from rock bottom and using the lessons forged in adversity to help others rise. Whether consulting early-stage founders, advising sales teams on high-performance strategies, or using the raw, unfiltered truths of his life in *Nobody's Legend* to inspire transformation, Jason's mission is clear: the key to your future isn't circumstance—it all boils down to how you think.

Today, Jason is a sought-after speaker and coach, helping individuals, teams, and organizations unlock breakthrough performance, build mental resilience, and create lasting change.

He connects with audiences across industries and backgrounds, proving that transformation isn't reserved for a select few—it's within reach for anyone willing to challenge their mindset, master their emotions, and take ownership of their future.

To learn more, visit **JFinspires.com.**

www.ingramcontent.com/pod-product-compliance
Lightning Source LLC
Chambersburg PA
CBHW061134120626
46546CB00005B/1774